The art of nutritional cooking

The art of nutritional cooking

Michael Baskette, C.W.C., C.C.E.
Eleanor Mainella, R.D.

 VAN NOSTRAND REINHOLD
New York

Library of Congress Catalog Card Number 91-27701
ISBN 0-442-00190-8

Printed in the United States of America.

Van Nostrand Reinhold
115 Fifth Avenue
New York, New York 10003

Chapman and Hall
2 – 6 Boundary Row
London, SE1 8HN, England

Thomas Nelson Australia
102 Dodds Street
South Melbourne 3205
Victoria, Australia

Nelson Canada
1102 Birchmount Road
Scarborough, Ontario MIK 5G4, Canada

16 15 14 13 12 11 10 9 8 7 6 5 4 3 2 1

Library of Congress Cataloging-in-Publication Data

Baskette, Michael.
    The art of nutritional cooking / Michael Baskette, Eleanor Mainella.
       p.   cm.
    Includes bibliographical references and index.
    ISBN 0-442-00190-8
    1. Cookery.   2. nutrition.   I. Mainella, Eleanor M.   II. Title.
TX714.B373 1991
641.5′63 — dc20   91-27701
                                                                  CIP

Contents

Foreword

Modern American Cuisine has finally turned the corner in regard to nutrition. No longer is nutrition viewed as a fad or style of cuisine. It is now recognized as an integral component of cuisine.

The Art of Nutritional Cooking by Michael Baskette, CWC, CCE, and Eleanor Mainella, RD, combines the artistic flair of the chef with the scientific orientation of the dietitian. Both are the recognized experts in their field, and this marriage of arts to science yields results that are beneficial to all of us. Far too long have these two respected professions gone their individual ways, ignoring the benefits to be derived from the natural alliance based on food. Once united, as in this book, the symbiotic relationship is obvious. While the chef maintains his mission in search of flavor, the dietitian sets parameters for individual health and wellness based on the latest creditable scientific data. However, this newfound partnership should not blur the lines between the professions. The chef should remain the practitioner of the art. The dietitian should remain as the source of information regarding health and wellness as they relate to individual diet. That both work together so well in the following pages is a tribute to the quality of the work contained herein.

Chef Baskette's perception of flavor and its relation to taste sets the foundation for the book. He addresses in depth all components of this sense. Mrs. Mainella puts this genius in a matrix of creditability that makes this volume a must for those who continually strive to expand their culinary horizons. It provides enough detail to be complete while still holding your interest. You are not overindulged with information that cannot be incorporated into your culinary repertoire.

This book will become a classic in the culinary classrooms all across America as well as a valuable addition to your personal library. It is well that it heeds its own advice, that of moderation, variety and balance. It does not preach nutritional dogmatism, but addresses the main facts of this science in a well-rounded and informative manner. The presentation of material is clear, concise, and necessary as a precursor to the recipes that follow.

Chef Louis Jesowshek, CEC, AAC
Chairman of Nutrition Projects Committee
American Culinary Federation

Preface

The science of nutrition was born out of the same craze for knowledge that underlies most of modern thinking; the burning desire to "understand" one's self and one's environment. Today "nutrition" is as much a way of life as it is a collection of data and scientific theories. Recognizing its importance on maintaining good quality in human life makes it the most sought after preventative facing the twenty-first century. What we eat and drink not only builds what we are today, it also determines in what shape we will find ourselves tomorrow.

The Art of Nutritional Cooking is both a guide and a tool to all who are interested in preparing healthy food. It is more than just a recipe book and much more than a "nutrition" text; it is an explanation of a new way of life. It combines both the tenants of science and the axioms of philosophy into an applied scientific culinary experience. Built upon a framework of cooperation and support between an experienced chef and a registered dietician (combined together for the first time in a single text) It opens up a new challenge for cooks, chefs, and dieticians to work hand in hand for a healthier tomorrow.

Good nutrition does not only heal the sick, protect the aged or build the young, it is what we all should strive to achieve in our quest for long and healthy lives. Eat well, but eat smart!

The recipes in the book are mere examples of the many culinary applications available for the cooks and chefs who undertake this new challenge. They represent ideas as much as formulas and procedures. If you read what is being said in the recipes as closely as you read the text then you will be better able to master the art of nutritional cooking.

Many of the recipes have nutritional or culinary footnotes attached to them to emphasize a certain nutritional aspect. Salt has been left out of most of the recipes to show the benefits of cooking for taste using natural ingredients and flavors. Then, if desired, a pinch of salt may be added.

Make adjustments in the seasonings and ingredients. Your cooking is only as good as your understanding of how to create and preserve good taste in all your food.

1

Exploring the past

S alts and fats played essential roles in food preservation for thousands of years before the invention of controlled freezing, refrigeration, and canning. Thus, over the centuries, these necessary ingredients often dominated food flavoring in the European regions from which we draw many of our culinary traditions. This historical dependency on salts and fats may help explain the reluctance of twentieth-century consumers to abandon these ancient culinary staples. The relatively new science of nutrition (less than three centuries old), however, shows us that good health is best achieved through the use of a variety of foods and tastes.

Taste is a pleasure — complicated yet primal, refined yet personal. We use it as a selector in our choice of what to eat. Frequently, the pleasurable tastes help us to escape from life's many inconsistencies — we may eat when we are happy and overeat when depressed. In anticipation of a hard day's work, we allow ourselves an extra food portion to fuel our physical machines. Chiffon pie becomes a prize for a job well done and peach cobbler a reward for honesty.

This helps explain why we are reluctant to give up some taste and variety in favor of better nutrition. Unfortunately, we often neglect nutrition until we begin to develop major health problems, which then require rigid dietary guidelines. Nutrition is thus often perceived as a concern of the sick and the elderly, and the young continue in over-consumption of the wrong foods.

It is difficult to change this mindset, which is based on centuries of traditions and lore. We must first explore the history of food to help reveal why humans became so dependent on salts and fats. More important, we must show that good nutrition does not necessarily mean the giving up of tastes. Rather, it is awakening the palate to many of the natural tastes disguised by improper seasonings and poor cooking methods.

Food preservation

Fats

Humans first learned through observation and experimentation what to eat and how to survive. Their eating experiments might lead to a better way or sometimes end in death, but in this way humans learned what foods to avoid.

They also learned how animals survived extremely cold climates and scarcity of foods by fattening themselves during the plentiful springs and summers. Bears, for example, would fatten themselves to three or four times their springtime weights and successfully sleep through the long winters. Ducks and geese, which seemed to prefer the colder climates, contained more fat than lean meat. These animals and birds used their own fat as a stored food supply and as insulation. It becomes easy to conjecture as to why ancient hunters preferred catching fatty animals, for they possessed qualities that humans desired. Early cooks soon used high percentages of fats in their cooking to reproduce these "healthful" qualities.

Early humans unexpectedly discovered that cooking animals with a high fat content or adding large amounts of fat when cooking leaner meats could also preserve them. Although they did not understand that immersion in rendered fat sealed out the oxygen necessary for most bacterial growth, humans came to associate the presence of pure fats with "wholesome" food. The absence of a fatty taste automatically triggered concern over the food's condition.

Fats were also used to supply moisture to dry foods such as sausages and meat puddings. This practice, dating back thousands of years, was the basis for an American Indian food called *pemmican*.

When Alexander MacKenzie became the first European to cross the North American continent in 1793, he carried with him a powerfully sustaining food called pemmican. Traveling unsettled lands was very treacherous and fresh game and wild vegetables were often scarce. Pemmican, a portable food supply, gave the traveler high-energy proteins and insulating fats and would not spoil, even in extreme conditions.

The recipe, which had been handed down for thousands of years, consisted of a paste made of dried lean meat and equal amounts of animal fat. The technique of drying thin meat strips in the sun and the wind had been used for centuries; the addition of fat not only preserved the mix but also lent it palatability. The paste was then wrapped in animal skins and sealed with tallow (a blend of beeswax and rendered animal fat). The Cree Indians, who aided MacKenzie's expedition, would have included chopped berries or nuts for variety and flavor.

Pemmican was so successful as a food for travelers that it was one of the first products used in a new canning process developed in the early nineteenth century by Nicholas Appert of France and Bryan Donkin of England (Tannahill 1973). Pemmican is still being used by explorers. William Steger, Jean-Louis Etienne, Victor Boyarsky, Geoff Somers, Keizo Funatsu, and Qin Dahe depended on pemmican when they crossed Antarctica by dogsled during a seven-month journey in 1989–90.

In many cultures throughout history — dating back to 3000 B.C. — the use of animal fat as a preservative kept food healthy. It was also used as an insulator and to give moisture to otherwise unpalatable foods. Foods necessary to sustain life . . . is that nutrition?

Salt

The use of salts as a preservative dates back to the time of the early Egyptians, who used them in body mummification. They believed that heavily salted flesh could be preserved almost indefinitely. Although there is not a clear connection, salted fish became one of the earliest foods exported by the Egyptians.

Another religious tradition fostered growth in the use of salted foods. The early Christian religion required that during Lent, under penalty of death, only fish be eaten. Because fresh fish was only available to people living near water, fish preserved through the use of salt was transported to many inland Christians.

By the Middle Ages (A.D. 500–1500), salted fish, poultry, and meat became a common food source. Few people could afford to slaughter a live animal every time they wanted meat, so most of the meat had to be preserved for later consumption. Farmers often could not afford to feed their animals through the long winter months and therefore slaughtered most of them in the fall, selling some of the meat fresh, making sausage and salamis out of the higher-fat-content meat, and salting and curing the rest.

Early cooking methods were concentrated on the roasting of fresh meats. With the development of ironworks came the use of great iron cauldrons in which cooks combined dried meats and root vegetables with large amounts of water to add moisture. Dried legumes were added to absorb some of the meat's saltiness and produce a more palatable meal. These stews and other soup-type meals became the daily meal for many people.

Smoking and drying

The third ancient preservation tradition was that of smoking and drying. Juices were first forced out of thin meat strips by pounding and crushing the flesh with large stones. In dry climates, the meat strips were hung outside in the sun and wind to dry. In moist climates, houses were built to store the meats and a fire inside the building was used to force out the remaining moisture.

The different combinations of woods used as fuel produced a wide variety of flavors. Through experimentation, people discovered which ones produced pleasant tastes. Smoking became so popular that even wines and cheeses were stored in smokehouses. A smoked, hearty red wine or a piece of smoked, aged cheese would become great accompaniments to the most ornate of meals.

Historically, sausages are the result of a combination of all three preservation techniques. To make sausages, cooks finely ground meats (originally hand-forced through sieves, thus the term "forcemeat") along with almost equal parts of fat, then combined this mixture with herbs, spices, and a significant amount of salt. The resulting product, when smoked slowly over a hardwood fire, would last, unrefrigerated, for several months. Variety could easily be achieved through the use of different kinds of meats; combinations of herbs, flavored seeds, and spices; and cooking methods.

Discriminating tastes

During the Renaissance in Europe, between the fourteenth and seventeenth centuries, the culinary arts began to develop. No longer satisfied with eating for mere sustenance, people experimented with flavor combinations of foods and ingredients. The more pronounced the flavors, the greater the acceptance of the recipe. Spices and seasonings from the Eastern countries were so prized that wars were fought over their procurement and great prices paid for their delivery.

Over thousands of years, humans so indulged the physical senses that society was forced to place certain restrictions on behavior. However, when it came to taste, a reasonably private sense, people were able to defend extravagance as a reward for controlling the other expressive senses. This practice became so popular over the centuries that taste and pleasure became synonymous.

According to Jean Anthelme Brillat-Savarin (1755 – 1826), the eighteenth-century gourmand:

It appears that taste has two principle uses:

1. *It invites us, by means of pleasure, to make good the losses which we suffer through the action of life.*

2. *It helps us to choose, from the various substances offered us by Nature, those which are suitable as food.*

(Brillat-Savarin 1984, p. 37)

Brillat-Savarin used two main arguments for the overindulgence of taste: for pleasure and as an assurance of wholesomeness. The second point is the one most easily discarded because the development of the processes of freezing, and later, refrigeration, negated the need for great amounts of salts and fats as preservatives. As fresh foods become more available throughout the world, these preservatives become less and less important. Brillat-Savarin's first point is now the only argument that could remain for maintaining these old culinary traditions.

Understanding these historical traditions gives us the strength to abandon them in the hope of new taste discoveries. New taste sensations can be created by using foods' natural flavors, combined with modern cooking techniques, to stimulate our senses. Rather than dominating taste, salts and fats can now take their proper place as equals to other flavors.

A brief history of nutrition

Health versus diet

For centuries, people attributed certain healthful properties to food, but their reasonings were almost always guesswork and often laced with legend and superstition. For example, the use of garlic to ward off demons arose from evidence that garlic and other herbs relieved people of common ailments that were thought to be the result of demonic possession. As the centuries progressed, and information regarding health and disease became more scientific, evidence was found to demonstrate a direct connection between diet and good health. Enough evidence had not been found, however, to define any specific relationships.

By the turn of the seventeenth century, sea captains had learned that by rationing citrus juice to their sailors they would be less likely to contract scurvy, a disease affecting the gums and the healing of sores. They didn't know why it had to be every day nor why other, cheaper fruits would not produce the same results. Scurvy is a disease caused by a deficiency of vitamin C, which is water-soluble and therefore needs to be consumed daily. The concept of vitamins was unknown in those earlier days, let alone the concept of water- and fat-solubility.

People at that time were just beginning to realize that not merely the quantity, but the types, varieties, and wholesomeness of foods were important for a healthy diet. The science of "nutrition" — the precise knowledge of foods' compositions and their effects on human development — was born in the early nineteenth century.

Food properties

In 1846, Justus von Liebig (1803 – 1873) became the first scientist to describe human and animal tissue, including food, as being composed of carbohydrates, fats, and *albuminoids,* later called proteins. He hypothesized that, together with liquids, these would be the "parts of foods" needed to sustain human life. Together with other nineteenth-century theorists, who linked the mechanisms of the human body to the same scientific principles in fuel-burning engines, von Leibig would conjecture that there existed a precise connection between the specific types of foods that were consumed and good health. These initial discoveries would, however, only lend support to the belief in the benefits of eating meats, fats, and starches, as fruits and vegetables were still considered supplemental foods.

During the same period, Louis Pasteur (1822 – 1895) was perfecting his theories on the existence of microorganisms, which he believed were evidenced through the "high" smell of rotten foods. This smell identified foods unfit for consumption. He was also intrigued by the process of fermentation, dating back thousands of years, which undoubtedly "stole" something from the air to trigger the transformation of malted grains and grapejuice into ale, beer, and wine. Thus began the search for living particles too small to be seen with the human eye. When Pasteur identified and studied these microorganisms, he raised theories that would later be used to perfect the process of canning, and would lead to the discoveries of pasteurization and controlled fermentation.

Vitamins were not discovered until the beginning of the twentieth century, when Dutch scientists began research into the causes for certain diseases such as beriberi. It is therefore easy to see why controversy still exists over the connection between certain food components and good health. That few organizations can agree on acceptable levels or even the types of cholesterol in our diets is evidence of the inexactness of nutritional science.

Everyone does seem willing to accept one nutritional premise: a healthy diet requires a balance of foods. Overconsumption of almost anything is now considered unhealthy. It is this new science of nutrition, which grows more exact every day, that threatens thousands of years of traditional food habits.

2

Taste with herbs and spices

The role herbs and spices played in the development of
civilization cannot be overemphasized. Today they play
an important part in providing new tastes to daily meals. In order to be
able to build taste sensations in food, a cook must understand the structure
of ''taste''—a harmony of flavors—and the relationship between taste
and smell.

Many different kinds of herbs and spices are available and can be used
in many different ways for today's discriminating tastes. At the end of this
chapter is a catalog of herbs and spices most commonly used in today's
professional kitchens, with some historical anecdotes.

Leaves, needles, flowers, blossoms, seeds, berries, fruits, bark, and roots are items to which you would not generally attribute much importance, yet their cultivation and trade have influenced the very shape of world history. The above represent a whole spectrum of flavorings known as herbs and spices.

The botanical definition of herbs, as defined by *The American Heritage Dictionary* (second college edition, 1985) is: "1. A plant that has a fleshy stem as distinguished from the woody tissue of shrubs and trees and that generally dies back at the end of each growing season. 2. Any of various often aromatic plants used esp. in medicine or as seasoning."; while spices shall include all "various aromatic and pungent vegetable substances such as cinnamon or nutmeg, used to flavor foods and beverages."

This seems to segregate herbs as a subcategory of spices. The culinary definition may be quite different simply because of a need to characterize like ingredients with like applications. Herbs are the leaves and needles of plants that have the greatest flavor value when fresh, and, in chopped or whole form, are added to the preparation usually during the final stages. Spices are all other vegetable aromatics, including the bark, seeds, and roots of some plants, which usually require a drying or curing process to enhance the flavor. Used in whole or ground form, they are added early in the preparation to fully release their characteristic flavors. For example, while the leaves of plants like fennel and dill are considered herbs, their dried seeds are considered spices.

Over the centuries, some spice varieties have had great value and importance. Cassia and cinnamon were bartered for fine silks and jewelry; sesame seeds were used to pay ransoms and taxes in ancient kingdoms. Anise, cumin, and marjoram were used in embalming practices by the ancient Egyptians; even Moses was instructed to make holy anointing oils and fragrant incense using spices:

The Lord said to Moses, "Take the finest spices: five hundred shekels of free-flowing myrrh; half that amount, that is, two hundred and fifty shekels, of fragrant cinnamon; two hundred and fifty shekels of fragrant cane; five hundred shekels of cassia—all according to the standard of the sanctuary shekel; together with a hin of olive oil; and blend them into sacred anointing oil, perfumed ointment expertly prepared.

(New American Bible, Exod. 30:22–25)

History of spices

The history of the spice trade helps explain the development of world cultures and civilizations. The route of the spice traders, from India and the Orient through the Middle East and into Europe, determined which ancient cities would last through the centuries and which would perish. Constantinople and Alexandria became great market centers for the collection of these precious spices and their further sale and transport into Europe. Venice owed much of her development as a major European city and political power to the spice trade. Situated at the head of the Adriatic, Venice became known for the maritime expertise of her citizens, who would control all shipping in the Mediterranean Sea, including the movement of spices from the East to the West.

The Portuguese

It was the search for another route to the land of spices, one by sea, which encouraged the Portuguese to sail south along Africa's western coast and, they hoped, around the great continent and back north to China and India.

Prince Henry of Portugal (1394 – 1460), known as the Navigator, was a learned man who had a keen interest in maritime adventures, astrology, and cartography (map-making). He was also a very shrewd ruler who knew that finding a sea route to the spice lands would secure for his country a dominating position in world trade.

Henry would have known of the writings of the Greek historian Herodotus (484 – 425 B.C.), who made extensive journeys through the Middle East and logged his travels in a masterful work of many volumes called *The History of Herodotus*. He recorded the stories of the people he visited, believed to represent true history, including a story of King Necho of Egypt (610 – 594 B.C.).

The Egyptian king wanted to open a direct route between the Red Sea and the Mediterranean Sea to enable him to carry expensive spices to the Europeans without using the Arab caravans. He first tried to dig a canal linking the two seas, but abandoned this attempt after the loss of thousands of Egyptian lives. Still determined to find a connecting passage, Necho commissioned Phoenician sailors to sail his ships around Africa, not having any idea how long it would take. According to Herodotus, those Phoenician sailors who were successful in their attempt finally reached the mouth of the Mediterranean Sea three years later.

Two thousand years later, much more was known of sailing and shipbuilding, and Prince Henry must have thought he could re-trace the route of those Egyptian ships, this time from Europe to the Orient, with much greater speed and diligence. He was determined to take the edge away from the rich Venetians, no matter what the cost or the dangers.

Prince Henry died 27 years before Bartholomeu Dias (1450 – 1500) rounded the Cape of Good Hope, and 37 years before Vasco da Gama (1460 – 1524) completed the journey to India with three small ships on May 20, 1498, but his dream was finally realized, and Portugal became a major player in the trading of priceless aromatics.

Christopher Columbus

The adventures of the famous Italian captain Christopher Columbus (1451 – 1506) were merely an attempt to beat the Portuguese in discovering a sea route to the spice lands. While the Portuguese were headed south, Columbus, believing that the world was round and that Spain and India were on the same parallel at the top of the sphere, was able to convince King Ferdinand V of Castile and Queen Isabella I, rulers of Spain, that the quickest route was to the west.

Columbus had no way of knowing that whole continents stood in the way of any direct western route. He even named the natives he found on these continents "Indians," thinking he had been successful in winning the race to India.

Columbus did find "spice islands," but the allspice of Jamaica was unknown and therefore unrecognizable to him and his men. He had to settle for the introduction of both sweet and hot capsicum peppers (bell peppers, chilies, pimientos), from Cuba and other islands to the Spanish king and queen.

History of herbs

The story of herbs may not have as romantic and adventurous a history as that of spices, yet their use in cooking and diets dates back to mankind's earliest culinary attempts. Before man was able to turn iron into long spears (spits) to hold the meat over a fire, he used leaves to wrap pieces of meat or vegetables, before placing them directly in the hot ashes. The leaves helped to keep the ashes off and moisture in, and tended to add different flavors. Some of those flavors were better than others, so the use of those more flavorful leaves continued. Thanks to the development of agriculture and herding, perhaps over 12,000 years ago, the search for enough food to feed everyone became less risky. Variety and flavor quickly gained importance. As the art of cooking progressed with the introduction of iron, first in the form of spits for roasting, then in large cauldrons (because metallurgy in the early years produced a crude and not very pliable product, the forging of smaller pots was not yet possible), strong-flavored roots and seeds were rubbed into the flesh of meats or tossed into the cooking liquids of ragoûts.

Availability and use

Today, spices are much more easily obtained. Herbs that were only available in certain regions are now found throughout the globe. At the local market, fresh, dried, and ground herbs are now available year-round; spices of a consistent flavor and freshness unheard of before the twentieth century are easily had. Yet, the use of herbs and spices in cooking is generally limited to a basic few. Some spices, such as cinnamon and mace, are mistakenly restricted to use in baking.

Herbs and spices can be easily adapted to flavoring any recipe. Traditions that prescribe rosemary for lamb, sage for turkey, nutmeg for spinach, and cinnamon for muffins should be disregarded. Creativity comes into play when the chef overcomes these restrictive traditions and tries other flavor combinations.

History shows that early cultures took full advantage of all the flavors at hand to create their food. Apicius, the great Roman culinarian, had recipes calling for cinnamon and ginger as the main flavoring agents in many meat and fish sauces. The Greeks have a national dish called moussaka that consists of layered noodles, ground lamb, cream sauce, and cinnamon. The people of India, a country that is home to many spices, naturally have no hesitation in using mace and nutmeg with rice and curries or cinnamon and cassia to flavor cabbage and turnips.

The chef need keep in mind only one restriction when creating new dishes: not to confuse the taste buds by using too many opposing flavors in the same recipe. A recipe that uses rosemary, thyme, tarragon, and sage may produce a dish that is simply too confusing to the palate and may give the impression of bad taste. Most recipes can produce great dishes when combining one or two of the strongly flavored spices and herbs with one or more of the gentler ones. Combining rosemary and thyme with cinnamon and mace can produce excellent results; using tarragon and sage with fennel and allspice can create exciting flavors in otherwise plain meat, poultry, or fish dishes.

With the easy availability of herbs and spices today, it is important only to use fresh ingredients. It is best to buy whole spices whenever possible, and to grind them just before using them. A pepper mill can be used to grind many more spices than peppercorns, and is particularly good for grinding seed-type spices such as anise, fennel, and caraway. Leafy herbs such as basil, thyme, and oregano should be bought fresh whenever possible. If not available fresh, they should be bought in dried-leaf form. Ground leafy herbs lose their flavors easily, and who knows how old the herb is when you buy it, even if enough is used to keep your stock rotated.

The use of a sachet should always be considered when flavoring stocks, soups, and sauces. A sachet is a bag used as a type of spice/herb infuser that can be easily pulled from the stock or sauce and discarded after it has released all its flavor. The bag is made from cheesecloth and is tied with a piece of butcher's twine long enough to reach the handle of the pot or pan. The bag is then tossed into the pot when the stock or sauce is simmering and should remain there for at least 45 minutes. If the entire cooking process is shorter than that, the spices should be fully crushed to release their flavors more quickly.

Taste

Taste developed through the use of herbs and spices depends on the combination of ingredients and their overall freshness. Any spice that is on the shelf for six months should be discarded, for it will not give the desired effect. Similarly, combining too many flavors will confuse the taste and the desired effect will be lost. Even though the sensation of taste is one of man's most basic senses, it still remains somewhat of a puzzle.

The extreme tastes (or "true" tastes as they are sometimes called) namely, sour, sweet, salt, and bitter, are detected directly when they come in contact with the tongue. These tastes give the most satisfaction, for they are detectable regardless of what other taste may be accompanying them and they easily give a sense of completeness. Customers do not usually want to add salt to ice cream or sugar to french fries, yet these complete flavors are very satisfying. These tastes also tend to linger on the tongue; they seem to bind other tastes together. In the absence of these tastes, the flavor seems unfulfilled and lacking in complete roundness. A word used to describe this phenomenon is "bland." In a recipe where the chef wants to reduce or eliminate one of these true tastes, he or she should consider adding or increasing one of the other three. For example, when reducing salt in a recipe the use of acid, such as found in lemon juice or cranberries, or the use of sweet tastes such as vanilla or anise could be increased.

The olfactory sense and taste

Whereas some tastes are merely enhanced through the sense of smell, others depend on it in order to be fully noticed. Biological evidence proves the importance of the nasal cavity's olfactory nerves to the tasting of segregated flavors. Herbs and spices that have highly volatile properties of smell must be handled in a way that ensures their scents are not released until they are needed; the longer they are exposed to the air, the less scent they emit, as these simply float away. In ground or powdered herbs and spices these scents dissipate even more quickly. It is important, therefore, to use freshly ground spices and fresh herbs whenever possible. It is also important to add herbs and spices only toward the end of the cooking process so that their flavors are not lost through evaporation. Even in cases where the chef wants the spices' flavors to penetrate the flesh of roasting meat, or to blend completely with other ingredients in a sauce (where he or she would want to add spices at the beginning of the cooking process), it is advisable to add more fresh spices at the end. Dried herbs and spices may need up to 30 minutes to fully release their flavors, whereas fresh herbs and freshly ground spices would only need a few minutes.

Smoking and the heavy drinking of alcohol affect tastes because they dull the olfactory nerves. Flavors become dependent on the extreme tastes for completeness: extra salt, more vinegar, and very sweet foods become taste satisfiers. This is why foods traditionally served at bars and taverns are more highly seasoned than those served in restaurants. The professional chef should not be offended when customers ask for more salt or say the pie is not sweet enough, for these customers are probably having difficulty with their natural tasting senses.

The chef can take advantage of the importance of smell to taste when trying to create new flavors or flavor combinations. As the chef is preparing the dish, the volatile aromas will permeate the air directly above the product. The chef can use this to tell the fullness or emptiness of flavor. For example, the chef might be interested in seeing what taste would develop by adding a certain herb or spice to a dish, but does not want to add it directly until sure that it will taste good. The first step would be to hold the herb or spice over the product and at the same time try and smell the aroma from the spice and the product together. Second, a small amount of sauce or liquid from the product could be mixed with a small amount of the herb or spice and tasted.

This test is crucial when the chef tries to follow nutritional cooking practices, reducing salts and saturated fats, while maintaining good taste, by using more herbs and spices. Experimenting with taste combinations and testing new flavors before serving them to guests is very important.

A catalog of the most commonly used herbs and spices

Allspice was relatively new to the Europeans that settled America, although it is one of the only spices native to the North American Hemisphere. Found abundantly in the Caribbean islands, it sometimes has been called Jamaican pepper. Allspice gets its common name because of its resemblance in flavor to a blend of other spices such as cloves, cinnamon, and nutmeg. It can be bought in dried berry form, which is preferable to crushed or ground, and can be easily ground in a pepper mill or crushed under a rolling pin before being added to a variety of dishes. Allspice is excellent in flavoring meat, poultry, and seafood stews and sauces, especially venison, rabbit, duck, turkey, shrimp, and mussels. It is also good in vegetable dishes, particularly those using greens or root vegetables.

Allspice   *Anise Seed*

Anise is a very old spice known throughout the Mediterranean region. It has been used to flavor everything from alcohol (anisette) to curries. Combined with mace, allspice, ginger, coriander, and cumin, anise adds character to many vegetarian dishes, which are a prominent part of the diet of eastern Indian and Arabic cultures. Anise can be bought as an extract, which is distilled with alcohol, and is excellent for flavoring cream sauces and puddings. Its seeds can be easily ground and used to flavor many stews and fricassees. It is also used in salad marinades in combination with dill and sweet peppers, or by itself with cucumbers and sour cream.

Basil is one of the most widely used herbs in the Mediterranean area. It grows very easily in most climates and its seeds can be stored for replanting the following growing season. Because basil is easy to grow in hothouses, it is available fresh year-round. Basil, part of the mint family, has a slight mint taste when first eaten. In dried-leaf form, that mint taste is almost lost, but its characteristic sweet flavor still remains. Besides its popular use in Italian tomato sauce and salad dressings, basil is also quite excellent as a seasoning for roasting meats, poultry, and fish. Basil is a good blending herb when used in combination with some of the more powerful-tasting herbs such as cumin and tarragon. Fresh leaves may also be chopped and mixed with salad greens or marinated eggplant.

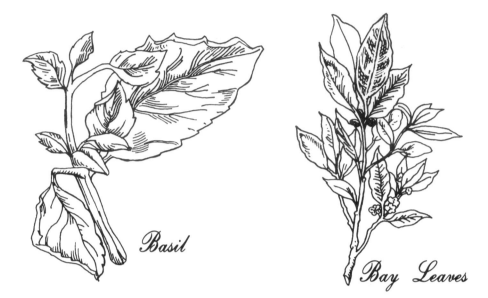

Basil

Bay Leaves

Bay, or laurel leaves, come from an evergreen whose cultivation dates back to ancient history. In Greece and Imperial Rome it's leaves were used as a symbol of wisdom and glory; it was often tied into a crown worn by emperors and kings (also a symbol for scholarship; the word "baccalaureate" means laurel berries). As a gardening shrub, laurels add a robust aroma to backyards throughout Europe. As a spice, bay is well known for its contributions to stews and meat pies. It gained this status because it has always been available, and in the cold winters when other herbs were unavailable and imported spices costly, cooks would merely pick a few leaves from their gardens to lend spice to their soups and stews. When fresh, bay has a very strong flavor, and only a few leaves are ever needed. The leaves can be fried in hot oil and then removed from a sautéed dish, leaving behind its aroma.

Cassia is a spice very similar in taste to cinnamon, yet a little more pungent. It also comes from the bark of an evergreen, and is harvested and dried in the same way as cinnamon.

Caraway is known to most Americans as "the seeds found in rye breads," which is unfortunate, because the flavor is an excellent enhancer for many other dishes. The Germans and Austrians use this seed in many of their native dishes. Goulash, for example, is a stew with caraway and paprika as the main flavoring agents; sauerbraten and sauerkraut both use caraway to provide a distinguishing taste. Caraway is an excellent spice for stronger-flavored dishes like these and others made with lamb or venison. It is also an excellent accompanying spice with sesame or sage.

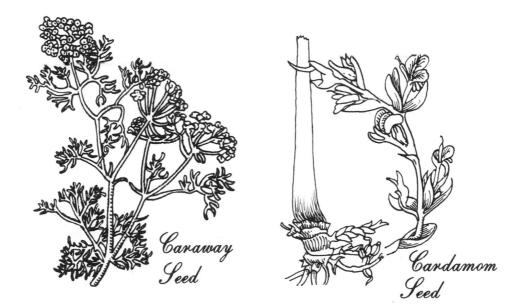

Caraway Seed

Cardamom Seed

Cardamom is very underestimated. It rarely is found in some bakery items and sausage recipes, but is generally forgotten. At one time this spice's use was so popular that its rich fragrance was incorporated into some of the more valuable perfumes and oils of ancient Rome. Cardamom comes in seeds that are easily crushed or ground as needed. It is excellent when used in dishes requiring a subtle, yet distinguishing, taste, such as rice pilaf or creamed onions, but also can be used in a combination of flavors for curries and meat pies. One of the original curry spices, it rightfully has a reputation as one of the great blending spices.

Cayenne pepper was one of the "spices" discovered by Christopher Columbus when his ships reached the Caribbean Islands. Belonging to the genus capsicum, cayenne is related to sweet bell peppers, jalapeños, and chilis. Cayenne pepper pods grow 3 to 4 inches long, narrow to a point, and are red. Their pods are first dried, then crushed (leaving the whole seeds and similar-size pieces) or are ground very fine. Like all spices, in ground form they will eventually lose their potency. This is not usually appreciated because they are extremely potent when freshly ground. Cayenne is also used to produce liquid hot sauces used as flavoring agents for soups and stews.

Celery seed, because of its close resemblance in taste to its mother plant, is used quite frequently as a spice. It is a very small seed that does not have to be crushed or ground to release its very concentrated flavor, which adds quick identification to almost any dish it is used in. It is excellent both in cold- and hot-food preparations. Celery seed offers a unique blending taste that can smooth out otherwise pungent tastes or enhance some of the most delicate flavors.

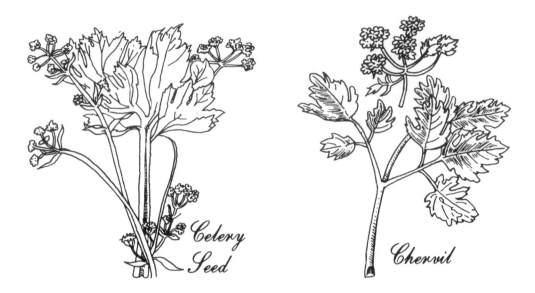

Celery Seed

Chervil

Chervil has long been considered one of the essential herbs in French and other Mediterranean cuisines. It shares a place with tarragon and parsley as one of the three *fines herbs* used in many basic French entrées, soups, and stocks. In dried form, it has almost no taste, and, therefore, has not gained much popularity in American cooking. Now that it is available in fresh form, its popularity is sure to rise. Chervil can be used in meat and vegetable dishes and has a very clean and refreshing taste. Its flavors are easily extracted when sautéed in oil or steeped in stock or sauces. It should only be added to the dish or soup just before removing it from the heat, as the delicate flavor dissipates very quickly.

Cinnamon has had one of the most romantic histories. The Arabs who transported this valuable spice from the East into Europe determined not to share its trade and created unbelievable stories about its collection and transport to scare off anyone even thinking of competing. A story recorded by Herodotus tells of a great bird in the far East who, high in rocky mountain peaks, built its nest out of sticks of this spice. In order to collect the spice, traders risked their very lives. Naturally, stories like these also kept the price very high.

Actually, cinnamon comes from the bark of a laurel-like evergreen found in Ceylon (Sri Lanka). It was not until the Portuguese captain Vasco da Gama reached India by sea in 1498 that these myths were finally put to rest. Cinnamon has been shackled by the idea that it can only be used in bakery items. Cinnamon actually has as much flexibility as any other spice. It is excellent for sautéed potatoes, June peas, carrots, sweet potatoes, or even brussels sprouts. Cinnamon has long been used in cream sauces for dishes such as moussaka or meat pies, or in a stuffing for turkey, quail, pheasant, or duck. It is also quite good when used in seafood stuffings for flounder or deviled crab. Cinnamon should be bought and used in stick form whenever possible; it can flavor a stock or sauce and then be removed and used over again. But where this is impossible, freshly ground cinnamon is quite adequate. Like any preground spice, its potency is quickly lost with age.

Cinnamon

Cloves are the dried, unopened blossoms of a tall evergreen. Its crimson buds are picked before they open and are dried on palm leaf mats until they turn reddish-brown. They can be purchased either whole or ground. When fresh, cloves release a flavor that is quite potent. Cloves, and especially their oil, have been used throughout the centuries as a cure for many ailments; they were used in medicinal teas to aid in digestion and reduce fevers. Cloves are traditionally used to flavor hams and spice cakes; however, their distinctive taste may flavor a variety of dishes, such as vegetable dishes or savory pies and fillings. Cloves are also one of the great blending spices. Traditionally used with cinnamon, nutmeg, or allspice, cloves also blend well with sage, fennel, caraway, anise, and bay leaves.

Cloves

Coriander also has a place in history. In the *Bible* book of Exodus there is a description of the life-saving bread called manna, which fell from the sky to help feed the Israelites in the desert; the bread tasted of coriander seed and honey. Coriander blends very well with whole grains, for they share a similarly nutty taste when roasted. The seeds are small and round, light-brown, with a thin shell and are easily ground or crushed with a rolling pin. Coriander is excellent in sausage recipes and savory dishes of all descriptions. It is used in some of the world's best chutneys and also blends well with most fish and shellfish preparations.

Coriander Seed/Cilantro

Cumin Seed

Cumin has long been recognized as one of the world's most widely used spices. Native to Egypt (which gives it one of the oldest histories of any spice used in cooking), it has a prominent place in the foods of the Near East and Latin America. It comes in seed and ground form. Cumin provides the characteristic flavor to chorizo, the famous Spanish sausage, and is one of the main flavors in two very different spice blends — chili powder and curry powder. Cumin has a fairly dominant flavor that blends well with sage, thyme, garlic, or ginger; it gives excitement to rice, beans, potatoes, vegetables, meat dishes, fish, and poultry. Freshly ground cumin seeds may also be used to flavor biscuits or wafers, lending a certain Mediterranean flare.

Dill can be used in either leaf or seed form, although the seeds are more pungent. A perennial, dill grows back every year from the seeds that fall to the ground. Dill provides the characteristic flavor in the world-famous dill pickle, and seems to do extremely well with other marinated preparations. Dill should be used with other dominant flavors such as those found in sour cream or vinegar dressings.

Dill

Fennel, or *finocchio* as it is referred to by the Italians, who worship the taste, has a flavor similar to anise. A little more delicate in taste, it is easily blended in various preparations. Fennel may be used for its leaves, like dill; for its seeds, which is generally the case; or as a vegetable, for it produces a stalk-like plant similar in texture to pascal celery, with a slightly rounder bulb at the root. As a vegetable, fennel can be used by itself, either braised, simmered, or sautéed, or as a flavoring for stews and soups. Its leaves and seeds can be used in any number of preparations. Fennel gives the characteristic flavor to Italian sausage and has gained popularity for its flavor in tomato sauces, especially pizza sauce. Fennel has also been found in European-style hearth breads, and should be considered for any assortment of rolls and breads.

*Fennel
Seed*

Garlic, which originally comes from Asia, enjoys as romantic a history as any herb or spice. Its amazing medicinal properties, although only scientifically demonstrated in the twentieth century, have long been associated with the warding off of evil and the promotion of lasting youth. A bulbous plant made up of several smaller cloves, garlic is generally used fresh, and is preferred in this form. Because of its popularity, it can also be found in several dried forms, from chopped and minced to flakes and powder. Garlic juice can also be used to flavor sauces and stews. Garlic's flavor changes drastically when cooked in hot oil, producing a much milder and sweeter flavor than in its raw or liquid form. If added too early to a sautéed preparation, garlic can easily burn, leaving behind unsightly black specks and an "off" taste.

Garlic

Ginger

Ginger is another almost-forgotten treasure of ancient cookery. Today, it is generally found only in cookies and Oriental cuisine, yet its history predates that of almost all other flavoring spices. Ginger is taken from the root of a plant that is easily grown in gardens or flowerpots. The Chinese used to carry potted ginger on long journeys to assure themselves of its fine flavor and medicinal properties. Peppery in taste, ground ginger gives curry powder its spicy, hot characteristic. The fresh root can be easily shredded, chopped, or grated, and is available the whole year. Ground, dried ginger loses most of its special characteristics and should be avoided. Ginger is excellent with summer and winter squash, celery, rutabagas, and turnips; it is also good with savory poultry and meat dishes and seafood stews.

Horseradish is also a root native to Eastern Europe, although it is found wherever root crops are grown. These tubers are first washed, then ground, skin and all; for the skin holds much of the characteristic tang. A small amount of water is added during the grinding process to give it a smooth consistency. Horseradish should be refrigerated to help retain its highly volatile properties. Grinding fresh horseradish releases vapors 10 times more potent than those released from an open jar, and may be too powerful for the average person to bear. Buy freshly ground horseradish from a reputable dealer. Unlike most other spices, horseradish loses its potency when cooked; its characteristic flavor literally vaporizes. It is therefore used mainly in cold sauces such as cocktail, barbecue, and mustard. It can be used in hot sauces but must be added only just before serving. Because of its great potency, horseradish is generally used as a condiment spice, but can easily be adapted in smaller quantities for any dish that requires a slightly different, tangy taste.

Juniper is a berry widely known for its use in the flavoring of some English gins. Its sweet, aromatic taste has been used for many years as an essential ingredient in game stews such as venison or rabbit, but can also be used to flavor vegetable dishes such as cabbage, broccoli, and onions. Its strong taste blends well with other highly flavored tastes without being lost.

Mace is the aril, or thin skin, around the nutmeg nut. It is removed, then dried and ground. Its taste therefore resembles the nutmeg, yet is somewhat milder. Mace is much more versatile than nutmeg because it is more easily blended with other tastes without overpowering them. Its delicate fragrance can enhance the most subtle of flavors. It can also be used to stimulate some of the more vibrant flavors, for its taste lingers in the mouth and on the nostrils, due to its sweetness. Naturally, mace is more expensive than nutmeg, as it is only a small part of the whole nut.

Nutmeg/Mace

Marjoram, which is sometimes called sweet oregano, is one of the most popular herbs of the southern Mediterranean region. A very hardy perennial, it grows wild almost everywhere dirt and sun are found. Marjoram also shares its taste with thyme, and can therefore blend very well with thyme and oregano. Whenever a dish calls for a subtle flavor of fresh herbs, marjoram is quite excellent.

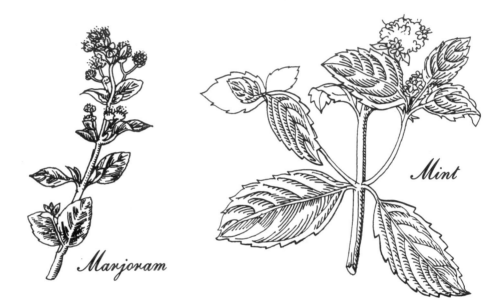

Mint has a very sweet and almost peppery taste. It, too, is a hardy perennial that renews itself every spring. Mint has quite a strong, characteristic flavor, which should be used in moderation in cooking. Whereas a little mint can enhance the flavor of some vegetables such as green peas, too much can totally dominate their delicate flavor. As a replacement for salt in vegetable cooking, a touch of mint can give both sweetness and a peppery spice.

Mustard, which is related to the cabbage family, is used both for its greens as a vegetable high in vitamin A, magnesium, potassium, iron, and fiber, and for its dried, pungent seeds, which produce the characteristic mustard taste. Mustard greens are quite delicious when cooked with onions and bell peppers, and finished off with a touch of lemon juice and olive oil; they can be served hot or cold. Mustard's more traditional flavor is fully released when the ground seeds are mixed with water and allowed to rest for 10 to 15 minutes; the water stimulates enzyme growth, resulting in the hot/volatile flavor. Mustard seeds are very small and can be easily crushed for making a sauce, or used whole to slowly develop their taste through longer cooking processes. In creating recipes, however, it is difficult to judge how much mustard to use because the flavor is not released until much later. Recipes should be tested thoroughly and adjustments made after the finished product has been tasted. Generally what happens is that too little mustard is used to give any value to the taste or too much mustard is used, overpowering the taste. When using mustard sauces for flavoring, it is best to make the sauce from ground seeds by adding water and allowing this to rest, or to use a good name brand that will be consistent in flavor and texture.

Nutmeg is the nut, or kernel, of a large fruit resembling a yellow plum. It grows on a large evergreen and is allowed to ripen and dry on the tree. When the fruits are dry, they split open, revealing a bright red aril, the mace, with the nutmeg in the center. Nutmeg has a strong, characteristic taste that easily can overpower other, more subtle tastes; a few specks of nutmeg can beautifully enhance the flavor of greens and potatoes, whereas a half teaspoon can be overwhelming. Nutmeg is excellent when used with some of the stronger-flavored meats and vegetables, such as venison, lamb, sweet potatoes, and cabbage, but in small amounts it can be used in almost all preparations. Nutmeg blends extremely well with cinnamon, mace, allspice, and an American spice blend commonly referred to as pumpkin pie spice, and can be used for other fruit, squash, or potato pies.

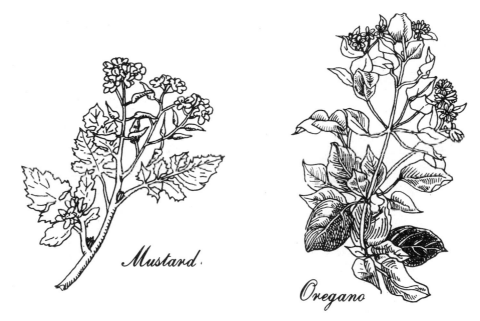

Mustard.

Oregano

Oregano, commonly referred to as the "pizza pie spice," is related to marjoram, yet has a much more pungent flavor. A perennial that grows wild throughout the southern Mediterranean region, oregano has been used in all types of recipes, from meat stews and pies to poached fish and shellfish chowders. Oregano's potency holds up very well when dried; however, fresh leaves are still preferred.

Paprika is the dried, ground flesh of a sweet, red capsicum pepper called pimientos. It takes its name from a Hungarian word meaning "Turkish pepper," for although Christopher Columbus was the first to bring these new fruits back to Spain, its full introduction as a spice did not come until much later. By that time, the Turks had gained control over a large part of the trade from the New World to Europe, and the peppers first found their way to Turkey, where they were dried and crushed, and then reintroduced into Europe. Today, there are Spanish and Hungarian paprikas, with the Spanish variety being a little less pungent. Although most people, who never actually taste the spice, believe paprika to have little or no flavor and therefore use it as a colorful garnish for pale foods such as poached eggs and baked fish, paprika does have a distinct flavor when heated in a sauce or other hot-food preparation. It should be used sparingly as a garnishing spice, for it can adulterate an otherwise delicate taste.

Paprika

Parsley

Parsley has been underrated as an herb and overrated as a garnish. Although parsley is not a perennial, it grows quite prolifically, with very little attention and is available fresh year-round. It has a sweet, mint taste when eaten fresh and should never be bought in dried form. Like all herbs, it should be used immediately after it is chopped. To dry chopped parsley for future use, place it in a cheesecloth bag and rinse with cold water, then, using the bag, squeeze the parsley dry and place it in a closed container with a few pieces of stale bread. The bread will act as a sponge, removing all the excess moisture. Parsley is one of the more eatable garnishes because it acts like a breath freshener, leaving the palate clean.

Pepper has long been one of the most prized of all the spices. It adds excitement to almost every dish, and is one of those tastes that is identifiable in any combination. Green, white, and black peppercorns are all from the same berry; green peppercorns are picked green and cured in brine, black peppercorns are picked green and dried in the sun; white peppercorns are taken ripe from the tree, and their outer skins are removed. Black peppercorns are the most pungent, whereas green are the least. Black and white peppercorns are usually cracked with the flat blade of a knife or ground in a peppermill for the most flavor. Because of the usually high amount of pepper used in almost every recipe, the practice of cracking or grinding your own may be too cumbersome. It is preferable to buy cracked or restaurant-grind peppercorns for a rich, peppery taste. Finely ground peppers should be avoided unless a recipe specifically calls for them. Ground white pepper is usually used to season white or blond sauces because black pepper will leave behind small specks. Red pepper should not be confused with these peppers. Red pepper is of the family capsicum, called cayenne (see cayenne pepper), which is related to the chili pepper and bell peppers.

Pepper *Rosemary*

Rosemary is most popular in the eastern Mediterranean area. Its leaves come from an evergreen that grows on the rocky coasts of Greece and Turkey. Its use, therefore, has been most associated with lamb preparations, although this is an unnecessary relationship. Rosemary has a very distinctive flavor that is excellent in any number of savory dishes. If used fresh, the leaves, which are available year-round, may be easily chopped and left in the preparation. In dried form, the leaves are very tough and should be removed from the dish before serving. A sachet may be needed for easier removal.

Saffron is composed of the dried stigmas from the saffron crocus, which grows throughout the whole Mediterranean region. Because of the delicate procedure needed to harvest the spice (the tiny stigmas must be picked by hand, with an estimated 750,000 plants needed for 1 pound of saffron), the price of this flavorful spice has always been extremely high. It is one of the primary spices used in the French seafood stew called bouillabaisse, and is also used to flavor many Spanish dishes, such as the popular paella. The beauty of the spice is that only a small amount is needed to give a recipe a unique, signature taste.

Saffron   *Sage*

Sage is another of those spices that traditions have locked into only a few culinary applications: turkey with sage dressing, and country breakfast sausages. In other areas of the world, sage is used more for its medicinal than its culinary properties. The people of the Mediterranean area believe that a tea made from fresh sage leaves can relieve almost every kind of digestive or intestinal problems. Sage does have a very distinctive taste, but that makes it even more versatile than the delicately flavored herbs and spices. Its flavor can enhance even the most powerful-tasting stews, pies, stuffings, and sausages. Sage is also quite good on its own as a flavoring for potato dishes, corn, carrots, celery, turnips, greens, etc.

Savory is an herb whose taste most closely resembles that of thyme, but is not quite as pungent. It can be used in a variety of savory dishes or as the primary seasoning for beans, peas, rice, leeks, or potatoes.

Savory

Sesame Seed

Sesame is a spice that has lost its allure over the centuries. At one time, the spice was so favored that it was believed to possess supernatural powers (recall the story of the Arabian prince Ali Baba who, searching for the city's hidden treasure, commanded the secret passage door to open by chanting the words, "Open sesame"). Sesame seeds, which are 60% oil, are used primarily today in the oil form as a highly flavorful cooking medium. Unfortunately, its other most popular use is for the topping of hamburger buns. Sesame deserves a more vibrant place among the world's seasonings, for its flavor is very unique, especially when roasted. It can be used to highlight the flavors of any stuffing or breading or to flavor salad dressings and marinades. The oil can be used not only in Oriental stir-fries, where it is commonly used, but also in sautéed lamb, venison, chicken, and veal preparations.

Tarragon has earned an important place among the world's seasonings for its very unique taste and versatility. Tarragon is not as easily grown as some of the other herbs, yet demand has created a world market for its fresh leaves as well as the preserved leaves in brine. Dried tarragon should be avoided because it tends to have a very "grassy" taste. Tarragon gained world recognition for its use in the popular béarnaise sauce and in cream sauces for poached fish and shellfish. A simple dish of toasted english muffin with gruyère cheese and crabmeat becomes an excellent luncheon item or appetizer when topped with fresh béarnaise sauce. Tarragon oil and vinegar is also a very popular item in salad making or for vegetable and meat marinades.

Tarragon

Thyme

Thyme is a very popular herb, for not only does it offer a good taste by itself, as in Cajun jambalaya, but it is also quite excellent in blending with other spices. Thyme has very small leaves that dry very well, but the dried herb has a much more pronounced flavor and can tend to overpower some of the more delicate tastes. Fresh thyme has a very distinctive flavor, yet it enhances other flavors, rather than hiding them. Thyme can be used in almost any type of dish, and is also quite excellent in flavoring biscuits, rolls, and muffins.

Turmeric is a spice with little flavor of its own and is generally used as a coloring spice in curries, soups, and rice dishes. Turmeric is sometimes used in place of saffron in paella and other dishes because of its very low cost; however, the taste is unforgivably dissimilar.

Vanilla* is not usually thought of as a spice, yet it fits both the botanical and culinary definitions. Vanilla is the pod of a climbing orchid grown in tropical America. This pod is dried very slowly in the sun, and is turned many times during the process. Vanilla is most readily available as an extract, which has been distilled with alcohol, yet its dried pods are much superior. The pods can be infused for their flavor in stocks or sauces, and then rinsed off and stored for later use. One single vanilla bean can last through several applications. Vanilla is another flavor that has been relegated by tradition to use in dessert applications, yet its versatility is much greater than that. Vanilla can be used in fish and seafood chowders or savory meat dishes, where a slight sweetness can enhance an otherwise unexciting flavor. Only a small amount is needed to turn the taste completely around.

---

* Pictures of all herbs and spices courtesy of American Spice Trade Association.

3

Natural flavorings

Any discussion of taste must include the natural flavorings. These represent a whole spectrum of flavors and taste combinations derived from the bulbous plants: garlic, onion, fennel, and celery, and from root sources such as ginger, parsnips, carrots, and turnips. Vegetable and animal fats, acid products, and vinegars also play a great part in the natural flavoring of food.

Using the same ingredient, a chef can employ various culinary techniques to create a wide range of flavors (i.e., the difference in taste between a sweated onion in a cream soup or a sautéed onion served with sliced steak). These flavorful ingredients, and the vegetable stocks made from them, can be used to replace fatty or salty ingredients in some basic recipes without sacrificing taste.

Along with herbs and spices, there exists a wide range of other natural flavorings that the chef can orchestrate into exciting taste sensations. These include a vast variety of bulb and root vegetables, flavored oils, vinegars, and fruit juices that contribute distinctive flavors as well as some very important vitamins and minerals to the final dish.

It may seem confusing to the student chef to talk about carrots, celery, and onions in the same way as basil, oregano, and marjoram, but the experienced chef knows and appreciates the flavors of these ingredients and the versatility they impart to recipes. No longer confined to using only regional ingredients, today's chefs can pick and choose the right combination of foods and seasonings for the greatest variety.

Flavoring vegetables

Chefs must keep in mind the importance of foods' natural flavors when creating recipes so as to enhance, rather than disguise, taste. Following the same tasting principles discussed earlier, as regards the four "true" tastes — sour, bitter, sweet, and salt — the chef should create flavor combinations using vegetables and other natural flavorings that will contribute the greatest overall taste sensation.

For example, of the root vegetables, the most flavorful are carrots, parsnips, and turnips. Carrots and yellow turnips (rutabagas) have a sweet taste, whereas parsnips and white turnips have a more bitter flavor. The chef who takes advantage of these basic tastes uses carrots and rutabagas to blend otherwise pronounced flavors and white turnips and parsnips to add spice and character.

Onions, celery, tomatoes, and bell peppers also have distinguishing flavors that add dimension to various preparations. These can be used in the same way as herbs and spices.

The onion family

There are many varieties of onions that can be used as seasoning vegetables: the round-bulb type, including Spanish onions (yellow), white onions, red Bermuda onions, shallots, and pearl onions; and the elongated bulb varieties, including green onions, leeks, and chives. Garlic is also a member of the onion family, but is treated more as an herb or spice than a vegetable because of its highly concentrated taste.

Onions have varying amounts of the same cysteine derivatives (a cysteine is a sulfur-laden amino acid), which are responsible for their distinctive tastes. These compounds are stored in the plant's cells in a relatively stable state until the cells are burst open through the cutting or chopping process. The end result is a mixture of ammonia, pyruvic acid, and a third compound that is later broken down into diallyl disulfide, the precursor of the garlic smell.

The hot, biting taste of onions and garlic is most prevalent in the raw, chopped state, and slowly loses this potency during the cooking process. A milder taste is achieved if these vegetables are used in whole or large-cut form. Finally, a sweetened, lighter taste can be developed through a dry cooking process (sautéed, pan-fried, grilled, or roasted), which helps caramelize the natural sugars. These three distinguishable taste variations help chefs create versatility in their cooking and baking.

An example of this is the production of many of the small sauces (derivatives of the five *basic* or *mother* sauces). The base for a lot of these is a well-made stock, in which large pieces of onions are used (usually no smaller than rough-cut, and many times simply halved or quartered) for the blending quality of their characteristic taste. On the other hand, for a more distinctive flavor in some finished sauces finely chopped shallots are often used in the final preparation.

Within each onion variety there exists a wide range of flavors and smells, depending on where they were grown and when they were harvested. Each type has a distinctive flavor and may not be interchangeable in all recipes. The Spanish onion has usually the strongest onion flavor (even this varies throughout the year, depending on storage time and geographic location) and the spring onion the slightest. Large white, Bermuda, and pearl onions lean towards a sweet taste, even when raw, and caramelize extremely well.

Celery and fennel

Both celery and fennel are stalk-producing, bulbous vegetables that are used both as vegetables by themselves, and as flavoring vegetables for a variety of dishes. Likewise, both vegetables produce seeds which in turn are used as spices either whole or in ground form.

Like members of the onion family, celery and fennel give different taste sensations depending on whether they are used raw or cooked. The experienced chef can use them both ways to create slight but interesting variations of flavor.

The pepper family

Capsicum is the genus name for a whole family of flavoring fruits, used as vegetables and seasonings in cooking, known as peppers. This diverse family includes all varieties of the sweet "bell" peppers (so called because of their bell-like shape) as well as the hot jalapeño and chili peppers commonly used in Mexican and Cajun cuisine.

Green, red, and yellow bell peppers are similar in taste, and are used quite regularly as flavoring vegetables throughout much of the Latin world. They are sweet tasting and blend well with some of the more pungent vegetables to produce a rounded taste.

Chili, jalapeño, cayenne, and Anaheim are all varieties of hot peppers. The volatile oils which create the burning sensation are present largely in the seeds and inner membranes of the pepper pods. Removing some or all of the seeds can produce even a greater variety of taste sensations. Cayenne pepper, the narrow-podded red hot pepper, is used to make liquid pepper sauces (Tabasco is one trade name), crushed red pepper, and ground red pepper; it is extremely hot.

Vegetable mirepoix

Professional chefs know the importance of vegetable flavors for sauces, stews, and roasts, for they are trained to use what is called a *mirepoix* of vegetables in the making of stocks for soups and sauces, and for lifting large pieces of meat or poultry off the bottom of a roasting pan while cooking. A mirepoix is a selection of rough-cut vegetables used primarily as a flavoring tool. A commonly used collection of vegetables could include one member of the onion family, from Spanish onions to leeks, celery, carrots, and turnips. Chefs may also add parsnips, ginger, or garlic to provide a distinctive flavor to a particular dish.

The vegetables' flavors are extracted slowly over a long and slow cooking process. The mirepoix is usually discarded at the end after most of the flavor and nutrients have been cooked out.

In all stocks, the strained liquid holds the blended taste of the vegetables plus the vitamins and minerals extracted from them. In pureed soups and sauces, the vegetables are sometimes left in the liquid and pureed into a very fine consistency, thus contributing all their nutrients to the final product.

As stated earlier, a mirepoix may also be used in lifting meats and poultry off the bottom of roasting pans to prevent them from frying in their own fatty drippings. When the cooking is over, the mirepoix can be used in the making of an accompanying sauce.

For white stocks or sauces, the mirepoix would not include carrots or yellow turnips, for the carotene color pigments would bleach out when cooked. Instead, it would contain the center stalks of celery, a cream-colored green, or celeriac — a white-fleshed tuber whose taste resembles pascal celery. The amount of onion would remain the same; the amount of turnips would most likely be increased to replace the flavors of the missing carrots.

For brown stocks, the mirepoix is usually browned along with the bones so that the vegetables' natural sugars would caramelize, adding more color to the final product. For white or neutral stocks, the vegetables are simply added, freshly cut, to the bones.

Sweating versus browning

Two taste variations from flavoring vegetables can be easily achieved through the cooking process. Vegetables that are cooked, uncovered, in hot oil, allowing the evaporated moisture to escape, will brown as their natural sugars caramelize under direct heat. These vegetables will add color and a slightly sweeter taste to the final product. Vegetables that are cooked in a covered pan will not brown as quickly because the evaporated liquids are trapped in the pan during cooking, inhibiting the coloring process. These liquids condense on the lid and fall back down onto the vegetables, thus the descriptive phrase *sweating*. These vegetables will have the most natural tastes.

Vegetable stocks

Vegetable stocks are an excellent substitute for the fatter meat stocks usually used in production kitchens. They can be used to create accompanying sauces to be served with almost all meats, fish, poultry, or vegetables.

Vegetable stocks may be used to form the braising liquid for tougher meat cuts, adding dimension to the final flavors rather than letting them be dominated solely by the meat juices.

In most situations when it becomes necessary to thin down an already prepared sauce, vegetable stocks can be used instead of the traditional chicken or veal stocks, for they have the same effect without the added fats and cholesterol.

Rice pilafs are excellent when made with vegetable stocks, eliminating the problem of the rice tasting like chicken when a chicken stock is used. Vegetable flavors added in these instances act as do herbs and spices for seasoning foods—as an accent to the dominant flavors.

Cream soups such as cream of broccoli or potato leek, which traditionally have had chicken or veal stock for a base, should be made with vegetable stocks; not only will this produce the same effects, it will also enhance, not hide, the flavors of the dominant vegetables.

Keeping in mind the same reasoning in relation to mirepoix and color, the chef can make either light or dark vegetable stocks by browning or sweating the vegetables. The types of vegetable combinations can also affect the color of the final stock, especially onions, which can be almost black in color and still have a clean, sweet taste.

Any variety of vegetable can be used for a stock, as long as the chef keeps in mind the taste he or she is looking for in the final product. Carrots, parsnips, turnips, celery, and onions create a very full-bodied vegetable stock. Tomatoes, bell peppers, and any assortment of vegetable trimmings or stems can also be used for different applications.

In place of sugar

Chefs may add a small amount of sugar to some of their recipes, such as tomato-based stews and sauces, to help cut the red tomatoes' acid taste. Carrots or sweet bell peppers can be used to do the same trick. When making a tomato sauce, the chef should sauté onions, carrots, and bell peppers until golden-brown (caramelization of the sugars not only adds color but also brings to the surface the vegetables' natural sweetness) before adding stocks and tomato product. The golden color actually blends well with the bright-red tomato color without changing it significantly, and the sugars help to mellow the acidic bite. If desired, the vegetables can be easily strained out before the final seasonings are added.

Some salad preparations, such as coleslaw or hot bacon dressing for spinach salads, also call for a sweetener to be added. Bell peppers or carrots could be used in these applications as well; even fennel (the bulbous vegetable) can add sweetness and character to some of these marinade-type preparations.

Oils and fats

Chefs can use many different oils and fats for cooking. The strongest-flavored oils are sesame, olive, any of the nut oils (hazelnut or walnut, etc.), butter, and margarine. The ways they can be used are almost endless. The chef can add a small amount of sesame or walnut oil to a stir-fry to accentuate the taste, at the same time reducing the amount of soy (a fermented sauce high in sodium) or other flavor enhancers normally found in these preparations.

Sautéed dishes or pan-fried items take on a whole new character when olive oil is the cooking medium; even omelettes cooked in a small amount of this ancient oil take on a slightly different character. Olive oil comes in at least three different forms, each with a varying degree of olive taste. Virgin olive oil comes from the first pressing of the olives and has the strongest olive taste. Plain olive oil is produced from the second pressing of the olives and, while still containing the same oil properties as virgin olive oil, does not have as strong an olive taste. A third form, called "light" olive oil, comes from the third and fourth pressing of the olives and is almost clear in color (as opposed to the shades of green found in virgin and plain olive oil) with almost no olive taste. In recipes requiring a strong olive taste one should use virgin olive oil, while in other recipes for which the benefit of using olive oil is desired — but not the taste — one should use plain or light olive oil. Virgin olive oil is of course the most expensive of the three forms.

Some chefs stay away from the highly flavorful oils because they believe their flavors will dominate the dish (sesame oil has an extremely dominating flavor; olive oil is a close second); however, they need to consider these oils as seasonings, rather than as frying mediums. In a recipe that calls for a fat for stir-frying, sautéing, or pan-frying, the flavorful oils can be used as a portion of the frying medium, with an oil with little or no dominant flavor such as canola oil, soybean oil, or sunflower oil as the primary oil. In this use, the strongly flavored oils act more as a spice.

Flavored oils

Flavored oils allow chefs to give their recipes a more complete taste by utilizing flavor-extraction techniques and the cooking medium to disperse the specified tastes evenly throughout the entire dish. Chefs make flavored oils by infusing the essence of their favorite herbs and spices into any of the pure cooking oils they would regularly use.

A garlic/tarragon oil can be made very easily, for example, by taking a safflower or soybean oil and adding crushed garlic cloves and fresh tarragon sprigs (approximately four cloves and two full sprigs per quart of oil). Allowing this mix to rest (at least 24 hours) will let the garlic and tarragon flavors be extracted into the oil. The oil then can be used for sautéing or pan-frying, or in a marinade or salad dressing to give the final dish a signature taste.

Fresh herbs and cracked, whole spices are best suited for this type of extraction process. If dried herbs or ground spices are used, the oil should be strained before use. The extraction process can be quickened by heating the oil slightly before adding the herbs and spices.

A black pepper/garlic oil may be excellent for sautéed shrimp or crabmeat dishes; a dill-flavored oil would accentuate the most ordinary of salad marinades without an overpowering dill flavor.

Some restaurant chefs keep chopped garlic and chopped shallots as part of the hot line *mise en place* (readied ingredients), and cover the chopped bulbs with fresh oil. If a recipe calls for a stronger garlic or shallot taste, they have access to the actual chopped product; when the recipe calls for just a hint of these flavors, they merely spoon off a tablespoon or so of the oil and add that during the cooking process, replenishing the oil at the end of the shift.

Olive oil and other flavorful oils can also be used for these herbal infusions, but the fact that the originating oil flavors will also dominate should be kept in mind. Just as they sometimes make their own restaurant blend of spices, chefs may develop their own herbal/oil blends that could be used for many different cooking procedures. These blends give character and depth to the most simple applications.

Butter and margarine

Two more fats to consider are butter and margarine. Today there is a definite concern with the amount of cholesterol and saturated fats in the daily diet, which translates into the necessity of reducing the use of these types of fats. Nutritional diets, however, do not dictate the total elimination of these fats (10% of total daily caloric intake should consist of saturated fats), but simply their reduction.

As cooking mediums, butter and margarine should be avoided because the same results can easily be achieved through the use of unsaturated oils. But when it comes to flavor, nothing tastes the same as fresh, whole butter. Margarine is merely vegetable oil that has been hydrogenized, making it solid at room temperature. Some products today have been flavored artificially to resemble the taste of butter without the cholesterol.

If the recipe calls for the taste of butter, then it should be used as a seasoning by adding a small amount at the final stages of cooking so that the pure taste remains with the final product. If the recipe calls for butter as the cooking medium, it can be replaced with a combination of unflavored oil and a smaller amount of butter.

Acid products

Sour is one of the four "true" tastes mentioned in the chapter on herbs and spices. It is distinguishable from other tastes in a dish, acting as an influencing flavor over them. Some type of acid product may be used in a recipe instead of salt to heighten the taste, having the same stimulating effect without the sodium. In some cases, the use of an acidic product totally eliminates the need for salt.

These products come in many forms, ranging from citrus juices such as lemons, lime, and orange, tomato products, and vinegars, to sour cream and yogurt. Each gives the chef great flexibility in his or her preparations.

The exciting taste that makes beef Stroganoff more than just beef stew is provided by the addition of sour cream to the final sauce; flounder à la meunière is a fantastic variation of sautéed flounder, with only the addition of a few drops of lemon juice making the difference. Using acid products as seasonings can transform tastes from average to gourmet.

Flavored vinegars

Flavored vinegars can be made in much the same way as flavored oils, by the simple infusion of herbal and spice essences into a favorite vinegar. Fresh herbs and cracked, whole spices offer the best results. A rosemary/thyme white vinegar gives extra definition to seafood marinades; a dill/garlic vinegar gives character to cucumber, potato, and pasta salads.

Fruit-flavored vinegars are also gaining popularity in the preparation of salad dressings and marinades. These vinegars use crushed berries or chopped fruit for flavor. Once the fruit flavor has been fully steeped out (three to four days) the vinegar is strained off and can be stored indefinitely. These vinegars can be made more rapidly for quick service by using fruit that has been finely pureed and by adding some of the fruit to the dressing; however, the presentation will be quite different and the versatility of use not as great.

Lean (defatted) stocks

Stocks are the bases of many soups and sauces, and are usually made from the bones of animals or fish or the shells of shellfish. Great care should be taken in making stocks so as to reduce as much as possible the amount of fat in the final product.

The best way to produce lean stocks is first to choose bones from lean animals (veal naturally produces a leaner stock than does beef; chicken parts should have all excess fat removed before using). Once the stock has been made it should be strained, cooled down in an ice bath, and refrigerated overnight. While the stock is cooling the fat will rise to the top of the liquid and can be skimmed off with a spoon or ladle. After the stock has completely cooled in the refrigerator the fat will solidify on the top of the stock and can be easily removed. Returning the stock to the stove a second time to repeat the process will release even more of the fat from the stock.

Do not salt your stocks. Salt can be added to a recipe as needed as a better way of controlling the amount of salt in the final dish.

4

Liquid flavor enhancers

Alcoholic beverages provide another way to enhance the flavor of foods. Although most people think of them only as drinks, they are used by the professional chef to impart unique tastes to cooked food or pastry items. There are many different kinds of beverages that may be used in this way, with wines, beers and ales, brandy, and various liqueurs being among the most common. Within each of these categories are different types that give different flavors to a dish.

When concentrating on enhancing flavors in food, the chef cannot afford to overlook the versatility provided by using nature's liquid flavor enhancers. These liquids — wines, beers, brandies, and liqueurs — represent both a concentration of a single flavor and the intricate blending and harmonizing of a variety of flavors.

As old as recorded history is the history of wine and beer. How they were discovered may never be known. Although humans have enjoyed the spirit (alcohol) of these drinks for thousands of years, they have also had a value in cooking and baking. Likewise, brandies and liqueurs can give extraordinary distinction to otherwise simple or plain tastes. These liquids can impart character and excitement to the simplest of preparations.

Nutritional components

Not only do wines, beers, brandies, and liqueurs impart their excellent flavors to foods, but many may add to the nutritional worth of a finished product. Alcohol, by itself, does not add nutritionally to the human diet (and, in fact, is usually reduced or even eliminated through evaporation during cooking), but the beverages containing the alcohol can contribute to nutrition.

Some wines contain potassium, calcium, phosphorus, magnesium, and iron, whereas most others aid in the absorption of these minerals and zinc, when made a part of a meal. Wine consumption has also been associated with raising the level of high-density lipoproteins (HDLs — the "good" cholesterol) in the blood system. Moderate wine drinkers (one to two glasses per day) have less chance of suffering heart attacks or strokes associated with high levels of LDLs (low-density lipoproteins, the "bad" cholesterol) in the blood arteries than do nonwine drinkers.

Beers contain traces of protein or amino acids, fats, and some B vitamins, which remain in the bottle from the yeast used in fermentation. Liqueurs are, in many cases, flavored with the essences of herbs and spices, and were originally created as medicinal cures; their contribution to health can be argued but not totally denied.

Wines

All of the four wine classifications: table, sparkling, fortified, and aromatized wines can be used in cooking and baking. Each, naturally, imparts its own special quality and flavor.

Table wines (or still wines, as they are sometimes called) are varietal wines whose fermentation has completely ceased before the bottling process. They may be named with a particular variety of grape (cabernet, sauvignon, merlot, etc.), or they may consist of a blend of many types of grapes and be known simply as red, white, or rosé table wine.

Sparkling wines are those wines which go through a second fermentation process once bottled, thus trapping inside the carbon dioxide produced by the growing yeast, which in turn creates bubbles (the "sparkle") when the bottle is opened. Only sparkling wines produced in the French province of Champagne are allowed to carry the family nomenclature.

Fortified wines are wines which have brandy added to them before bottling to help raise the alcohol content of the wine. Familiar types of fortified wines are madeira and marsala.

Aromatized wines are wines, sometimes fortified and sometimes not, which have been flavored by herbs and/or spices. Vermouth is the most familiar of the aromatized wines.

It is important to use wines for cooking or baking that would be considered good for drinking as well. Quite often, chefs try to use inferior wines in the kitchen as a way to save money, never realizing that they are also saving on taste and quality. The opposite, however, is not necessarily true — using only the most expensive wines will not always produce a better end product.

Many young chefs make the mistake of substituting a similar wine for the specific wine called for by the recipe. In more than just a few restaurants, the kitchen staff is given the two- or three-day-old open bottle of wine from the bar, lest it go sour, to use in cooking. This practice naturally dictates the substitution of many types of wines so long as they are similar in color (red versus white) and in the degree of sweetness or dryness. But there are so many other discriminating differences between varietal wines, even between similar varietals produced in different regions or countries, that this practice leads to inconsistency in taste and quality. The right wines should be selected for the right dish.

France, Italy, Germany, Spain, Portugal, Australia, and the United States all produce excellent wines — from the very common table wines to the sophisticated varietal and sparkling wines. The only way to learn the proper use of these different wines is to taste them.

France

The French winemakers have worked hard and long to develop an excellent tradition. It is wise to spend a lot of time tasting the different, available French wines when choosing the right wine for the kitchen.

All of France's six main wine-producing regions — Bordeaux, Champagne, Burgundy, Alsace, Rhône, and Loire — offer a variety of excellent wines. Each region is further divided into distinct districts producing their own types and qualities of wine.

Bordeaux, for example, is subdivided into nine districts: Médoc, Graves, Saint Emilion, Pomerol, Sauternes, Premières Côtes de Bordeaux, Côtes de Bourg, Côtes de Blaye, and Entre-deux-Mers. Wines produced in each of these regions and subdistricts have distinct characters varied enough from one another to make the task of choosing the right wine very difficult.

Although complex, the task of choosing the right French wine can also be educational and fun. It may be best to start with the Bordeaux region, which is well-known for its red wines from Médoc and Saint Emilion, and with Burgundy for its world-famous whites, especially from the Chablis and Mâconnais districts.

To mellow the bitter taste of turnips or parsnips or to flavor a cool fruit and berry dessert, for example, a sweeter wine, such as one of the whites from Sauternes, would be appropriate. These wines are produced from overly ripe grapes that are almost to the point of being raisins. In these grapes, the juices have partially evaporated, leaving behind a very high concentration of sugars, increasing the glycerine and thus reducing the acids. The resulting wines will be fruitier and sweeter than most other varieties.

Champagnes, when used in cooking, give a light body to many sauces, especially berry and other fruit sauces served with duck, lamb, or pork. Although the effervescence is lost during cooking, the character of the excellent wines used in the making of champagne remains on the palate. When Dom Pérignon, the seventeenth-century Bénédictine monk, invented the bubbly wine, he insisted on using only the finest white wines for the base. The true champagne producers of today still insist on this excellent tradition.

Italy

An excursion through Italy's wine regions would be exciting and educational. Perhaps because of the great influence (and financial support) of religion, especially of Catholicism, on the production and distribution of wines, Italy can boast of having one of the finest collections of wines in the world.

Wines are produced almost everywhere in this country, from the Piedmont, one of the northernmost regions, to Sicily, the southern island that is the home of the marsala wine.

Some of the best red wines come from Barolo, a town in the northern Piedmont. The noble grape of this region is called the nebbiolo. Barbera and grignolino grapes are also important in the Piedmont and Lombardy regions for producing a wide range of reds. These wines are excellent cooking wines whose strength of character withstands the longer cooking methods.

The white grape trebbiano, also grown in the north, is the base grape for soave, one of Italy's most popular white wines. Soave is excellent for use in poultry dishes or seafood sauces and stews.

From Tuscany comes the very popular chianti and chianti classico. Although perhaps the most famous of the Italian wines in America, because of the familiar straw-wrapped bottles easily identifying chianti governato, its culinary attributes are few. This particular chianti is intended to be drunk while quite young and is sold in the popular straw *fiaschi* more for decoration than anything else. However, because of its youth, chianti governato cannot contribute a full-bodied character to sauces or stews. Many chefs believe, therefore, that chianti does not make a good cooking wine. The other varieties — chianti vecchio and chianti classico riserva — are excellent cooking wines. These wines, aged from two to three years, acquire a more developed character suitable for cooking and marinades. Chianti classico riserva is the perfect flavoring liquid for braising rabbit and quail and for shellfish ragoûts and sauces.

From Sicily come some very great wines used in kitchens around the globe. Although very destructive to human life, the volcano, Mount Etna, on the eastern end of the island, which has been semi-active over the centuries, has contributed a fertile volcanic ash to much of the island. This ash is a perfect grape vine fertilizer. The best wines are produced from grapes grown directly on the volcano's slopes and bear its name: Etna bianco, Etna rosso and Etna rossato.

Perhaps the most famous Sicilian wine is marsala, a fortified wine, which means brandy is added after the fermentation has ceased to raise the alcohol content. The volcanic soil in which this wine's grape is grown gives marsala an acid undertone that withstands the highest cooking temperatures. Marsala is not only popular for cooking, but also for drinking. The sweet marsala makes an excellent dessert wine; the dry marsala is most generally used for cooking.

Germany

Germany is also divided into several wine-growing regions. The three most famous are the Rheingau, Rheinhessen, and Rheinpfalz.

From Rheingau come some of the most famous wines in the whole world. Johannisberg, hallgarten, and rauenthal are but a few of the most popular. This region's wines have excellent body, flavor, and character and are among the longest-lived of any German wines. They are generally fruity in nature and can add great depth to many sauces, marinades, and desserts.

From the region of Rheinhessen come the most popular liebfraumilchs. Liebfraumilch is neither a district nor a vineyard, but is rather a blending of wines. Liebfraumilch is an excellent drinking wine that may be used as an apéritif (before dinner cocktail), with the meal, or as an after-dinner wine. Liebfraumilch's consistent flavor makes it a great cooking wine for soups, stews, and sauces.

Rheinpfalz is Germany's largest wine-producing region. Although much of this region's wine is consumed by Germans, its excellent white and red table wines make good cooking wines, when available in this country. Table wines are generally of less character than varietals; in Rheinpfalz, this is not the case.

Spain

Spain's southernmost wine region, Andalucía, is the home of the country's most prized vinicultural possession, sherry. The lands that produce the finest of these wines are situated between the Guadalquivir and the Guadalete rivers. Jerez de la Frontera is the primary shipping port for this fine beverage.

The sherry we know today is the product of soil, fruit, and the intricate solera system. Solera is a controlled blending system that takes 7 to 10 years to complete. It is begun by placing several casks of a particularly fine wine in a long line on the ground. This wine is not touched for a minimum of seven years. The following year, more casks are filled with new wine and placed above the first line of casks. In succeeding years, similar casks are placed on top of those from the previous years until the number of *criaderas* (reserves) matches the number of years decided upon by the particular house producing the sherry (houses may vary the number of years of the solera from 7 to 12). When the solera is completed, one-third of the wine in the bottom casks is drawn off to be bottled. This bottled wine is replaced by a similar quantity of wine from the casks stored directly above. In a similar fashion, wine from each of the higher rows is drawn to replace wine in the lower casks. The top row is then filled with new wine produced that year. The best sherries for cooking are the *finos,* which range from the very dry manzanilla, to the pale dry amontillado, which also has a slightly nutty flavor. The sweet sherry wines—oloroso, cream, and brown—may be used in dessert sauces and fillings.

Portugal

Of all the wines produced in Portugal, the fortified port is most prized in the culinary arena. Port is fortified before fermentation has completely ceased, which leaves some of the unused sugars behind. Port is, therefore, always a sweet wine. Port's significant character gives distinction to sauces and stews.

Port comes in three types: vintage, ruby, and tawny. Each of these wines is excellent for drinking and as flavoring liquids for cooking.

Vintage port is produced only during exceptional years when nature has cooperated fully with the wine growers. If rain, sun, and the soil work together, through the entire growing season, an exceptional wine full of character, bouquet, and flavor can be achieved. This usually occurs about every three to four years. Vintage ports need several years to fully mature in the bottle, and may be too costly for regular kitchen use. However, for the special occasion or feast, there is no substitute.

Ruby and tawny ports are aged in wooden casks, giving character to these otherwise young, fruity wines. They are usually blended wines, which ensures a consistency in style and quality similar to that achieved in the sherry solera system. Tawny ports, which are blended and well-wooded (aged), are generally more consistent and thus better for culinary use.

Another Portuguese wine, although produced on an island 535 miles south by southwest of Lisbon, is the very popular madeira, which takes its name from the island on which the grapes are grown.

The name of Madeira means the "wooded isle," and this place was found by Portuguese sailors on their way around Africa in search of the spice islands and India. Captain João Gonçalves of the Portuguese navy was given the task of settling the island and setting it up as a resting place for other ships. Finding the island to be completely covered by a very dense forest, and being short of manpower and time, he decided to burn the trees as a quicker means of clearing the land. However, it took nearly seven years for the fire to go out.

Captain Gonçalves was later rewarded for his deed. The volcanic island heaped upon by a thousand years of decaying organic matter was now completely covered by several feet of freshly consumed potash. Captain Gonçalves accidentally made Madeira one of the most fertile islands in the world. This combination of volcanic soil, organic debris, and potash was perfect for the cultivation of grapevines and, later, sugarcane. One of the oldest domesticated grape varieties, the malvasia candiae, was transplanted from Crete to this new, lush home. Before long, Portugal had a thriving, wine-producing colony.

When shipping madeira became a profitable business, it was accidentally discovered that the wine actually improved its flavor and body during long voyages. Especially if the ships passed through tropical waters, a noticeable difference came to the character of the wine, making it even more delightful to drink. Today, madeira is matured in *estufas,* hothouses lined with hot-water pipes. This system keeps the temperature of the room where the casks are stored between 95°F and 120°F, thus reproducing the effect of the heated casks in the hulls of ships.

Madeira outlives most other wines. It is said to be quite excellent even after 100 or more years. By law, vintage madeira is aged in casks for a minimum of 20 years. Madeiras are produced following the same solera principles used in Spain. This ensures consistency in quality and taste year after year. There are four types of madeira — sercial, verdelho, bual, and malmsey. Sercial is the driest and suitable in most culinary applications. Malmsey is the sweetest, almost liqueur-like in consistency and taste.

Other wine-producing countries

Excellent wines are produced today in many other countries. Austria, Greece, Hungary, Switzerland, Australia, Brazil, and the United States are all fine wine producers. Chefs should not halt their wine exploration before tasting a few examples from each of these countries.

Aromatized wines

As their names suggest, aromatized wines are those that have been made more "aromatic" by the infusion of herbs, spices, and other flavoring ingredients. Primarily used as apéritifs, some aromatized wines also make excellent cooking wines. Aromatized wines are almost always fortified with brandy.

Vermouth is perhaps the most popular aromatized wine used in the kitchen. It is made from some of the finest white wine grapes and is aromatized with between 20 to 50 different herbs, plants, roots, seeds, barks, flowers, and citrus-fruit peels. Using vermouth in the kitchen in place of white wine adds the flavor of a well-protected spice blend. Vermouth is produced both dry and sweet; each has different advantages.

Other aromatized wines that may have a place in the kitchen pantry are the French dubonnet, which is excellent for dessert sauces and currant pies; campari from Italy, which accents the most delicate of salad dressings or chutneys; and cynar, whose flavor comes from the artichoke and can add softness and elegance to a variety of cream sauces and vegetable dishes.

Other fruit wines

Grapes are not the only fruit whose juices are made into wine. Apples, pears, cherries, plums, and various berries are all capable of producing some very fine wines. These specialty wines do not contain the tannins and other acids of grape wines, and therefore need to be drunk while still very young. They are usually fortified with brandy made from a similar wine; for example, pear wine is fortified with pear brandy. Always sweet, these wines are excellent flavoring liquids for fruit sauces, soups, and desserts.

Beers and ales

Beers and ales are fermented beverages that use grains instead of fruit to feed the alcohol-producing yeast. Grains are complex carbohydrates that must be transformed into simple carbohydrates for the yeast to feed upon. Today, this is done by sprouting the grains. When the grains germinate, they produce an enzyme called *amylase,* which then converts the starches into the sugars maltose (malt) and dextrin. The germinated grains are then roasted in kilns to stop further growth of the sprouts. This also dictates the color and sweetness of the particular beer.

Beer is produced in varying degrees of lightness and body. Lager is the clearest and lightest. Lagers are effervescent, which is caused by an artificial carbonation before bottling. Most of the American beers are of the lager type. Stout, on the other hand, is a very dark beer that takes its color from the roasted malt and the addition of roasted barley to the brew. Stout is slightly bitter tasting, with no effervescence.

The history of beer is as unclear as that of wine. No one really knows who first discovered beer or perfected its brewing. There is evidence that the Egyptians brewed a beer made from corn, but little is known about the process, and no one can really say what the beer tasted like.

Beers and ales have been used in cooking and baking throughout Europe, but not as much as wine or brandy. Perhaps in the past this was because of beer's bitterness, or more likely, because most beers were home-brewed and lacked taste and color consistency. Beers also do not age as do wines, and therefore had to be drunk or used right away.

Beer production has become more scientific today, and its consistency in taste, body, and color can be guaranteed brew after brew. In fact, little change has occurred in their taste for over 100 years. Also, with new bottling techniques, beer can be stored for a longer time.

Some European chefs are fond of using the darker ales and stouts for cooking and baking. Several of the most flavorful roasts and stews can be made even more tasty with the addition of a good ale to the marinade or sauce. Sauerbraten, the German version of potted roast, can be accentuated with a bottle or two of dark, malty ale.

Beers are also excellent as part of the poaching liquid for highly seasoned meat sausages and blood puddings and for steaming strongly flavored vegetables such as cabbage, mustards, and kale.

In bread baking, beer not only contributes taste and color, but also aids in the dough's fermentation. In fact, no one knows for sure which came first, the discovery of raised bread or of fermented beer. More than likely, they were simultaneous.

Brandy

Brandy is a distilled beverage taken from a variety of host wines. Although the science of distillation dates back thousands of years, the art of commercial brandy making was not realized until the sixteenth century.

Brandy can be made from any of the fruit wines: grape, cherry, apple, pear, or even berry. Retaining some of the characteristic flavor of the base wine, brandy can also be a great flavoring liquid in cooking.

Because of its high alcohol content (from 80 to over 100 proof), brandy burns off very quickly, leaving behind its distinctive flavor without further poaching the cooked product.

Brandy can be added right to the sauté pan just before plating the food. Once the brandy has flamed (burned down), the sauce can be finished in seconds.

Liqueurs

An invention of the alchemists, liqueurs, distillations flavored with all kinds of herbs, seeds, roots, and other spices, were supposed to help prolong life beyond normal years. Many times, they were prescribed as medicinal cures and even love potions.

To help this "medicine go down," liqueurs were always sweetened with the addition of one or more types of sugar. Liqueurs contain anywhere from 2½% to 35% sugar by weight. Liqueurs, therefore, must be used quite sparingly in cooking.

Here is a list of some of the more widely used liqueurs and their flavoring agents:

Amaretto — almond flavor achieved through crushed apricot stones.

Anis or *Anisette* — aniseed; used in Italian cookies and candies.

Bénédictine — perhaps the oldest known liqueur, developed in the early sixteenth century, made from 27 different herbs with a cognac brandy base.

Coffee liqueur — based on the coffee bean; kahlua and tia maria are two types.

Crème de cacao — flavored from cacao and vanilla beans.

Crème de cassis — black currant-flavored liqueur.

Crème de menthe — white or green (with food color added); made primarily from peppermint.

Crème de noyaux — also almond-flavored, derived from crushed fruit stones.

Curaçao — flavored from the dried peel of green oranges; comes from the island of Curaçao.

Drambuie — made from old, Highland, malt Scotch whiskey and heather honey.

Galliano — Italian made, from flowers and herbs.

Gran marnier — orange curaçao liqueur with a cognac brandy base.

Kümmel — caraway-flavored liqueur; made in Germany.

Pear liqueur — made from fresh pears.

Peppermint schnapps — also a mint-flavored liqueur, usually with a higher proof than Crème de menthe.

Sambuca — a licorice, candy-flavored liqueur from the elderbush.

Sloe gin — although called a gin, it is a sweetened liqueur flavored from the sloe berry.

Triple sec — a white, orange-flavored liqueur.

5

Menu planning

Nutrition is not something that is likely to disappear from the consumer conscience, but instead it will become an even stronger influence on future consumer choices. Professional chefs play a crucial role in supplying nutritionally sound menu choices for their customers. When planning a menu, chefs now consider nutrition in addition to equipment availability, the versatile use of products, and modern trends. Cooking/preparation methods can be slightly modified to increase the nutritional worth of menu items without significantly changing their taste or presentation, and menu-planning strategies can be developed with customers' health in mind.

A great deal of work, thought, and time goes into the planning of a menu. More than just a collection of delicious-sounding food choices, a well-designed menu is the outline for the restaurant's whole concept. It sells the restaurant; it is the restaurant.

Many chefs are reluctant to change or adapt their menus to the many food fads that quickly come and go. Others may, at best, add a few "specials" to their regular menus to please their experimental customers, but are unwilling to make what they consider to be drastic changes. Although a few restaurant owners will take advantage of a specific fad to create a whole menu concept, they know the restaurant's life span will be brief. But is nutrition a fad?

Nutrition: fad or trend?

Food *fads* and food *trends* are two very distinct manifestations of consumer choices in restaurant and home cooking. Fads are exciting food choices, completely new or resurfaced food preferences that catch on for a while but then lose their popularity as quickly as they started. Trends, on the other hand, are evolutions in the philosophy of cooking that lead to changes in general eating habits. Trends may, in fact, have been influenced by several different fads, but are sure to continue after those fads have long subsided.

To clearly show the difference between fad and trend, the following is used as an example of a relatively new American consumer trend — the appreciation of American regional cuisines — born out of the success of different fads.

"California" cooking caught on throughout the country under the guise of "nouvelle cuisine," and made its way to the menus of the least and the best restaurants. The very sleek array of crisp vegetables and lean portions, which symbolized this new cuisine, made the cover of all the major food publications as testimony to its popularity.

A second regional cuisine, Cajun/Creole cooking, became faddish and captured the general public in a fiery display of Louisiana tastes and name products: crawfish pie, Cajun popcorn, blackened redfish, jambalaya, etc. Louisiana kitchens were opened in a variety of places, from New York to Moscow. Their distinct spice blends lined grocery store shelves in all 50 states, and everyone experimented with the new "blackened" technique.

"California" and Cajun/Creole became America's hot-spot cuisines for a time. They were new, exciting, and clearly different, but have already begun to lose their popularity. Yet, in their wake was born a new trend towards regional cuisines that continues to shape America's eating habits.

Some chefs believe that nutrition is merely a fad. It is a mistake to make this assumption.

Nutrition is neither a fad nor a trend, but a way to pursue the oldest dream of all: the human desire to live as long as possible. Throughout the ages, humans have sought any way possible, through science or magic, to increase their life spans. After thousands of years, the search for the fountain of youth finally includes the basics of good eating.

There will always be a place for the traditional foods that predate nutritional science —

the creams, the fats, etc., but more customers will more frequently choose the healthier foods simply because it will help them live longer, healthier lives.

Nutrition is a relatively new buzz word, yet mankind has long searched for the correct combination of foods to preserve health and, ultimately, life itself. Professional chefs who understand this may create for themselves an unquenchable market; the chefs who do so first will be considered pioneers.

The chef's role

Chefs have a specific role to play, when planning their restaurant menus, in guaranteeing the rights of their customers to be able to make nutritional choices. Although not every restaurant patron is counting calories or fighting high blood pressure, those who are should have the option of choosing a menu to meet their specific needs.

The chef has a dual role in the presentation of nutritional choices: first, in the construction of the menu through a variety of items, and second, in the design of the recipes and the training of the staff who will ultimately produce and serve them. Both roles can be guided by an understanding of basic nutritional guidelines and aided by simple culinary substitutions that can transform traditional recipes into formulas for good nutrition.

The menu

The word to use over and over again in menu planning, representing the whole concept of customer choice, is *variety*. Variety can be achieved in three ways: through the *style* of cooking, the cooking *methods,* and creating a particular taste.

Other than for specialty restaurants (e.g., Italian restaurants serving only Italian food) a well-planned menu is one that offers a variety of cooking styles for the educated and adventurous customer. Customers with varied backgrounds and experiences should feel comfortable coming to the restaurant over and over again. They will keep coming back as long as they can find menu items of distinction.

Consuming food is one way the adventurous consumer can experience foreign cultures through the tastes associated with their cuisines. It is also a way that chefs can offer nutritionally prepared foods, low in salt and saturated fat, without having to label the items with consumer health flags. Many of the ancient cuisines, through years of trial and error, now embody the same nutritional guidelines proposed in this text. These can be offered as part of the menu: The Oriental-style stir-fries, the Indian curries and vegetarian entrées, the Mediterranean pasta dishes with their olive oil and herb sauces, and even American Indian cuisine, with its legumes and wild rices, are just a few examples.

These excellent examples explain in part the survival of entire civilizations through the development of smart eating habits. Perhaps this development was mere coincidence, resulting from the use of fresh foods available in each region, as opposed to the twentieth-century compulsion toward processed foods. In any case, these natural cuisines survived through their use of basic, good nutrition.

Modern chefs have the added advantage of selecting menu items representing as many of these food styles as they want. These choices offer customers variety and excitement in their dining experiences.

The use of a variety of cooking methods is essential to the task of supplying good nutrition to customers without taking away from the pleasure of eating. Ideal nutritional cooking would use steaming or poaching as the primary methods, and offer simple fruits for dessert, but who would want to base his or her whole diet on these? Chefs must offer their customers a choice of menu items prepared in many different ways. This will allow them to create their own balanced meals while in the restaurant, and to balance menus with their other daily meals.

As many cooking methods as possible should be employed in each menu category: appetizers, soups, salads, entrées, and desserts. Perhaps not all of the methods can be used in each category, but variety is the key. Menus that have only fried appetizers or broiled and sautéed entrées become too restrictive for the average customer. Not everyone likes the thin, ''healthy'' consommés, broths, or vegetable soups; hearty, thick soups also have their place in a nutritional menu.

Even in desserts choices are possible. The word is balance, not elimination. Not all desserts need be on the heavy side; a good selection of sherbets, yogurt, sponge cakes, and fresh fruit pies should be an option for customers who still have room left for a little taste of fun.

To create an exciting menu for customers who come for a complete meal, and especially for repeat customers, who are always looking for different experiences, the chef should always consider *taste*. This one, simple way to create variety in the menu uses as many different flavors as possible in recipes.

Taste may be dictated by the herbs and spices in the dish, so the chef should avoid using the same herbs and spices as dominant flavors more than once on the same menu. Marinated basil chicken kabobs for an appetizer, basil vinaigrette for a salad, pesto for the fettuccine, and wild mushroom sauce with basil for the broiled flounder will be too much. The main ingredients — the chicken, lettuce, fettuccine, and flounder — are only a part of the taste sensations; taste is the collection of all the different flavors.

Tastes are also dictated by the other flavoring ingredients used, so the chef needs to be careful that everything does not end up tasting like olive oil, garlic, or bell peppers.

Another way to orchestrate variety is through the accompanying vegetables and starches. Many chefs tend to oversimplify the preparation of these accompaniments as though they were unimportant fillers. The most adventurous standbys become buttered carrots, cauliflower mornay, broccoli hollandaise, and rice pilaf, but these are so unimaginative that they take away from the full effect of the dining experience. With some creative planning, these accompaniments can become an integral part of the overall impressions of a well-executed meal. A few examples are sesame-seed carrots, cinnamon noodles, turnips with dried figs, or brown rice with dates and toasted almonds.

The recipe

Just as important as menu selection is the development of the individual recipes. Procedural and ingredient substitutions can be made that will ensure the product's quality and, at the same time, offer more nutritional choices.

The use of herbs, spices, and other natural flavoring ingredients as taste enhancers has already been discussed. In some cases where the amount of salts and saturated fats were reduced, the dish's flavors were increased through the addition of these other flavorful ingredients. In recipes where some of these ingredients were already included, it was simply a matter of adding more during the final cooking or marinating stages to ensure their dominant presence. Freshly chopped herbs or freshly ground spices stirred into a dish just before service give character to the overall flavors. A small amount of wine, liqueur, or brandy laced into a soup or sauce before plating can enliven flavors without overpowering the main ingredients.

Substituting for fats

Although butter and lard have been traditionally used in cooking and baking, new information regarding the use of vegetable oils makes substitutions, in most cases, a very simple process. Margarine has already been substituted for butter, and vegetable shortening for lard, but these hydrogenated fats have the same ill effects on health as the saturated ones. It is better to use one of the many liquid vegetable oils whenever possible.

Olive and sesame-seed oils are very ancient in origin, but many chefs shy away from using them because of their pronounced flavors. New techniques in oil extraction have given the chef a greater variety of vegetable oils to choose from.

The one obvious problem with using liquid oils instead of the hydrogenated ones is in their lower smoking points (the temperature at which the oil will burn and give off an unpleasant taste). For frying, a simple solution is to trim down the size of the foods and remove bones whenever possible so that they cook quicker at the lower, safe temperatures. When this is not possible, the items can be completed in a very hot oven, which will finish the cooking process and retain the desired crisp texture.

The lower smoking point also means the fat in the oil breaks down quicker and must be replaced sooner. This is a small expense that can easily be passed on to the customer.

For baking, vegetable oils are not as easily substituted in all cases. In rolled-in doughs and pastries, such as puff pastry, danish, and flaky pie crusts, the substitutions do not work. In cakes, muffins, and breads, oils work just as well as butter or shortening, with only a slightly lower volume. The difference in volume can sometimes be overcome with the addition of whipped egg whites before baking.

Although replacing butter with oil is nutritionally better, the lost buttery taste will need to be replaced with a taste from some other flavorful ingredients, such as pureed fruits or vegetables, vanilla, extracts, or liqueurs.

Marinating meats and poultry is another way of replacing the saturated animal fats with vegetable oils and increasing taste at the same time. The exterior fats can easily be trimmed, and fatty skins removed before cooking. These leaner meats, however, tend to become dry and lose their flavor. Marinades that consist of vegetable oils, flavoring liquids from wine to lemon juice, and herbs and spices allow the products to be cooked quickly under the higher temperature broilers, thus sealing in more of the meat juices. They also let flavors penetrate throughout the flesh because of the tenderizing effect of the marinades' acids.

Substituting meats

In some cases, it is possible to substitute one meat for another in a particular recipe and still have a quality product. Much like milk, which can be purchased in whole form and also in less fatty forms, and coffee, which can be purchased in regular and decaffeinated forms, so can some meat recipes allow substitutions of meats with lower fat concentrations and, at the same time, let customers eat their favorite meals.

Casseroles, stews, sausages, stuffings, and many meat sauces are good examples of recipes that can use meat substitutions. If complete substitution makes too great a change, then partial substitution is a possibility. (If you really do not like to drink skim milk, 2% milk is still better than whole milk.) The end results will be much lower in fats and cholesterol, but will still have great flavor and appearance.

Turkey is one of the best meats for substitutions because it seems to take well to most cooking procedures and taste combinations. For example, half the amount of ground beef or pork in a recipe can be replaced with ground turkey without a noticeable taste difference. Venison and other game meats, which are naturally more lean than most domesticated animals, also make excellent substitutes. Game meats may be more expensive, but customers who are concerned about their meat consumption will not hesitate to pay a higher menu price.

6

Nutritional guidelines

Nutrition has to do with the impact on our health of the food we eat. Various foods contain proteins, carbohydrates, fat, vitamins, minerals, and water. These nutrients are essential for building tissue, regulating bodily functions, and providing energy. The culinary professional and the home cook need to understand the basics — the major nutrients — in order to prepare balanced menus for guests and families.

The science of nutrition is still very young and much still needs to be learned. With all the claims and counterclaims regarding the amounts of fats, sweets, and vitamins and minerals needed for proper health, the professional, as well as the amateur, cook is understandably confused. It is simply best to say "everything in moderation and balance."

Protein

Proteins are those nutrients needed for building body tissue and rebuilding body cells. Most foods contain some protein. Those that contain the largest amounts are meat, poultry, fish, shellfish, eggs, dairy products, and legumes. Second to these are grains. Vegetables and fruits also contain small amounts of protein.

Choosing protein foods

The best protein foods to use are ones that are low in fat, salt, and sugar (skim milk, lean meat, fish, skinless chicken, and beans are good choices), as these help the consumer avoid cardiovascular disease, cancer, and obesity. (In addition, individuals who avoid obesity can help lessen the possibility of getting diabetes, gout, and arthritis.) In general, fresh protein foods are less salty than processed protein foods. Examples of protein foods that contain sugar are ice cream, custards, flavored yogurts, some sausages, cold cuts, and cured ham.

Examples of lean meat cuts are the shank, brisket, flank steak, and top round. Because they are lean, these cuts are also tougher than fatty ones. They can be tenderized before or during cooking by grinding, pounding, slow-cooking, braising, and marinating.

U.S. Dietary Goals for protein are 12% – 15% of one's daily calorie intake. Because it is known that each gram of protein has 4 calories, recommended intake can be easily calculated.

> *Example:* **Recommended daily protein intake, given an intake of 2500 calories per day.**

> 2500 calories/day
> $\times 15\%$ (recommended percentage of protein)
> 375 calories of protein recommended
> $\div 4$ calories per g of protein
> 93.75 g of protein recommended

TABLE 6-1.

Calories per Portion for Various Food Items

Food Type	Portion Size	Grams of Protein per Portion	$\left(\begin{array}{c}\times 4\ Calories\ per \\ Gram\ of\ Protein =\end{array}\right)$	Calories per Portion
Meat, poultry, fish, eggs	1 oz	7		28
Legumes	½ cup	7		
Milk (whole and skim)	8 oz	8		32
Bread	1 slice	2		8
Starchy food	½ cup	2		8
Vegetable	½ cup	2		8
Fruit	½ cup	0.5		2

See Table 6-1 for a listing of various food items and their calorie counts per portion. Table 6-2 lists a typical day's protein intake.

Another method of calculating minimum protein requirement is to use the formula $0.8 \times$ adult body weight in kilograms. The example on page 56 calculates this protein requirement for a person who weighs 150 lbs.

The method in the example on page 54 is based on the Recommended Dietary Allowance of the Food and Nutrition Board, National Academy of Sciences, National Research Council, and tends to yield a lower figure than the 15%-of-calories formula. One should not have less than this lower recommendation. Having in excess of the 15% would not be harmful to healthy persons, but eating too much protein would probably mean a lower carbohydrate intake, resulting in an unbalanced diet.

TABLE 6-2.

Sample Daily Protein Total

Food Eaten	Amount	Grams of Protein
Breakfast		
Eggs	2	14
Toast	2 slices	4
Margarine	2 tsp	0
Milk	8 oz	8
Cereal	½ cup	2
Orange juice	8 oz	1
Lunch		
Bread	2 slices	4
Tuna	2 oz	14
Mayonnaise	1 T	0
Medium peach	1	0.5
Cola beverage	8 oz	0
Dinner		
Sautéed chicken	4 oz	28
Rice	1 cup	4
Broccoli	½ cup	2
Watermelon	1 cup	1
Tea	1 cup	0
Sugar	1 tsp	0
Snack		
Milk	1 cup	8
		90.5 Total Grams Protein

Example: **Recommended daily protein intake for a 150-lb individual.**

150 lbs
÷2.2 kg/lb
68.1 kg body weight
×0.8
54.5 g of protein recommended

There are times when more protein is needed. Pregnancy and lactation require an additional 20 g and 30 g, respectively. Infants, children, and teenagers need more protein than adults to allow for growing bones and muscles.

For example, a baby needs 2.2 g of protein per kilogram of body weight in the first six months of life and 2 g of protein per kilogram of body weight for the second half of the first year. A baby will have tripled his or her weight by the first birthday.

Protein does not account for all a food's calories. Flesh foods, even lean meats, have fat. Fat can also be found in whole and partially skimmed milk. Carbohydrates are found in bread, vegetables, and fruits. All kinds of fat contain 9 calories per gram, carbohydrates contain 4 calories per gram.

Nuts and beans are plentiful sources of protein. Nuts, however, contain large amounts of fat. Beans have virtually no fat, but contain carbohydrates in amounts equal to those in starchy foods.

Sugars, jellies, syrups, honey, and sweet drinks have no protein. Neither do fats and oils. Alcoholic beverages do not contribute to protein intake.

Digestion and absorption

Protein foods are digested in the stomach and the small intestine. When food reaches the stomach, a hormone called *gastrin* stimulates the production of hydrochloric acid. The acid activates an enzyme called *pepsinogen;* the pepsinogen then converts into *pepsin,* which in turn breaks the protein down into smaller parts, called *polypeptides.*

The enzyme *rennin,* found naturally in the stomach, coagulates milk and begins to digest the milk protein *casein.* There is a question as to whether rennin exists in adults, but it is definitely the milk-digesting enzyme for young children. Rennin obtained from calves' stomachs is used in the cheese-making process to curdle milk. Another stomach enzyme, *gelatinase,* liquifies gelatin, an animal by-product.

Some of the still-intact proteins, some polypeptides, and a small amount of amino acids leave the stomach and enter the upper portion of the small intestine, the duodenum. Duodenal hormones stimulate the release of pancreatic hormones, which break down the proteins that were still intact. Other intestinal juice enzymes break down the polypeptides into amino acids, the final protein break-down. Magnesium, zinc, copper, and manganese are all essential for this enzyme activity. These minerals can be found in foods such as meats, grains, and vegetables.

The amino acids are then absorbed through the lining of the small intestine into the bloodstream. These acids then enter the portal vein and go into the liver and from the liver go to the tissues.

Amino acids: the building blocks

Amino acids are white, crystalline, sweet, and usually tasteless (they are sometimes bitter). They are the building blocks of protein. Most proteins are comprised of 12 to 20 amino acids locked together in one large molecule. Some proteins contain up to 280 amino acids.

The human body needs 20 amino acids for proper nutrition (Fig. 6-1). Twelve of these can be generated through the digestion of dietary nitrogen from various protein sources. The other eight cannot be made in the body and must be ingested directly from the appropriate food sources. These eight are called *essential amino acids*. The other twelve are known as *nonessential amino acids*. All eight essential amino acids must be present at the same time to be used for building tissue. For vegetarians, this means that grains, nuts, beans and seeds should be eaten during the same meal periods so they will combine through digestion to supply them.

All the essential amino acids are present in animal foods (such as pork, beef, lamb, veal, chicken, fish, eggs, and milk) — with the exception of gelatin, an animal food product. Plant foods, with the exception of soybeans, tofu, and soy milk, do not have a good balance of the essential amino acids. Almonds, brazil nuts, buckwheat, and wheat germ have a better balance of these acids than most plants.

Essential Amino Acids	_Nonessential Amino Acids_
Phenylalanine	Glycine
Methionine	Alanine
Leucine	Serine
Valine	Cystine
Lysine	Tyrosine
Isoleucine	Aspartic acid
Threonine	Glutamic acid
Tryptophan	Proline
	Hydroxyproline
	Citrulline
	Norleucine
	Hydroxyglutamic acid

Figure 6–1. The 20 amino acids needed for proper nutrition. (Source: The Importance of Proteins in Health and Disease, CIBA Pharmaceutical Company, Summit, NJ, circa 1964. Used with permission.)

Buckwheat has an amino acid composition that is nutritionally superior to that of other cereals. It is high in *lysine,* the limiting amino acid in wheat and rice. (A limiting amino acid is one which is provided in an unsufficient amount, thereby causing the food to be categorized as "less than complete." Adding the limiting amino acid to a deficient food will put the eight essential amino acids in a proportion that will foster rapid and optimal growth. If two foods having the same limiting amino acid are eaten together, the resulting complete protein value is less than that for either food alone.) Buckwheat grows in cool-weather areas and its flour is well-known as a pancake ingredient. It is even more delicious when used in the groat form (the hulled grain). Buckwheat comes in coarse, medium, and fine groats. When coated with egg or oils, the grains cook up separately. They are then cooked in water or stock and can be used in a variety of soups, casseroles, and stuffings. Uncoated buckwheat groats can be cooked into a soft cereal of the same consistency as oatmeal.

Nonessential amino acids are as important as the essential ones. They make up 40% of the tissue-building proteins and also supply nitrogen for the synthesis of body compounds such as enzymes, hormones, and antibodies.

All proteins contain the elements carbon, hydrogen, oxygen, and nitrogen. Carbohydrates and fats do not contain nitrogen. Nitrogen, the distinguishing element in protein, can be used to make nonessential amino acids. Some proteins contain sulfur or other minerals such as iron, iodine, and cobalt. The human body uses these mineral-rich proteins to make DNA, RNA, antibodies, enzymes, hemoglobin, and certain hormones (insulin, thyroxine, and adrenaline). Protein is also necessary for regulating the water balance.

"Less complete" proteins can be used to supply energy after the nitrogen is removed. The nitrogen can be excreted through the urine, or the body can use it for the production of nonessential amino acids. These less complete proteins can be combined with complete proteins or combined with other less complete proteins, which then supply the limiting amino acid. Less complete proteins that, when combined, form complete proteins are called *complementary proteins* (Fig. 6-2). For example, wheat contains very little of the amino acid lysine, whereas legumes have a lot of it. When eaten together, legumes "complement" the wheat. Legumes, on the other hand, do not have much of the amino acid methionine, which is found in generous quantities in wheat.

Evaluating protein nutrition

Two ways to evaluate the quality of protein in a particular food are PER (Protein Effectiveness Rating) and NPU (Net Protein Utilization). PER is the protein's ability to support growth and NPU rates protein according to its nitrogen content. The United States Department of Agriculture (USDA) evaluates the PER of food. Figure 6-3 lists several foods in decreasing order of PER.

Nitrogen balance and excess dietary protein

"Nitrogen balance" occurs when the nitrogen obtained from the daily food intake equals the nitrogen output in the urine. This is the ideal state of protein nutrition. If the body is not getting

Grains and Milk

Bread and Cheese
Rice and Milk (pudding)
Cereal and Milk
Cheese-Rice Casserole
Macaroni and Cheese
Manicotti
Blintzes
Bread Pudding
Tacos
Pizza

Grains and Legumes

Pita Bread and Falafel
Rice-Bean Casserole
Wheat-Soy Bread
Rice and Lentils
Corn-Soy Bread
Wheat Bread and Baked Beans
Rice and Peas
Corn Tortillas and Beans
Toast and Pea Soup
Bread and Legume Soup
Bread and Peanut Butter
Rice and Chick-peas
Bean Burritos
Peanut-Butter Cookies
Rice and Tofu
Rice and Black-Eyed Peas

Legumes and Milk

Bean Soup and Milk
Chick-peas and Cheese Sauce
Peanut-butter Soup made with milk

Seeds and Grains

Seeds and Bread
Sesame Seeds and Rice
Sesame Bread Sticks
Baklava

Seeds and Legumes

Sesame (Hummus) and Chick-peas
Sesame Seeds in Bean Casserole

Seeds and Nuts

Sunflower Seeds and Nuts

Nuts and Grains

Granola
Baklava

Fig. 6–2. *Some common complementary proteins.*

enough protein, then muscle tissue is broken down to supply the nitrogen the body needs. When the body uses its own tissue because of a lack of adequate protein intake, the result is "negative nitrogen balance." More nitrogen will be excreted in the urine than is taken in.

On the other hand, if more nitrogen is retained than is excreted, the term used is "positive nitrogen balance." Positive nitrogen balance can occur during growth, pregnancy, lactation, and the healing of wounds and burns. These conditions require extra dietary protein so that nitrogen balance can be sustained.

Protein-Containing Foods

Egg (whole)
Milk (whole, human)
Milk (whole, cow)
Egg albumin
Corn germ (defatted)
Liver (animal)
Meat (beef)
Fish (muscle)
Wheat germ
Soybean meal (low-fat)
Rice (whole)
Casein
Wheat (whole)
Potatoes (white, raw)
Wheat (gluten)
Oats (whole)
Barley
Yeast (dried brewer's)
Cottonseed meal
Corn (whole)
Rye (whole)
Buckwheat flour
Peanut flour
Peas and beans (dried)

Fig. 6 – 3. A list of protein-containing foods, in decreasing order of Protein Effectiveness Rating. (Source: **The Importance of Proteins in Health and Disease,** *CIBA Pharmaceutical Company, Summit, NJ, circa 1964. Used with permission.)*

If the body takes in too much protein on a regular basis, there is a good possibility of dehydration. During the digestive process, water is required to split amino acids that are joined together. This is called hydrolysis. If protein intake increases and water intake remains the same, dehydration may occur. Fad diets promoting excessive amounts of protein, therefore, are not recommended.

Athletes may consume extra protein, believing that it is needed for strengthening or building muscles. Muscle is about 75% water and only about 25% protein. Consequently if a weight lifter, for example, were trying to increase his muscles by 4.4 lb a month, he would need only 1 extra ounce of protein a day. If the weight lifter eats more protein than is necessary for muscle growth, it is wasted. The body will simply turn the protein into carbohydrates by removing the nitrogen. The nitrogen is excreted in the urine, and the carbohydrates would be used for energy. Natural carbohydrates would have been a more efficient use for energy in the first place.

Insufficient dietary protein

Protein deficiency disease is not often seen in this part of the world. The symptoms of a mild protein deficiency include lackluster hair and nails. More severe protein deficiency leads to thin, weakened, and dyspigmented hair. The parotid glands, located below and in front of each ear, become enlarged. Moderate protein deficiency may also cause the liver to become enlarged.

Kwashiorkor is the protein deficiency disease usually encountered in underdeveloped parts of Africa where the diet consists primarily of plant proteins. It is characterized by retarded growth, edema, peeling skin, anemia, and susceptibility to infection. The mortality rate is very high. Skim milk powder can be used to provide protein and alleviate the deficiency. To help reduce the incidence of the disease in these populations, farming of soybeans and education about the combining of plant proteins to create the eight essential amino acids is necessary.

Protein cookery

Eggs, milk, and flesh foods — the major sources of protein — need to be properly cooked. A general rule for cooking protein is to use low to moderate heat. Too high heat will make eggs rubbery, milk curdle, and meat tough.

High heat draws water out of the protein and leaves a dry, tough product. Custard cooked at a high temperature will weep, a classical example of overheated protein. Meats cooked at high heat will not only be tough but will also lose a great deal of volume. Their excreted juices collect in the bottom of the pan and evaporate.

Tender meat cuts such as the tenderloin, rib roast, and sirloin contain a high amount of collagen. Collagen and elastin are the two types of connective tissues in muscles. Collagen takes on water (hydrolizes) when cooked and changes to gelatin, which has a tenderizing effect on meat. Elastin does not react with water and must be ground or chopped to soften. Meat in which the collagen dominates can be cooked at higher temperatures, but only for a brief time such as in broiling or grilling.

Carbohydrates

Carbohydrates are the nutrients needed to supply the body with energy; they are the body's fuel. Carbohydrates consist of starches, sugars, and fiber. (Table 6-3 lists some common food items and their carbohydrate content.)

Starches and sugars are the body's main energy source and are well-absorbed. Fiber is a carbohydrate that is not digested and, therefore, cannot be absorbed. Cows and sheep can digest fiber; humans simply excrete it.

TABLE 6-3.

Carbohydrate Content of Some Common Food Items

Food/portion	Starch	Sugar	Fiber
Milk (1 cup)	—	12 g (lactose)	—
Meat, poultry, and fish	—	—	—
Eggs	—	—	—
Seeds (½ cup)	30 g	Trace	3 g
Beans (½ cup)	20 g	Trace	3–6 g
Nuts (¼ cup)	20 g	Trace	4–5 g
Fruits (½ cup)	—	10 g (fructose) and other sugars	1.5–3 g
Vegetables (½ cup)	An average of 5 g	Some vegetables have small amounts.	Some
Bread (1 slice) and cooked grains (½ cup)	15 g	Trace	Whole grains are the better source than 1–3 g processed flour products.
Sugar (1 tsp)	—	5 g (sucrose)	—
Fat	—	—	—

Starches and sugars

Examples of starches are foods made from grains, such as bread, pasta, and cereal, as well as beans and potatoes. Examples of sugar-containing foods are milk, fruit, juices, honey, and, of course, products made with sugar (beet sugar, corn syrup, and/or sugarcane) such as candy, cakes, and sweet chocolate.

Over half of the daily calorie intake should come from carbohydrates. If the proper amount of carbohydrates is lacking in the diet, the liver will convert fatty acids and amino acids to carbohydrates to supply energy. However, if less than 15% of a person's total daily calories comes from carbohydrate foods, the brain will not be supplied with nourishment quickly enough. Eating a high-protein diet that is low in carbohydrates often leads to a headache, dizziness, and fatigue.

All carbohydrates must be broken down to single glucose units before the body can use them for energy. Starches, called polysaccharides, have many glucose units that must be broken apart. Sugars are simpler units and can easily be broken down.

Starches come in two different forms: branched (*amylopectin*) and unbranched (*amylose*). Starch digestion begins in the mouth with an enzyme called *salivary amylase*, or *ptyalin*. This process hydrolyzes cooked starch into the sugar *maltose* (raw starch, such as uncooked macaroni, cannot be digested). Food does not remain in the mouth long enough for much digestion to take place. The salivary amylase that mixes with the food continues to work in the stomach so that as much as 50% of the starch can be broken down. When the food lowers the acidity of the stomach, no more starch digestion can take place there.

Starch digestion continues when the chyme, the liquefied food, enters the duodenum. There, an enzyme called *pancreatic amylase,* secreted from the pancreas, breaks the un-branched starches into maltose, a disaccharide (a two-unit sugar). Branched starches, which can contain up to 2000 units of glucose, are broken down into dextrins, which have six units of glucose each. The dextrins are then further broken down into disaccharides, which are then finally broken down into monosaccharides, or simple sugars — the smallest carbohydrate unit. There are specific enzymes for each disaccharide, as illustrated in Figure 6-4. The three simple sugars pass through the villi of the small intestine (the intestinal structure through which nutrients enter the blood).

Enzyme deficiency (lactose intolerance) Sugars can only be digested when the proper disaccharide enzyme is present. Diseases that damage the intestine's lining, such as celiac disease, are associated with enzyme deficiency. Aging is also accompanied by a decrease in enzyme abundance.

The disaccharide *lactose,* found in milk, may cause problems such as bloating, cramps, gas, and diarrhea in some individuals. People who live in parts of the world where milk is not a safe food or where it is not available show a diminished amount of the lactose enzyme *lactase.* Lactose intolerance then becomes a genetic condition and passes to future generations. Much of the world's population is lactose intolerant.

Lactose intolerance can easily be verified by a hydrogen breath test. Milk is given to the patient and the breath is then tested for hydrogen; its presence (not usually found in the breath) indicates lactose intolerance. The flatulence (gas), nausea, bloating, diarrhea, and cramps are partly due to the osmotic activity (water entering the intestine to dilute the sugar) and partly due to bacterial fermentation. Intestinal bacteria form lactic acid, fatty acids, and hydrogen gas. The fatty acids are absorbed by the intestine and are an energy source. When the lactose concentration of the small intestine exceeds the bacterias' ability to digest it, osmotic pressure results in increased motility, pain, and diarrhea.

Disaccharide		*Enzyme*		*Monosaccharide*
Maltose	+	Maltase	→	Glucose and Glucose
Sucrose	+	Sucrase	→	Glucose and Fructose
Lactose	+	Lactase	→	Glucose and Galactose

Fig. 6 – 4. Disaccharides and their corresponding enzymes and monosaccharide products.

Most lactose-intolerant persons do not develop symptoms before ingesting the amount of lactose in two glasses of milk, about 24 g. The lactose-intolerance test, when it is given, uses the amount of lactose in about a quart. Lactose is mostly found in the whey (the liquid part of the milk); therefore, hard cheeses made from the curds have little lactose. Cream, ice cream, and milk chocolate contain large amounts of lactose. Whole milk is better tolerated than skim milk, and milk causes less problems if it is taken with a meal. Yogurt is well-tolerated if it has active cultures; freezing, however, destroys this tolerance for lactose-intolerant persons, as it destroys the *lactobacillus* bacteria, which would otherwise ferment the lactose to lactic acid. The culture used in acidophilus milk also does not help those with lactose intolerance, as it does not grow in the milk but rather is added after having been grown in a medium, and thus does not ferment the lactose to lactic acid.

The lactose enzyme lactase, in the form of a liquid or a pill, can be added to milk or ingested along with it. Although calcium absorption is not influenced by lactose intolerance, milk products are usually avoided by those who develop symptoms. Calcium-rich foods other than milk include collard greens, turnip greens, kale, small fish with bones (sardines, for example), salmon, beans (particularly soybeans), and tofu.

Absorption and storage Glucose (sometimes called dextrose) travels directly from the blood to the tissues to be metabolized into energy. The hormone insulin is needed to clear glucose from the blood. Fructose and galactose are converted to glucose in the liver. The liver can also make an emergency supply of starch called *glycogen*. One-third of this glycogen is stored in the liver and the other two-thirds are stored in the muscles to give the body a three- to four-hour emergency energy supply.

Athletes engaging in endurance sports know the importance of carbohydrate foods. It is also possible to manipulate the diet to increase the glycogen content of athletes' muscles. Research shows that stripping the muscles of glycogen allows them to be replenished with an increased amount. There are various methods to glycogen load. One two-phase method is as follows:

Phase I	Phase II
1. Exercise heavily.	1. Rest from exercise.
2. Eat only 100 g of carbohydrates a day.	2. Eat large amounts of carbohydrates.

Each phase is three days long, and the total number of calories consumed in each phase should be equal.

A sample daily diet containing approximately 4000 calories might contain as much as 16 servings of starchy food (8 cups) during the loading phase, whereas the stripping phase would have as much as 18 oz of animal protein and 12 T of fat. Both phases would have moderate servings of fruits and vegetables and adequate liquids. It is easy to see why this diet, possibly high in cholesterol and saturated fat, is subject to criticism. Several precautions must be taken if the diet is used at all. The stripping phase should have at least 100 g of carbohydrates to prevent hypoglycemic symptoms. The loading phase should not contain candy and sweet sodas, which may cause stomach bloating.

There is controversy concerning the merits of glycogen loading for athletes who are better able than most of us to turn fatty acids into glucose. It must be remembered, also, that glycogen will hold water, and this reserve in the muscle will cause a tight, stiff feeling. A small advantage might be having water on hand, which may be needed by the athlete.

Sweets An overload of simple sugar in the gastrointestinal tract will also cause bloating and diarrhea. This is due to excessive water, which will be drawn into the intestines to decrease the concentration of sugar. Sugar (which is the disaccharide *sucrose*) and honey both break down into the simple sugars glucose and fructose. Therefore, excessive amounts of these sweets should not be taken before participating in sports events.

An example of a weight-reduction diet that resulted in deaths from osmotic diarrhea was one that promoted fruit as the main food. The major nutrient in fruit is the carbohydrate fructose — a simple sugar. Although fruit contains vitamins, minerals, and valuable fiber, it should be eaten in moderation, not as the sole food source in the diet. Refined sugar is a source of energy, but it has no other nutritional advantage. It is without vitamins and minerals and contributes to tooth decay, a major health problem in children.

Fiber characteristics and health benefits

Fiber can be divided into different types: *lignin, cellulose, hemicellulose, gums,* and *mucilage.*

Lignin comes from the woody part of plants. Although classified as fiber, lignin is described by some as a noncarbohydrate with no known role in human nutrition. There are, however, sources that claim that it has use as a digestive regulator and protects against diarrhea. On the other hand, cellulose, found in the cell wall, and hemicellulose, found in both the cell wall and cell contents, bind water and thereby increase stool bulk and decrease its transit time. They have laxative characteristics. Frequent evacuation of waste from the colon may help in preventing colon cancer. Wheat bran and corn bran contain considerable amounts of hemicellulose, but less than psyllium. Psyllium seed fiber is the active ingredient in the drug store product Metamucil.

The gums, mucilages, and pectins are water-soluble fibers, which means that they dissolve in water after being extracted from the plant. The gums and pectins increase fecal transit time but do not increase stool bulk. They bind water in food but not in the gastrointestinal tract. They also may play a role in reducing the risks of colon cancer by binding carcinogens.

Pectins are found in many plants, and are usually extracted from citrus products for commercial use as a thickening agent. Natural sources of pectin include orange pulp, sweet potatoes, apples, and other fruits and vegetables. The chemistry of pectin is very complex. Purified pectin and guar gum develop a gummy, glue-like material when added to water. Purified pectin is not palatable and causes nausea if taken in generous amounts. Commercial pectin is usually extracted from oranges and used as a thickener in products such as yogurt, jellies, and fruit pies. Oat gum is extracted from oat bran, and guar gum is a storage polysaccharide extracted from the Indian cluster bean.

Locust bean gum Another gum is locust bean gum. Locust bean gum comes from the endosperm of the locust bean, also called carob. It is not from the same part of the plant from which the chocolate substitute, carob, is obtained. (That comes from the husk.) Carob is, however, high in pectin and in lignin. It comes from trees grown in the Middle East, Spain, Morocco, Greece, and Cyprus, as well as in southern regions of the United States. It takes 15 years before the tree bears the carob fruit, which is a glossy, brown pod 4 to 12 inches in length and 1 to 2 inches wide, with numerous hard seeds and a sticky, sweet fruit.

In research studies, locust bean gum has been reported to decrease LDL and VLDL cholesterol by binding bile acids, but it has no effect on glucose. In large amounts, it causes temporary flatulence and increased stool bulk. In ancient times it was used as a laxative. The other gums do not seem to have this water-holding capacity. Locust bean gum is used as a food additive and helps the texture of commercial products by making them thicker. An example is ice cream, which may have gum agents added.

Soluble fiber The oat bran advertised as water-soluble fiber is not the only food with this value. Oat bran is better accepted in the diet because it can be incorporated into tasty baked goods. Beans also have water-soluble fiber. If eaten in quantity, beans create flatulence and belching in most people. Rice bran has half the soluble fiber of oat bran and can be found in the form of cakes and cereals. Corn and barley also contain soluble dietary fiber.

Cholesterol-lowering properties The pectins, gums, and mucilages carry away some of the bile salts and some fatty acids. Bile salts contain cholesterol and are recycled back to the liver. Removal of cholesterol by fiber obviously can aid in controlling cholesterol levels. (See the section on cholesterol later in this chapter.)

Another decrease in cholesterol is attributed to the water-soluble fiber in oats and beans because they lower high-density lipoproteins (HDLs) and low-density lipoproteins (LDLs) in a favorable proportion. Pectin, guar gum, and oat gum have these unique, cholesterol-lowering properties.

Neither cellulose nor hemicellulose have significant cholesterol-lowering effects. It is the high viscosity of the gums which is responsible for lowering cholesterol in the blood (the hypocholesterolemic action). Pectin and guar gum are five times less effective than the medicine cholestyramine in binding bile salts.

Blood sugar control There have been studies that possibly link fiber to the control of blood sugar in diabetes. A highly processed diet is rapidly absorbed in the upper small intestine, creating a rapid rise in blood sugar. The presence of fiber in the diet delays sugar absorption. All types of fiber impede the outward passage of sugar from the intestine, but the most effective are the viscous fibers guar and traguncanth.

Pectin and methylcellulose (a gummy product resulting from the introduction of the methyl group into cellulose) are also viscous, but in research studies, the use of a special crisp bread made with guar provided the best results. In tests done with natural foods, beans were found to lower blood sugar better than breads and grain products. Diabetics on a diet of high-fiber foods such as whole-grain cereals, vegetables, and legumes are able to reduce their intake of insulin. Whole grains are not processed to remove the fiber that is in the bran, whereas white flour has most of the fiber removed.

Diverticulosis There is definitely evidence that fiber helps prevent diverticulosis, a condition in which pockets are formed in the colon. These diverticuli, little herniations, may become inflamed and can rupture. Fiber increases the stool volume, which expands the colon; the filled, expanded colon is better able to withstand pressure from outside the colon, which can be the cause of the diverticuli.

Weight control No calories are retained from fiber. Therefore, many weight-control schemes have advocated fiber bulk, which is filling and has no calories. As research goes, there are pros and cons as to whether fiber-filled menus increase satiety and result in weight loss.

Fiber is found in fruits, vegetables, nuts, beans, and whole grains. Dates, figs, prunes, and raisins are very high-fiber foods, but have many calories due to their high-sugar content. Melons and berries also have a high-fiber content, but have less sugar. Beans have a lot of fiber, but also are high in calories because of their large starch content. Nuts have a lot of calories because of their oil content. The lowest-calorie fiber foods are lettuce, celery, cucumbers, mushrooms, zucchini, string beans, and other watery vegetables.

Phytates A much-discussed disadvantage of fiber is the *phytates*. Phytates in fiber are necessary for the synthesis of the cell wall starch during the plant's germination. In humans, the phytates bind minerals (such as iron and zinc), calcium, and copper. In countries where the diet is marginal for adequate nutrition, the phytates are a problem, but in healthy diets, mineral absorption is more dependent on the total amount of minerals in the meal than on the presence of phytic acid. Phytates are found in whole-grain breads and cereals. The problem is easily solved in whole-grain breads by the addition of yeast, which inactivates the phytates. In any event, there is evidence that the body adapts to phytates in a short period of time. There is no phytate problem with sprouted grains.

Animal fiber For all practical purposes, animal products do not contain fiber. Meat, poultry, fish, eggs, and milk products are generally considered fiber-free foods. Of some interest, however, are indigestible polysaccharides of animal origin called chitin and chitosan; these are found in the skeletons of insects and aged beef as well as in tempeh and shellfish, and chitosan can be synthetically prepared. These viscous substances can be used as thickeners and stabilizers in processed food.

Best choices The best carbohydrate choices, those that should make up the bulk of the carbohydrates in our diet, are whole grains and vegetables. Choosing whole grains can raise the fiber intake to the 25 to 40 g per day recommended by the American Cancer Institute. The B vitamins found in whole grains are necessary for the chemical processes that turn carbohydrates into energy. Enrichment puts back only vitamins B_1, B_2 and B_3. Enrichment does not put back vitamin B_6 and pantothenic acid, another B vitamin. Milk should be taken in

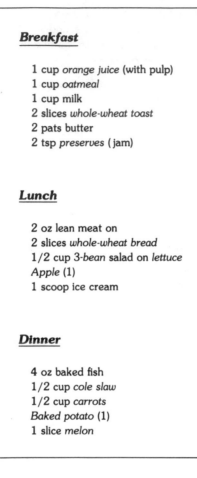

Breakfast

    1 cup *orange juice* (with pulp)
    1 cup *oatmeal*
    1 cup milk
    2 slices *whole-wheat toast*
    2 pats butter
    2 tsp *preserves* (jam)

Lunch

    2 oz lean meat on
    2 slices *whole-wheat bread*
    1/2 cup *3-bean* salad on *lettuce*
    Apple (1)
    1 scoop ice cream

Dinner

    4 oz baked fish
    1/2 cup *cole slaw*
    1/2 cup *carrots*
    Baked potato (1)
    1 slice *melon*

Fig. 6–5. Sample high-fiber diet.

amounts appropriate for age. Fruits should be eaten in moderation. Figure 6-5 shows a typical day's menu in a high-fiber diet.

Fats and oils

There is great emphasis today on the quality and quantity of fat in the diet. However, there is no question that fat plays a very important role in regular bodily functions. Fats are needed for cushioning the body's organs, insulating against the cold, and transporting the fat-soluble vitamins, and as a source of stored energy. Fats also aid in the satiety levels of our meals because they are digested slowly thus giving a sense of fullness for a longer period of time.

    Fats consist of *glycerol,* transparent syropy liquid formed by hydrolysis of fat, and *fatty acid chains* of various lengths. Fatty acid can be saturated, monounsaturated, or polyunsaturated. The degree of saturation has to do with the number of double bonds in the carbon chain. The following is an example of a carbon chain with two double bonds:

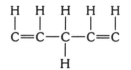

Saturated fatty acids have no double bonds, monounsaturated fatty acids have one double bond, and polyunsaturated fatty acids have more than one double bond. Polyunsaturated fat is essential for humans. It is needed for prostaglandins, healthy skin, normal liver function, membrane fluidity, and eicosanoid synthesis for immune function. Most of the fat in our diet consists of *triglyceride*, a glycerol attached to three fatty acid chains that do not have to have the same saturation.

The fatty foods that we eat are made up of a combination of saturated, monounsaturated, and polyunsaturated fatty acids. The particular fatty acids that predominate in a food are important because certain fatty acids are implicated as contributory agents in cardiovascular disease.

Cholesterol

Cholesterol is one of the substances found in the plaque that produces arteriosclerosis, hardening and thickening of the arterial walls. Cholesterol is a sterol made by our liver. Much more is made by the liver than the body gets from food. Food sources high in cholesterol are brains, eggs, shrimp, fatty meats, fish roe, sardines, and products that contain milk such as butter, cheese, and ice cream.

Although much is said about the health risks associated with high cholesterol counts, cholesterol has many positive functions, too. It is necessary for hormone production, for completing the active form of vitamin D, and for making bile. It is found in human milk, demonstrating its importance for infant growth.

Some individuals can eat liberally from those foods that have a high level of cholesterol and not have any health problems; others may have problems. It is advisable to have a blood test to evaluate the cholesterol level.

The type of cholesterol that health professionals are concerned about is found in LDLs. LDLs are a byproduct of VLDLs (very-low-density lipoproteins), which are made in the liver. The liver makes VLDLs from fatty acids that come from the food that was eaten and digested. The VLDL from the liver enters the blood and is broken down into IDLs (intermediary density lipoproteins) and then into LDLs (low density lipoproteins). LDLS are 50% cholesterol and are associated with coronary heart disease. It seems that less LDLs result when the diet is high in polyunsaturated fat. Monounsaturated fat also reduces LDL levels.

Palmitic fatty acid found in large amounts in palm kernel oil and in coconut oil is a very highly saturated fat that raises the LDLs. Research also has found that high LDL levels are caused by genetically produced faulty proteins that carry LDL in the blood. It is prudent to cut back on palmitic fatty acid. The food industry is beginning to respond by replacing the coconut and palm oil in processed foods and cereals with more desirable fats. Palm kernel oil is much more saturated than palm oil. It is similar in composition to human milk fat and in studies does not raise cholesterol levels.

Another saturated fatty acid, stearic acid, found in meat and chocolate, does not appear to raise LDL levels. This is not the only fatty acid in meat or chocolate. Chocolate contains from 15% to 35% cocoa butter as fat. No food has just one type of fatty acid. Stearic acid comprises about one-third of the saturated fatty acids in beef, pork, and poultry, 34% of the fatty acids in cocoa butter, and about one-fifth of those present in fish.

The liver also makes HDLs (high-density lipoproteins), some are made in the intestines also. HDLs act as receptor cells for clearing cholesterol from the blood. HDLs cycle the cholesterol from LDLs back to the liver. HDLs are important in the prevention of cardiovascular disease. Persons at risk for coronary heart disease have inadequate amounts of HDLs. Aerobic exercise such as running, biking, dancing, swimming, and walking will increase levels of HDLs.

Omega 6 and omega 3 fatty acids

It has been discovered that *omega 6 polyunsaturated fatty acids (linoleic acids)* lower HDL levels as well as LDL levels. Earlier programs promoting ingestion of large amounts of oils with linoleic fatty acid uncovered other problems, such as weight gain and gall bladder problems. Tumor growth attributed to this fatty acid have been found in animal studies.

A diet high in grains is high in omega 6 fatty acid. Grain-fattened animals have much higher levels of saturated fat compared to the much leaner animals eaten years ago, when animals were mainly fed by grazing.

Monounsaturated fat, on the other hand, lowers LDL, but not HDL levels. The main monounsaturated fatty acid is *oleic acid,* which is found in all fats. The body itself produces oleic from acetic acid. Animal fats vary in oleic content from 20% to 40%. Vegetable fats range from 12% to 75% oleic. The richest source of oleic acid is olive oil, followed by canola oil, and then peanut oil. No health problems have yet been associated with this fatty acid. Many studies have been done on olive oil and it has been recommended as a replacement for corn oil in the effort to reduce LDL cholesterol. Canola oil is also being promoted as a good choice, particularly because it has a mild odor and flavor. No studies have been publicized to confirm or refute any possible benefits from peanut oil.

Another seemingly beneficial fatty acid is found in fish oil. It is an omega 3 fatty acid called *eicosapentaenoic acid.* Epidemiological evidence shows that Eskimos, who eat a generous amount of salmon, do not have heart disease. The omega 3 fatty acids in fatty fish may prevent the development of coronary heart disease by competing with omega 6 polyunsaturated fatty acids (linoleic and arachidonic, an essential fat produced in the body from linoleic) in the cell membrane and reducing the conversion of omega 6 fatty acids to thromboxane, a regulator of cellular function. The net result is to decrease platelet aggregation, which may cause blood clotting, and increase dilation of the blood vessels. Both are helpful in preventing arterial disease.

It may be good to eat fish such as salmon, mackerel, herring, albacore tuna, lake trout, bluefish, Atlantic halibut, sardines, and anchovies. Continued research is needed. For the present, it is best not to take supplements of fish oil in the form of liquids and tablets. One study found that noninsulin-dependent diabetics developed impaired insulin secretion and increased glucose output after one month of taking 18 g per day of fish oil concentrate. Another problem is the risk of cancer associated with fatty fish, which pick up more pollutants from the waters in which they live than leaner fish. (Cautions on contaminated fish are issued by state health departments.)

Plant sources of omega 3 There is a plant source for omega 3 fatty acid, alpha linolenic. Omega 3 fatty acid converts in the body to eicosapentaenoic acid, which also converts into docosahexaenoic acid, which is needed for the central nervous system. Walnuts are a plentiful source of linolenic fatty acid. Four teaspoons of chopped walnuts or $1\frac{1}{4}$ tsp of walnut oil gives the equivalent of 300 mg of omega 3 fatty acid. Walnuts do, however, have omega 6 fatty acids. Canola oil, which is made from rapeseed, a relative of the mustard family grown in Canada and the northwestern United States, with similar large yellow flowers and small round black oil-rich seeds, has 60% oleic, 24% linoleic, and 10% linolenic fatty acids. The predominance of monounsaturated fat and the benefit of linolenic acids make canola oil a good choice. In the past, rapeseed oil was banned by the Federal Department of Agriculture (FDA) because it contained erucic acid, which in studies was found to cause cardiac lesions in animals. Rapeseed oil at that time contained 30% to 60% of its fatty acids as erucic acid. Today, erucic acid makes up only 2%.

Soybean oil also has linolenic fatty acid, in addition to generous amounts of linoleic. Because linolenic fatty acid has three double bonds, it can become rancid. Oxygen reacts with the double bonds in unsaturated fatty acids to form peroxides, which break down into ketones and aldehydes and cause objectionable tastes and odors. Heat and light accelerate this process. The food production industry partially hydrogenates soybean oil when it is processed (see the following section). Such fats stand up better for restaurant cooking and frying. Because hydrogenation removes most of the linolenic acid from soybean oil, the nutritional benefits of the linolenic acid are lost in shortenings and margarines made from this oil. An ounce of cooked soybean sprouts gives a generous amount of linolenic fatty acid and avoids the hydrogenation issue.

Hydrogenation

Unsaturated fat can be hardened and thereby partially saturated through a manufacturing process called *hydrogenation*. An example is margarine, which is partially hydrogenated to allow this vegetable oil to gain the spreading consistency of butter. Another example is shortening. Changing a liquid oil into a semisolid gives the product a higher melting point and better keeping qualities.

The hydrogenation issue presents some concern. The negative point of view, and it is a minority one, fears that *trans*-isomers, which are formed during hydrogenation, do not act in the same manner as normal fatty acids, which occur in the *cis* form. (If the hydrogen atoms are on the same side of the carbon chain at the double bond, the arrangement is called *cis,* and if the hydrogen atoms are on opposite sides of the carbon chain at the double bond, the arrangement is called *trans*.)

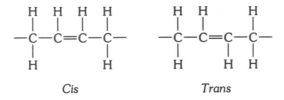

Cis   *Trans*

It is feared that mistakes can be made by the body when it is presented with abnormal fat. The body tries to incorporate the new *trans*-fat with its different spatial arrangement but then discovers that it is the wrong shape. A study on pigs given hydrogenated fat with 50% *trans*-fatty acids found that they developed lesions of the aorta. Some stick margarines contain 25% to 35% *trans*-fatty acids. Tub margarines contain 13% to 20% and hydrogenated oil contains 10% to 20%.

The second concern about hydrogenation is based on the shifts in the location of double bonds in the fatty acid chains and the decrease in the amount of polyunsaturated fat in the hydrogenated product.

Food products containing partially hydrogenated vegetable oils continue to be impor-tant sources of essential fatty acids. Studies by Ohlrogge et al. ("Food Fats and Oils," Institute of Shortening and Edible Oils, Washington, DC, 1988, pp. 9, 10) show that all of the partially hydrogenated vegetable oils are metabolized and do not accumulate abnormally in human tissue. In addition, although it is generally regarded that *trans*-isomers are unnatural, these forms do appear in nature. Cows may consume plants from which *trans*-acids are secreted into the milk. Microbial hydrogenation of the unsaturated fatty acids within the cow also contrib-utes a share of *trans*-acids to butter.

Oxidation

Many experiments confirm that cholesterol is not a problem unless it is oxygenated, and this is a consideration in the whole diet/heart issue. Cholesterol can be oxidized in food and in our bodies.* Oxidation is a process that occurs normally in all body tissues. In food, cholesterol is oxidized when heat and air are mixed in during the processing of some items such as powdered eggs, powdered milk, and whey. Many products contain these ingredients. The

---

* Imai, H., et al. "Angiotoxicity and Atherosclerosis Due To Oxidized Cholesterol," Arch Path Lab Med. 100:565–72.
Gorringe, J. "Why Blame Butter: Discussion On Paper," The Royal Society of Medicine, 79:661–663.
Addes, Paul B., "Coronary Heart Disease, An Update With Emphasis On Dietary Lipid Oxidation Products," Food and Nutrition News, Vol. 62, No. 2, p. 8.

high heat used in making evaporated milk, and smoked fish and meat can possibly cause oxidation. Without doubt, oxidation occurs in oils used for deep-frying. Fresh eggs probably do not contain oxidized cholesterol, but cooking methods that incorporate air together with heat such as in making hollandaise sauces and soufflés can cause oxidation. The cholesterol in scrambled eggs, for example, is more likely to become oxidized than the cholesterol in boiled eggs. Most food, however, has not been analyzed for oxidized cholesterol.

There is no certain answer to preventing oxidation yet. The use of antioxidants, natural and artificial, are possible future interventions. EDTA, BHA and BHT are some of the artificial antioxidants. Vitamin E and selenium are some natural antioxidants. (See the vitamins and minerals sections in this chapter regarding cautions on the use of these nutrients as dietary supplements.)

Prostaglandins

Prostaglandins are yet another factor in the diet/heart issue. Prostaglandins are produced every few seconds in the body. Linoleic acid (omega 6) converts with the help of enzymes into arachidonic acid, a precursor for various prostaglandins. In heart tissue, prostaglandins work in harmony — one dilating (PGI2) and the other constricting (TXA2) vessels. When the latter one is produced in excessive amounts, too much clumping and constricting occur, and a heart attack can follow.

It appears that fish oil (omega 3) can decrease the production of arachidonic acid by inhibiting the enzyme that makes it from linoleic acid. An important question that needs to be answered is how much omega 6 and how much omega 3 fatty acids are correct amounts.

The fatty acids also produce prostaglandins that regulate the functioning of the immune system. These immune prostaglandins cause inflammation at the site of injuries. Precise dietary recommendations for those with inflammatory diseases, such as arthritis, asthma, psoriasis, etc., are not yet available.

The fatty acids involved in the prostaglandins that regulate the heart and the immune system are linoleic, arachidonic, alpha linolenic, and eicosapentaenoic and docosahexaenoic.

Summary

Currently, the status of the fatty acids has to do with what we know about their role as precursors for substances that affect heart health and the immune response. Not enough information is available on how much of each fatty acid should be part of the diet of healthy individuals. Translating this meagre information into specific dietary recommendations is difficult, therefore.

Much more research needs to be done before pronouncements can be made concerning the correct amounts in the diet of certain fats. It may be prudent to replace some of the omega 6 fatty acids with omega 3 fatty acids. That is to say, more soy oil, olive oil, canola oil, walnuts, and fish should be used. It is not prudent to use supplemental doses of these fats. Prolonged bleeding and lessened disease immunity could result, especially with fish oil.

Another, very important consideration is the fact that food contains a mixture of several fatty acids and all fatty acids are high in calories. Excess calories can contribute to weight gain, and obesity is an independent risk factor for some of the same conditions the fatty acids are used to alleviate. It is boring to preach moderation, but it is also safe.

Comparison
*High-fat and Low-fat Meals

High Fat	Low Fat
Breakfast	**Breakfast**
Juice	Juice
Cereal	Cereal
Whole milk*	Skim milk
Biscuit*	Toasted bread
Margarine*	Jelly
Coffee	Coffee
Cream*	Skim milk
Sugar	Sugar
Lunch	**Lunch**
Salami* and bologna*	Lean roast beef
Croissant*	Rye bread
Mayonnaise*	Mustard
Salad with dressing*	Sliced tomato on lettuce
Ice cream*	Frozen fruit ice dessert
Soda	Soda
Dinner	**Dinner**
Fried chicken*	Baked chicken
French fries*	Baked potato + 1 tsp. butter
Spinach in cream sauce*	Spinach
Apple pie*	Apple sauce
Snack	**Snack**
Cookies*	Low-fat yogurt with fruit
Fruit	

Vitamins

Vitamins, organic compounds that the body must obtain from food, are necessary for good health. Without them, symptoms and sicknesses appear, leading to poor health, physical deformities, and even death. In proper amounts, vitamins are essential for growth and life. The name comes from *vita,* which means life, and *amine,* which indicates the chemical structure.

The discovery of vitamins was a very slow process. In the 1700s, it was accidentally discovered that oranges and lemons prevented the disease scurvy from affecting sailors, and later that other foods besides white rice were needed to prevent beriberi disease in sailors in the Far East. At the time, it wasn't known that vitamins were the substances responsible for these "cures," but the groundwork was being laid.

Studies were conducted on animals, who were given purified diets of carbohydrates, protein, fat, and minerals. These studies revealed that an unknown food factor was necessary for the maintenance of their good health. Very slowly, between 1925 and 1955, each of the vitamins was isolated and discovered.

The body's need for a vitamin to prevent health problems does not establish the function of that vitamin. The studies of vitamins' functions still continue. Vitamins are very specific and work as cofactors with enzymes in many different capacities and in each cell. Not all species need the same vitamins. For example, dogs do not need vitamin C. Their bodies can manufacture it, whereas human bodies cannot.

Vitamins are classified into two categories — *fat-soluble* and *water-soluble*. The fat-soluble vitamins need dietary fat for absorption; excess amounts of fat-soluble vitamins are stored in fat tissues or in the liver. The water-soluble vitamins are excreted in the urine when the body tissues are saturated. The fat-soluble vitamins are A, E, D, and K. The water-soluble vitamins are C and the B group (eight of them).

High intakes of both types of vitamins can create imbalances and some can cause toxicity. It is the excess intake of fat-soluble vitamins A and D that creates the most serious problems. Fat-soluble vitamin E is not toxic but can create imbalances with vitamin K. Excess vitamin K would not be a problem, except in the synthetic form, which is available only through prescription. Vitamins B_3 and B_6 are the two water-soluble vitamins that cause toxicity if taken in excessive amounts.

Vitamin A

Vitamin A is fat-soluble and is needed for growth. Taking supplements of vitamin A could lead to toxicity and cause severe headaches, skin rash, and hair loss. The vitamin is destroyed by oxygen, and proper care in preparing and storing food is needed to prevent losses. Air-tight storage containers, lids on pots, and quick preparation help. Vitamin E helps to prevent oxidation of vitamin A in the body. Vitamin A is more stable when heated than most vitamins. A vitamin A deficiency in the body may occur if the nutrients that help metabolize and transport it — zinc, protein, and fat — are not in the diet.

Vitamin A is necessary for the occurrence of a chemical reaction that allows day vision to switch to night vision. In fact, night blindness is one of the symptoms of inadequate vitamin A intake. Vitamin A is necessary for keeping epithelial tissue moist. This tissue lines the body. It is the skin on the outside of our bodies and the mucous membrane on the inside. A moist mucous membrane helps prevent infection. There is a theory that some types of tumors may begin when epithelial tissue dries out and becomes abnormal. Research done on animals, using large doses of a detoxified vitamin A, indicates that the vitamin is effective in combating this type of tumor.

Food sources of vitamin A come in two types. The preformed type comes from liver, egg yolks, milk-fat products (such as butter, cream, cheeses, ice cream), and cod liver oil. Neither muscle meats nor grain foods are a good source. Fruits and vegetables, on the other hand, are often a good source of the second type of vitamin A: the provitamin, a precursor called carotene. Carotene is a yellowish-orange pigment. Generally, chlorophyll masks carotene, and green as well as orange-colored fruits and vegetables are rich in carotene. These include sweet potatoes, carrots, cantaloupes, oranges, spinach, collard greens, peas, kale, romaine lettuce, as well as all other produce that is colored all the way through. Fruits and vegetables that have color only on the peel or in the outer leaves are not good sources.

In the United States, vitamin A deficiency is rare, but it is the most widespread deficiency in other parts of the world, where many children are blind because of it.

As a rule, nutritionists do not recommend vitamins as cures for medical problems unrelated to nutrition, but vitamin A derivatives have been used for years for acne, and a new topical form is being used as a short-term treatment to lessen wrinkles in middle-aged skin.

Vitamin A is listed sometimes as international units (IU) and sometimes as retinol equivalents (RE).* One IU of vitamin A equals 0.3 micrograms (μg) of retinol or 0.6 μg of beta carotene.

In the past, the recommended daily allowance was reported as 5000 IU for adult men. This was thought to consist of 2500 IU each of β-carotene and retinol, because incomplete data suggest that retinol esters and β-carotene provide equally for total vitamin A activity in foods. In terms of retinol equivalents, 2500 IU $\div$ 3.3 $\approx$ 750 μg due to retinol, and 2500 IU $\div$ 250 μg as β-carotene for a total of the present recommended dietary allowance of 1000 retinol equivalents per day for adult men. The allowance for women is less and calls for 4000 IU or 800 RE.

Vitamin E

Vitamin E, a fat-soluble antioxidant, is a family of vitamins called *tocopherols*. Alpha tocopherol is the most effective vitamin E and is sometimes included in the ingredient list of processed foods containing fat. The antioxidant properties of vitamin E prevent fat from becoming rancid. In the body, vitamin E prevents oxygen from destroying vitamin C and vitamin A. Nearly all foods have some vitamin E. The U.S. Recommended Daily Allowance (RDA) is based on the average intake of polyunsaturated fat in the diet (12 mg to 15 mg). Oils in the form of salad dressings, cooking oils and margarine, supply most of the polyunsaturated fats in our diets. Oils are also the richest source of vitamin E. Wheat-germ oil is a potent source of vitamin E, but some brands of wheat germ have the oil removed, and consequently the vitamin E. Other excellent oil-containing foods are seeds and nuts. Green, leafy vegetables also have high vitamin E counts.

---

* From Alpers, D., Clouse, R., Stenson, W., *Manual of Nutritional Therapeutics,* Little, Brown and Company, Boston, MA, 1983, p. 34. Used with permission.

Vitamin E has been the subject of many claims, especially those promoting disease cures and athletic performance but there has not, to date, been any proof to support them. There may be, however, a connection between vitamin E and the prevention of the formation of nitrosamines, carcinogens formed from nitrites and amines. The nitrites are normally found in the soil, in plants, in saliva, and in foods protected with nitrite preservatives. (Sodium nitrite is effective against botulism formation in anaerobically packaged food such as vacuum-packed cold cuts and canned meats.) Nitrites can combine with amines, which occur naturally in our bodies and in food.

Vitamin E is being used in pharmacological doses to treat fibrocystic breast disease, although there have been studies both pro and con. Vitamin E also is currently being used in the treatment of ulcers, wounds, scar tissue, and circulatory problems of the legs. Again, the usefulness of this treatment has not been proven. Large doses of vitamin E can upset the stomach, but there are no cases of toxicity from this vitamin. There is the possibility of upsetting the balance with vitamin K because too much vitamin E can compete with vitamin K's vital clotting activity.

Vitamin E is routinely given to premature infants, who are born in a relative state of vitamin E deficiency and, when exposed to oxygen, may develop an opaque membrane on the posterior surface of the lens of the eye. This disease known as retrolentive fibroplasia can cause blindness in premature babies.

Vitamin K

Vitamin K is a fat-soluble vitamin produced by plants and bacteria, and synthetically in laboratories. It is the only vitamin that cannot be bought over the counter. The bacteria that produce it in the intestines supply 50% of the body's daily requirement. Food sources include pork liver, soy beans, cabbage, and spinach. Vitamin K is needed for the blood clotting process. Injections of vitamin K may be given before surgery or to an infant following birth. Oral supplementation may be needed if one has been on a long-term antibiotic that may have killed the good vitamin K-producing bacteria. Persons on blood-thinning medication may need to avoid eating large amounts of food containing vitamin K.

Vitamin D

Vitamin D is fat-soluble and also toxic, if taken in large amounts. The RDA is 400 IU. One could get sufficient vitamin D if the hands and face were adequately exposed to the sun's rays for an hour a day. As insurance, however, milk is fortified with vitamin D to ensure intake. Milk was chosen because vitamin D works to help metabolize calcium, the mineral that builds bones and teeth and milk is the best source of calcium. Inadequate intake of vitamin D in children can lead to rickets, which causes the bones to soften at the ends and flare out, producing bowed legs and distorted rib cage. Too much vitamin D can cause headaches, constipation, and a hardening of soft tissue. Food sources of vitamin D are egg yolks, liver, and cod liver oil.

The B vitamins

The water-soluble B vitamins all function as coenzymes in the metabolism of other nutrients. Indirectly, they are necessary for normal functioning of the nervous system. Early symptoms of vitamin B deficiency are irritability, grumpiness, and nervousness.

The B vitamins are spread throughout the basic four food groups (see Fig. 6-6). Unfortunately, they have been processed out of some grain products. Some flour products that have been enriched will contain vitamins B_1, B_2, and B_3. Enriching also returns B_1 and B_3 to white rice (B_2 causes a yellowish color and is not used). These are the major B vitamins needed for metabolizing carbohydrates.

Vitamin B_6 and pantothenic acid — a B vitamin found in all natural foods — are not put back through enrichment. This is probably because B_6 is needed also for metabolizing protein as well as carbohydrates, and all of the protein foods are good sources of this vitamin.

The effectiveness of vitamin B_6 in providing relief from premenstrual symptoms (PMS) has not been proven. Because toxic levels of B_6, which cause nerve damage, are possible, it is questionable whether the vitamin should be recommended for relief of PMS. Use of the birth control pill, however, does increase the need for vitamin B_6. Some athletes, believing that

---

Vitamin B_1 *(Thiamin)*

*Pork
*Peanuts
*Sunflower seeds
*Liver
*Wheat germ

Note: Thiamin is made unavailable by an enzyme in raw fish (thiaminase).

Vitamin B_{12} *(Cobalamin)*

*Organ meats
*Clams
*Oysters
(All other flesh and dairy products)

Note: Cobalamin refers to cobalt-containing carrinoids that have biological activity for man.

Vitamin B_2 *(Riboflavin)*

*Milk
Ice cream
Cheese
Dark green leafy vegetables
Meat

Folacin

*Green leafy vegetables
*Organ meats
*Bananas (excellent availability)
*Lima beans
 Oranges

Note: There are 213 different forms of folacin (polyglutamates).

Fig. 6–6.   Excellent food sources of the B vitamins. Asterisk distinguishes foods that are the best sources for that particular vitamin.

Vitamin B₃ *(Niacin)*

*Tuna fish
*Peanut butter
*Chicken
*Bran cereals
 Meats
 Fish
 Grains
 Fruits
 Vegetables
 Seeds
 Nuts
 Brewer's yeast
 Coffee
*Liver
 Heart

Note: Tryptophan is a precursor for niacin. 60 mg tryptophan = 1 mg niacin. Milk is rich in tryptophan, an amino acid.

Vitamin B₆ *(Pyridoxine)*

*Beef
*White meat chicken
*Peanuts
*Bananas
 Fish
 Pork
 Dark meat chicken
 Potatoes
 Cauliflower
 Whole wheat bread
 Avocado
 Sunflower seeds
 Yeast
 Liver

Note 1: Pyridoxine is found in plant foods. Related pyridoxal and pyridoxamine compounds are found in animal foods.

Note 2: Canning causes 50% losses of this vitamin.

Pantothenic acid

*Egg
*Liver
 Beef
 Pork
 Bran
 All foods

Note: Lost in canning.

Biotin

*Liver and organ meats
*Yeast
*Egg yolk
*Soybeans
 Muscle meats
 Dairy
 Grains
 Nuts
 Fruits
 Vegetables

vitamin B_6 will enhance performance, have been known to ingest toxic amounts. Vitamin B_6 is required for cellular multiplications, protein synthesis, and antibody formation. It is also being studied in the treatment of certain skin cancers. Large amounts of vitamin B_6 disrupt the functioning of glucocorticords in melanoma (skin cancer) and kill the cancer cells.

Folacin is a B vitamin that comes in over 200 forms and is hard to analyze. It is extremely important in preventing anemia and is especially needed during pregnancy. Lima beans, bananas, and green, leafy vegetables are good sources.

Vitamin B_{12}, called cobalamin, is also needed to prevent anemia. The absorption of B_{12} requires an intrinsic factor, which is made in the stomach. Vitamin B_{12} is made by bacteria that are found in animal products — meat, fish, poultry, milk, and eggs. Strict vegeterians could develop a deterioration of the spinal cord if a supplement of B_{12} is not taken. This deterioration begins with numbness in the extremities and progresses to a loss of muscle coordination and paralysis. Memory problems caused by vitamin B_{12} deficiency reverse when the deficiency is corrected.

Biotin, another B vitamin, is produced by the intestinal bacteria and is not a dietary concern. Antibiotics, however, may kill these bacteria. Also, some other medications have caused deficiencies. Avidin, found in raw egg whites, binds biotin and could cause a deficiency if taken in large amounts.

All of the B vitamins are soluble in water, and care should be taken in preparing food. Use of minimal amounts of water, waterless cooking methods, the saving of cooking liquids, and avoidance of soaking should be adhered to. The B vitamins are destroyed by baking soda, and this should not be added to cooking vegetables, a "trick" to keep vegetables' green color from fading.

Vitamin B_2 (riboflavin) is lost when exposed to light. Opaque containers, lids on pots, and quick preparation help conserve this vitamin. Milk is the best source of B_2. Vitamin B_2 is involved in cell respiration and the health of tissues such as the esophagus lining. Deficiency begins with fissures or cracks that radiate from the corners of the mouth onto the skin and can extend into the mucous membrane. This symptom is called *angular stomatitis* and is followed by *cheilosis,* painful cracks on the upper and lower lips. Another classical symptom of vitamin B_2 deficiency is *magenta tongue,* the red, sore, swollen, glossy tongue. Other body areas affected by vitamin B_2 deficiency are the eyes, which feel gritty and burn or itch; the nostrils, which develop weepy, crusty lesions; the scalp, which develops a patchy discharge of the fatty lubricant, and the genitalia, where itchy, scaly dermatitis develops on the vulva of the female and the scrotum of the male.

Two vitamin B-deficiency diseases, beriberi, a disease of the nerves, digestive system, and heart, and pellagra, which affects the skin, stomach, and central nervous system, have been prevented in this country by enrichment of food. The former is caused by lack of thiamin (B_1) and the latter by lack of niacin (B_3). Thiamin is the most unstable of all the B vitamins. A synthetic version is more stable. Early deficiency symptoms involve the mouth and tongue. Because this is the most important vitamin in carbohydrate metabolism, a deficiency will result in loss of appetite and weight loss. Beriberi, if left untreated, can lead to death. Thiamin- and other B-deficiency diseases are found in alcoholics. Vitamin B therapy is a necessary part of an alcohol recovery program.

Niacin deficiency is accompanied by disorientation, confusion, and psychotic symptoms. Niacin has been used pharmacologically (and effectively) to reduce VLDL cholesterol synthesis. High doses of niacin have unpleasant side effects of flushing and itching, and niacin is not a good choice for those with diabetes or gout.

There is evidence that B complex vitamins appear to have supportive roles in maintaining immune system functions that can aid in preventing tumor growth. Vitamins B_1, B_2, B_3, B_6, and B_{12}, as well as folic acid, are needed for healthy tissues. More cancers are seen in those who have diseases in which deficiencies of these vitamins occur. Folic acid and vitamin B_{12} are included in a class of nutrients called *lypotropes*, which also include the B vitamin choline and the amino acid methionine. (Choline is made in the body and does not need to be obtained from food.) Lypotropes are essential to metabolic processes involved in cell proliferation and the maintenance of tissue integrity.

Vitamin B_{17}, laetrile, is not a vitamin; it is a drug derived from apricot pits that is 6% cyanide and usually kills the patients before the cancer for which it has been taken. Vitamin B_{15}, pangamic acid, is also not a vitamin. It is extracted from apricot kernels. It is widely used and promoted by enthusiasts in locker rooms and gyms but there is no valid scientific test to show that it improves oxygen uptake in the cells or that it removes lactic acid from the muscles. Any improvement in physical performance is due to the training itself.

Some overlooked foods that are fine sources of B vitamins are:

- Liver (B_1, B_2, B_3, B_6, B_{12}, folacin, pantothenic acid, biotin)
- Yeast (B_2, B_3, B_6, folacin, pantothenic acid, biotin)
- Wheat germ (B_1, B_2, B_3, B_6, folacin, pantothenic acid)
- Peanuts (B_1, B_3, pantothenic acid)
- Soybeans (B_1, B_3, biotin)
- Heart (B_2, B_{12}, biotin)
- Kidney (B_1, B_{12}, biotin)

Vitamin C

Vitamin C is water-soluble. It is destroyed by baking soda, copper, and iron and is unstable at warm temperatures and when exposed to oxygen. Foods rich in vitamin C should be kept in tightly closed jars and refrigerated. They should be cooked quickly and without water, if possible. Microwave cooking retains most of the vitamin C. Figure 6-7 lists some important food sources of vitamin C.

This vitamin's most important function is the formation of collagen, the intercellular cement. It is necessary in the supporting tissues, particularly in capillaries, the body's smallest blood vessels. Extra vitamin C is needed for the healing of cuts and wounds and particularly after surgery. The recommended allowances for vitamin C include enough to allow for storage of 1500 mg for a five-month reserve, if taken at 60 mg a day. Vitamin C is definitely necessary

Fruits	Vegetables
Oranges	Green Peppers
Grapefruit	Red Peppers
Lemons	Cabbage (raw)
Limes	Cauliflower (raw)
Strawberries	Broccoli (raw)
Cantaloupe	Spinach and all green leafy vegetables
Guava	*Peas
Mango	*Potatoes
Papaya	
Persimmons	
Pineapple	
Kiwi	
Peaches	
Nectarines	

Fig. 6-7. Excellent food sources of vitamin C. Asterisk indicates that vitamin availability is reduced significantly by cooking.

for the immune system. However, studies do not support the claims made for vitamin C in the prevention of colds. In very large doses, it does act as an antihistamine.

Mild deficiency of vitamin C causes fleeting joint pains, irritability, poor wound healing, susceptibility to infection, and easy bruising. Severe deficiency results in the deficiency disease scurvy. Symptoms include swollen gums, loosened teeth, anemia, hemorrhage of the blood vessels of the skin and mucous membranes. Death can result.

Too much vitamin C causes a rebound scurvy. Taking over 250 mg a day leads to dependence on a high dose, even though the blood stream levels are the same as on a normal dose. Too much vitamin C causes inaccurate blood glucose tests and blood in the stool, which may lead to false diagnosis of medical problems.

There are reports of kidney stones, decreases in copper and in selenium absorption, and adverse effects on growing bone caused by too much vitamin C. There are conflicting reports on the possible adverse effect of excess C on vitamin B_{12}.

Orange juice is the most popular food associated with vitamin C. Kept frozen, it retains its vitamin C for a year. The pasteurized, waxed container keeps well for a month, whereas freshly squeezed juice, kept tightly bottled, keeps for about three weeks. Flavor retention is a good indicator of vitamin content.

It is good to have a food rich in vitamin C every day, as the water-soluble vitamins leave the body more quickly than the fat-soluble ones. Some studies have found that it doesn't matter if the vitamin is taken every day, at every meal, or every four days. It does matter when the consideration is the absorption of nonheme iron from eggs and plant foods. This form of iron is much better utilized by the body when vitamin C is present in the meal.

Summary

There are special considerations to be taken into account when preparing foods so as to minimize loss of vitamin availability. Table 6-4 outlines some of these considerations.

When used intelligently and to their full potential, vitamins can be crucial both in maintaining good health and in counteracting the debilitating effects of certain circumstances such as illness or old age.

Minerals

Minerals are inorganic compounds. Some minerals play as important a role in maintaining good health as the vitamins. These minerals are obtained from food and are absorbed in the

TABLE 6-4.

Special Considerations in Food Preparation

Vitamin	Preparation
Vitamin A	Cover food during storage and cooking to prevent oxygen losses. Cut with, not across, the grain to prevent "bleeding of the vitamin" (ex: julienne carrots and green beans).
Vitamin C	Keep food tightly covered to prevent oxygen losses. Eat raw, if possible, as losses occur when heated. Cook using waterless, quick methods.
Vitamin B_1 (Most unstable of the B vitamins)	Do not soak food. Cook in as little water as possible. Save and use all cooking water in sauces, stocks, or gravies. Steam rather than foil food.
Vitamin B_2	Avoid exposure to light by using opaque containers and lids on pots. Prevent water losses, as for thiamin.
Vitamin B_3 (Stable to air, light, and high temperatures)	Prevent water losses.
Vitamin B_6	Prevent water losses. Fifty percent of this vitamin is lost in cooking and processing (avoid high heat).
Vitamin B_{12}	Prevent water losses.
Pantothenic acid	Prevent water losses. Lost in canning.
Folacin	Prevent water losses. Eat raw if possible; simmer, if cooking. Boiling causes 80% loss; steaming and frying cause 90% loss.

stomach and through the intestines. Excess minerals are excreted in the urine, in the stool, and in sweat. The minerals that the body needs in the greatest amounts are called *macrominerals;* those that the body needs in lesser amounts are called *microminerals.* If the body were completely burned, what would be left is a 5-lb bag of mineral ash, most of which would be calcium and phosphorus.

Phosphorus

All foods from plant and animal sources contain phosphorus and phosphates are part of all cells. Most of the body's phosphorus is in the bones and teeth, where it is tied up with magnesium and calcium to provide strength and rigidity to these parts. The remaining phosphorus is in the cells and body fluids. Phosphorus is necessary for energy production. The monosaccharides must be phosphorylated and turned into adenosine triphosphate (ATP), which gives energy to the body. The B vitamins that act as enzymes in carbohydrate metabolism are also phosphorylated. RNA and DNA, the carriers of genetic code, are phosphorylated; and some lipids (fats) combine with phosphophids such as lecithin, which becomes part of all cells. Other fats are connected to phosphorus to be transported through the blood. Phosphorus is one of the nutrients that helps to regulate the body pH.

Ideally, phosphorus should be in a 1 : 1 ratio with calcium. Excessive amounts of phosphorus upset this balance. Because phosphorus is so abundant, deficiency rarely occurs. If protein intake is adequate, so is phosphorus intake. Recommendation for a daily allowance is difficult because efficiency of absorption varies with the source of phosphorus and the ratio of calcium to phosphorus in the diet. Vitamin D, which has hormone action, also stimulates phosphorus absorption. Other hormones, particularly parathormone, influence the regulation of phosphorus in the blood. Because the kidney has a major role in regulating the body's phosphorus levels, patients with kidney insufficiency can develop toxicity (hyperphosphatemia).

Manganese

Manganese has an important role in enzyme functions in the carbohydrate, protein, and lipid metabolism pathways.

The best sources of manganese are whole grains, nuts, and legumes. Tea and cloves contain manganese. Blueberries are the best in the fruit and vegetable category, which is a moderate source of manganese if the soil content is good.

The minimum daily recommendation is 2 mg to 5 mg for adults and 1.0 mg to 1.5 mg for children.

Manganese deficiency has not been identified in humans. In animals, malformations of the young are among the list of manganese deficiency symptoms. Animal studies also show manganese to be important in antibody production.

Molybdenum

Molybdenum functions as part of the enzymes sulfite oxidase and xantine oxidase, which are involved in oxidative and reductive reactions. The best food source of molybdenum is legumes, followed by grains, leafy vegetables, liver, kidney, and spleen. Fruits, berries, and most root or stem vegetables have some molybdenum. Brewer's yeast is also a source. The food content depends on where the food was grown, because soil is an important factor.

The adult daily requirement is 75 to 250 μg. Young children need 25 to 75 μg, and children ages 7 to 10, 50 to 150 μg daily.* Excess molybdenum is suspected of decreasing the body's copper levels. Molybdenum toxicity is possible. As always, it is never recommended to supplement one's food intake with over-the-counter nutrients, as imbalances and excesses can be the result.

Recently, the importance of molybdenum to humans was made apparent after a patient on eight months of intravenous feeding developed molybdenum deficiency. The symptoms were severe headaches, night blindness, nausea, vomiting, edema, lethargy, disorientation, and coma — all reversed with 300 μg of molybdenum. Lack of the sulfite oxidase enzyme, which contains molybdenum, results in severe nervous system problems, as described in this case history.

Other research indicates that molybdenum helps degrade nitrates in the soil. The nitrate and nitrite concentration of plants is higher when there is a soil deficiency of molybdenum. After the plants are eaten, nitrates can be converted to nitrosamines, which are known carcinogens. Additionally, more vitamin C is found in foods grown in soil with molybdenum fertilizer.

Calcium

Calcium's main function in the body is the making, repairing, and maintaining of the bones and teeth, a process called mineralization. Mineralization involves the combining of calcium and phosphorous to make calcium phosphate, which is deposited in bones' protein matrix. The skeleton contains 99% of body calcium. Calcium also binds with protein for other vital functions such as blood clotting and muscle contraction and calcium helps to release neurotransmitters in the brain and to activate digestive enzymes. Too much calcium in the blood would lead to respiratory or cardiac failure and too little would result in tetany, a condition marked by muscle spasms. The muscle contraction of the heart depends on the calcium in the fluid around the cells.

The body regulates calcium so that when it is too low, a hormone called parathyroid is released, causing the body to take calcium from the bones. When calcium is high in the serum, a different hormone, calcitonin, causes calcium to be deposited in the bone.

---

* *"Molybdenum Deficiency in TPN," Nutrition Review,* vol. 45, no. 11, Nov. 1987, pp. 337–341.

Without question, the richest food sources of calcium are milk and milk products such as cheese and yogurt (see Table 6-5). In areas of the world where milk is not a prominent food, calcium is provided by soy products such as tofu and miso, edible seaweeds, oysters, and small fish with soft, edible bones (sardines). Legumes other than soybeans and dark green leafy vegetables, particularly collard greens, turnip greens, mustard greens, and kale, are high in calcium. Vegetable calcium is less available than that from animal sources. Bio-availability is influenced by the chemical form of a nutrient and the presence and amounts of other nutrients in a given food source, which can affect the absorption rate during digestion.

The RDA for calcium is 1200 mg for the young and 800 mg for adults. The elderly may need 1000 mg to 1500 mg to prevent osteoporosis, a condition where the bones become brittle and fragile. Calcium absorption decreases in persons older than age 60. The RDA is set higher than the actual calcium need because of the high protein and phosphorus content of the American diet (high meat, low dairy). The urinary excretion of calcium is higher in this type of diet. No deficiency results in most people in other countries, where 400 mg to 500 mg represents the daily intake.

Osteoporosis has become a major problem in recent times. Longevity has increased the number of cases. Preventive measures, such as good calcium and Vitamin D nutrition in early years and exercise, are the ideal approach. Estrogen replacement in women is another preventive measure that may be used in individual cases under medical supervision.

The popularity of calcium supplements has engendered much research. Calcium carbonate, calcium acetate, calcium citrate, calcium gluconate, and calcium lactate are different forms of these supplements. There are no significant differences in absorption of the various forms, according to some studies but taking these supplements with meals does increase

TABLE 6-5.

Calcium Content in Some Common Foods

Food	Calcium Content
Milk	280–300 mg/cup
Cheddar cheese	213 mg/oz
Cottage cheese	196 mg/cup
Ice cream	200 mg/cup
Custard	300 mg/cup
Sardines	330 mg/3 oz
Salmon	270 mg/3 oz
Greens	220 mg/cup
Other vegetables	<50 mg/cup (avg.)
Nuts	90 mg/3 oz (avg.)
Grains (refined)	18 mg/cup
Fish	21 mg/3 oz
Meat	9 mg/3 oz

absorption. Other studies support the fact that calcium is best absorbed from milk, because, it is thought, of the lactose in milk. An 8-oz glass provides 290 mg of calcium.

Overdoses of supplements can cause problems in persons with kidney problems. Calcium supplements also reduce the iron absorption from a meal. It probably is better to get calcium from normal foods.

Copper

One of the most important functions of copper is its role as a catalyst in hemoglobin formation. Hemoglobin is necessary for carrying oxygen to the body tissues, and a deficiency of copper could be the cause of anemia. Another aspect of copper's relationship to iron is copper's presence in ceruloplasmin, which transports stored iron and is also necessary for oxidation of ferrous (Fe^{+2}) to ferric (Fe^{+3}) iron (which is in turn the precursor of transferrin, the form in which iron circulates in the plasma).

Copper influences iron absorption and movement from the liver and other tissue stores. Copper-containing enzymes such as tyrosine (tyrosinase + copper) become dopa, which becomes melanin. Melanin is necessary for color, especially in the hair. Dopa with copper becomes norepinephrine, which is vital to central nervous system function. The mylein sheath that covers nerve fibers depends on copper. Copper also acts as part of enzymes that make the cross-links in bone matrix and in hair and blood vessels. Copper is important in respiration. Copper acts as an antioxidant and protects cells.

Deficiency of copper can cause anemia, as previously stated, osteoporosis, depigmentation of skin and hair, and weakness of elastic tissue in the blood vessels and central nervous system. Central nervous system abnormalities include apnea (difficulty catching breath), hypotonia (a deficiency of tone or tension), and psycho-motor retardation. Deficiency occasionally is seen in children who have a diet mainly consisting of milk. (Milk is low in copper.) A rare disease in which an infant is born with an inherited defect in copper absorption does not respond to copper supplements because in this disease, called Menkes steely hair syndrome, the copper cannot get into the tissues. The condition results in death in about 4 to 5 years.

The RDA for copper is 2 mg to 3 mg. Excess copper, which can cause restlessness, insomnia, and elevated blood pressure, competes with absorption of other minerals. Evidence exists for psychiatric symptoms from copper toxicity.

Oysters are one of the richest food sources of copper, with 3623 mg in a 100-g portion. Liver is the next richest source, with 2450 mg of copper, followed by dry beans, with 960 mg. Nuts, peas, whole rye and wheat, and avocados have very high levels of copper, compared to other foods. (Table 6-6 lists various foods and their copper content.)

Iron

The main function of iron in the body is the manufacture of hemoglobin, which is in red blood cells and transports oxygen to every cell. Hemoglobin also carries carbon dioxide from the cells to the lungs. (Normal hemoglobin should be from 14 to 16 g per 100 cc of blood.) The blood contains 55% of the body's iron. Iron is also an essential component of myoglobin, which

TABLE 6-6.

Dietary Sources of Copper (μg per 100 g of edible portion)

Food	Copper Content	Food	Copper Content
Asparagus	141	Liver	2450
Avocados	690	Mackerel	230
Bananas	200	Oats	738
Beans, dry	960	Oysters	3623
Beans, lima, dry	915	Peas, dried	802
Bread, white	205	Prunes, dried	291
Corn	449	Rye, whole	656
Eggs	253	Spinach	197
Flour, whole-wheat	435	Sweet potatoes	184
Kale	328	Wheat	787

Source: *Heinz Nutritional Data*, 7th Ed., distributed by H. J. Heinz Company, Pittsburgh, PA, 1990. Used with permission.

is a receptor and storage point for some of the oxygen in the muscles. Iron is stored in the liver, spleen, and bone marrow as ferritin and hemosiderin. Hemoglobin is made in the bone marrow from an iron-containing pigment called hematin and a protein called globin (and some lipid). Copper acts as a catalyst in the process of hemoglobin formation and cobalt is also necessary. Iron also is part of many enzymes. Too little or too much iron can increase susceptibility to infections.

Iron is needed by neutrophils and lymphocytes for good immunity, but large doses of supplemental iron will hasten bacterial growth. Iron supplements can also interfere with copper absorption.

There are two types of dietary iron — heme iron and nonheme iron. (Figure 6-8 shows foods high in heme and nonheme iron.) Heme iron is obtained from animal sources and is about 15% to 30% assimilated. Half the iron in meat, poultry, and fish is heme iron, which comes from the myoglobin and hemoglobin in these food items. The rest of the iron from these sources is nonheme iron, which is absorbed at the rate of 3% to 8% (some sources state ranges from 2% to 20%). Nonheme iron is found in eggs and accounts for all of the iron in plant foods. It is better absorbed when vitamin C is present at the time of intake and when taken with meat. For example, a meal that contains sweet potatoes with orange juice and meat will enhance the absorption of iron from the sweet potato. Orange juice will enhance the absorption of the nonheme iron in the meat. Meat will enhance the absorption of iron in the juice. (Sweet potato = nonheme iron; orange juice = nonheme iron + vitamin C; meat = heme iron, nonheme iron.)

Tannin in tea inhibits the absorption of iron by binding nonheme iron. Heme iron is absorbed by a different mechanism and is not affected by tea. Polyphenols in coffee inhibit iron absorption. Oxalic acid in spinach, rhubarb, and chocolate, phytates in whole grains and soybeans, and phosvitin in egg yolks bind iron. The preservative EDTA and antacids, if consumed in large amounts, also inhibit iron absorption.

Foods High in Heme Iron

Clams   Dark-meat poultry
Oysters   Light-meat poultry
Liver   Tuna
Beef   Sardines
Pork   Salmon
Lamb   Whitefish

Foods High in Nonheme Iron

Egg yolks   Peaches
Dark green leafy vegetables Grapes/Raisins
Legumes   Plums/Prunes
Nuts   Figs
Sweet potatoes   Dates
Peas   Brewer's yeast
Carrots   Blackstrap molasses
Broccoli   Enriched grains
Watermelon   Whole grains
Apricots

Fig. 6–8. Foods high in heme and nonheme iron. Breakfast cereals are sometimes fortified to give the entire RDA of iron in one serving.

The RDA for iron is based on the fact that iron is lost from feces, urine, and sweat at the rate of 1 mg a day. Because only one tenth of iron is absorbed, the allowances are set at 10 times the losses for men, which comes to 10 mg per day. For women in the reproductive years, the allowance is larger — 15 mg per day — to cover iron losses in the menstrual flow.

Iron deficiency anemia is common in women. The usual symptoms are pallor, weakness, easy fatigability, labored breathing on exertion, headache, palpitation, and persistent tiredness. During pregnancy, iron is very important and iron supplements are often necessary. Many women are iron-deficient even before pregnancy. An infant should get enough iron before birth to accumulate a five-month supply. Nature prepares for the fact that the infant's early diet is milk, which is low in iron. Human milk, although low in iron, has a type that is five times more efficiently absorbed than that in cow's milk. An infant would have adequate iron nutrition if its mother supplied adequate storage iron during pregnancy and followed up with breast-feeding. Most formulas are fortified with iron to prevent iron deficiency anemia. Many toddlers and school-age children do not get enough iron-rich foods. Iron deficiency affects the child's ability to learn and to fight off infections.

There are four laboratory tests for iron deficiency anemia: plasma ferritin estimates iron stores, transferrin saturation estimates iron supply to the tissues, red cell protoporphyrin indicates inadequate iron for the developing red cell, and the hemoglobin test, the test most often performed, measures depletion of the iron stores by measuring the level of hemoglobin.

Aluminum

There is no nutritional requirement for aluminum. It is included in this section because of the concern about aluminum and its possible role in dementia.

It has been suggested that aluminum may cause Alzheimer's disease, but the bulk of the scientific evidence suggests that this is unlikely. Aluminum toxicity does cause dementia in dialysis patients as a result of a high concentration in the water used to prepare the dialysate. The accumulation of aluminum seen in Alzheimer's possibly occurs as a result of a defect, rather than as a cause. There are more Alzheimer's cases in areas where drinking water has high aluminum levels.* Recommendations to avoid using aluminum cookware, aluminum-containing drugs, aluminum-type antacids, and food additives with aluminum are not upheld by most researchers.

Some aluminum-containing foods are pickles, artificial creamers, and dry mixes. The aluminum additives keep the moisture out of packaged mixes and in pickles, and impart a crisp texture.

Fluorine

The great benefit of fluorine is that it prevents tooth decay. Tooth decay rates have dropped 50% in the last 20 years because of fluorine addition to community water supplies. The National Institute of Dental Research has been pro-fluoridation. Only one part per million (ppm) of water fluorine is enough to promote dental health. Some areas have a naturally high fluorine content in the water, about 2 to 4 ppm. At ages 8 to 10 (or 12 to 16, if the third molar teeth are considered), is the crown calcification period of tooth life. The average diet provides 0.25 mg to 0.32 mg of fluoride. This is raised to 1.0 mg to 1.5 mg of fluoride for adults and 0.4 mg to 1.1 mg of fluoride in children 1 to 12 years of age, if water with 1 ppm is ingested. Dentists recommend a 1-mg daily dietary fluorine supplement if the water supply is not fluorinated. The application of 2% sodium fluoride solution directly to the child's teeth is also effective in preventing dental cavities. Babies are shown to have a range of 0.1 mg to 1.0 mg per day. The normal body contains fluorine in the blood and saliva. Fluorine is excreted in the urine, sweat, and feces, with 80% excreted in the urine.

---

* Martyn, C. et al., "Olographical Relation Between Alzheimer's Disease And Aluminum In Drinking Water Faucets," 1:59–62, 1989.

Water is the major source of fluorine today. The water used to prepare food will greatly influence the fluoride content of the diet. Intake can vary from 1 mg to 4 mg per day, depending on the water supply. The water used in commercial processing can also increase the fluoride content. Second, where the food is grown is more important than the type of food. Fluorine deficiency does not occur in humans because fluorine is present in all water, plants, and animals.

There are those who argue against water fluoridation. There is a very fine line between the amount of fluorine that prevents tooth decay and the amount that causes mottling. Although most fluoridated water only supplies 1 ppm, 1% of the population using water at this concentration have at least two mottled teeth, according to one study. Mottling, which consists of paper-white opaque areas of the teeth, is not dangerous, but it disfigures. At fluorine levels of 1.8 ppm, brown stains begin to appear. Mottling is proportional to temperature and humidity. Allergic reactions, usually hives, from normal fluorine concentrations in fluoridated water and toothpaste, are alleviated when the fluorine is discontinued.

More serious concerns are that fluorine may be increasing the risk of diseases such as cancer, heart disease, and genetic mutations. At .5 g of fluorine, hemorrhage of the stomach can occur. Fluorine concentrations of 2.5 g to 5 g are fatal. Fluorosis symptoms include arthritis, muscle pains, and lesions in the nervous system, eyes, and gastrointestinal tract. Degeneration of heart muscle fibers can occur. These symptoms result from fluorine's blocking of enzyme systems.

Animals grazing in areas close to toxic industrial wastes suffer the effects of fluorine toxicity. Fluorine studies conducted on rodents found bone and mouth cancers in rats, but not in mice. Very large doses of mineral were used. (All testing done on animals employs large doses because animals have a short life-span, and the large dose is used to approximate a life-time of human exposure.)

Fluorine therapy has been tried in the treatment of osteoporosis. There is no convincing evidence that this is beneficial. The procedure is to alternate six months of calcium and vitamin D therapy with six months of fluorine therapy. The theory was to create new bone with calcium and vitamin D, and then harden it with fluorine. If enough calcium isn't supplied, fluorine actually causes bones to be demineralized. Bone diseases are high in areas with very high fluorine levels (7 ppm). In the healthy body, fluorine is necessary for bone and tooth enamel. (It is incorporated into the crystalline structure of hydroxyapatite.)

Zinc

Zinc is needed for healthy hair and nails and a sizeable amount of body zinc is found in those parts. Twenty percent of the total body zinc is found in the skin. Most of the zinc in the body is bound to enzymes and is associated with carbon dioxide metabolism. At least 40 different enzyme systems require zinc. Zinc appears to have a major role in the synthesis of nucleic acids, including DNA and RNA, and in protein synthesis and is necessary for wound healing. No good method is available for assessing body stores.

Strict vegetarians are at risk for zinc deficiency but this is rare. Zinc deficiencies are more apt to be the result of genetic defects, disease, or burns. Deficiency results in a rash on the face and limbs, poor growth, loss of taste and smell, loss of hair, infertility, and loss of sexual function in males, poor wound healing, and depression. Zinc deficiency is also associated with a lessened insulin response to glucose. Zinc is necessary for a healthy immune system because it is needed by neutrophils and thymic hormone, both part of that system.

Oysters are the best food source of zinc. The old wives' tale about oysters and sex could stem from this fact, as zinc is important in sperm production. Herring is the next highest source. Other good food sources are milk, meat, eggs, seeds, whole grains, and brewer's yeast. Human milk has the most bioavailable forms of zinc. Cereals lose zinc during the milling process.

The requirement for zinc is 15 mg per day. Zinc absorption averages about 40%. Pregnancy and lactation require extra zinc. Children need about 10 mg and may not get enough if they eat refined cereals. In general, the zinc intake is proportional to the protein intake, seafood and meat having the highest amount in the foods normally eaten.

Toxicity from zinc is not seen, as dietary excess is unlikely. In addition, the body has a very efficient mechanism for regulating zinc levels. Too much zinc, 10 times the requirement, could cause interference with copper and iron. A zinc excess is also thought to impair immune response. In animals, excess zinc affects some activities of the liver.

High calcium and high phosphate intakes decrease zinc absorption. In supplement form, zinc is absorbed differently and less effectively than when taken in the daily diet. Zinc losses occur mainly in stool and sweat and also during menstruation.

Chromium

Chromium functions with nicotinic acid and amino acids in the body as a complex named glucose tolerance factor. This factor aids the attachment of insulin to cell membranes, helping the cells to take up glucose. Chromium also stimulates fatty acid and cholesterol synthesis. Chromium may help prevent cardiovascular disease, as well as diabetes. When there is adequate chromium in the diet, glucose tolerance test, cholesterol, triglycerides, and HDL levels all improve.

Of all the foods, it seems that brewer's yeast provides the most chromium, but it is seldom eaten by most people. Spices have been mentioned as having a high chromium content, but these are eaten in minute quantities. Mushrooms probably are an important source, but probably are not a regular part of most diets. Oysters and liver, rich sources of many nutrients, are also an excellent source of chromium. Eggs, meat, raisins, nuts, and some beer and wines, along with whole grains, bran, seafood, and chicken, are mentioned in the references that cite sources of chromium. Potatoes may have more chromium than most vegetables, if the skin is eaten. A nonfood source is stainless-steel cookware, which leaches this mineral into the food if some acid such as tomato, vinegar, molasses, or citrus juice is used in the preparation. It is not known whether the body can use this form of chromium.

The recommended intake for chromium is 50 μg to 200 μg per day. There are data to show that the typical American diet is not adequate in chromium, but other evidence supports the theory that individuals with less than the recommended intake do not have an imbalance. However, because only 1% to 2% of chromium intake is available, urinary chromium levels are not good indicators of chromium status. Most of the chromium is lost in the stool. The hair contains 990 ppm of chromium at birth and falls to around 440 ppm at age three. Hair analysis is not accurate for adults because of outside contaminants. The best way to check for chromium deficiency in suspected individuals is to look for diabetic-like symptoms. If the symptoms lessen with the addition of chromium to the diet, the chromium deficiency diagnosis is made.

No chromium toxicity is seen in humans. In animals, toxicity is associated with lung tumors. Studies on runners show that, after running, chromium losses in the urine are increased. Physical traumas produce this same finding.

Selenium

The main function of selenium is its protection of cell membranes from oxidative damage. Selenium's role is as part of the enzyme glutathione peroxidase, also known as "the selenium glutathione reductase system." In addition, selenium is part of proteins found in plasma, which carries selenium and acts as a defense against oxidant status. Selenium also plays a role in electron transfer functions. Selenium protects against cadmium and mercury toxicity.

Foods high in selenium are seafood, meat, liver, and kidney. Rice and whole grains have selenium concentrations that vary, depending on the soil concentration where the plants are grown. Fruits and vegetables are poor sources of selenium, with tomatoes and cabbage having the highest levels. Limited data exist regarding processed and refined foods. Milling causes loss of selenium in grain foods.

The Food and Nutrition Board (National Academy of Sciences, National Research Council) established 50 μg to 200 μg of selenium per day to be a safe intake. About 70 μg is a good amount to replace losses and maintain body stores. Excesses of selenium are toxic. Cattle grazing in high-concentration-selenium pastures develop symptoms of hair loss; erosion of the joints of the long bones, causing lameness; blindness; and liver disease. Animals sometimes die from selenium toxicity. Humans develop problems with only 10 times the maximum intake. Higher incidence of dental caries occurs in seleniferous areas. Liver failure caused by selenium toxicity can lead to death.

Heart abnormalities (Keshan disease) have been reported in Chinese children ingesting less than 38 μg of selenium daily. Muscle weakness is a symptom of selenium deficiency seen in hospitalized patients who are unable to eat and in those where it was not added to the parenteral (other than intestinal) feeding.

Research on cancer and selenium has led to conflicting opinions. There are a number of studies that discount the role of selenium deficiency as a cause for cancer.

The FDA has limited trials to 200 μg of selenium because of its toxicity. Selenium toxicity is, however, dependent on other factors, even with dietary sources. There are fish-eating populations in Japan ingesting 750 μg a day without any toxic results. In animal studies, researchers have used 20 to 60 times the nutritional requirement to demonstrate its effect against cancer. Work is still needed to determine maximum safety intakes and to prove its effectiveness in humans.

Magnesium

Magnesium is necessary for the efficient use of amino acids in the formation of protein. Magnesium is a co-factor in many enzyme systems, particularly in carbohydrate metabolism. About 60% of the magnesium present in the body is in the bones. Soft tissues contain more magnesium than calcium. Although little magnesium is in the serum and serum magnesium is not a good indicator of body stores, extracellular magnesium is important in neuromuscular transmission. When the body gets too much magnesium, it absorbs less. When it doesn't get enough, absorption is increased.

The most practical source of magnesium is nuts, especially cashews and almonds. Whole grains provide much more magnesium than do refined grain products. Vegetables that have chlorophyll also will have magnesium in moderate amounts. Protein foods, such as soy beans and other legumes, contribute magnesium. Flesh foods have smaller amounts, but their contribution is important. In general, dairy products are lower sources, as are most fruits. Hard water has significant amounts of magnesium.

Requirements are about 200 mg per day because the mineral is only 30% to 40% absorbed. The RDA is higher to account for individual differences and proposes 350 mg per day for men and 280 mg per day for women.

Deficiency produces vasodilation and hyperirritability, with convulsions and death in experimental animals. In humans, magnesium deficiency is rarely related to poor dietary intake. Diuretic use, alcoholism, and medical conditions that lead to urinary losses are likely causes. Severe deficiency from these conditions also causes calcium deficiency, as it impairs calcium absorption. Calcium deficiency in turn creates magnesium deficiency. Muscle twitching, tremors, numbness, and tingling are early symptoms of this deficiency. These symptoms can be followed by muscle weakness, convulsions, depression, delirium, and irregular heartbeat. Magnesium is important to the heart. In soft-water areas, there is a greater incidence of heart attacks and stroke. Toxicity is seen in patients with kidney failure.

Potassium

Potassium and sodium have interrelated roles. They have the same function, except that potassium functions inside the cell and sodium functions outside of it. They regulate normal water balance, conduction and transmission of nerve impulses, muscle contraction, heart action, and functions of some enzyme systems. Through excretion and conservation, healthy kidneys maintain steady levels of potassium and sodium. The fluid between the cells always has a high concentration of sodium and chloride. The fluid inside the cells always has a high concentration of potassium and phosphate.

All natural foods, except oil, contain potassium. (See Table 6-7 for a listing of some common foods and their potassium content.) Fruits and vegetables provide the most potassium, followed closely by milk and meats. Whole grains have more potassium than refined grains. Some medications and some salt substitutes contain potassium. One should not take a salt substitute without approval from a physician, especially if there are heart or kidney problems. Potassium also finds its way into food as additives that stabilize and preserve processed food products.

TABLE 6-7.

Potassium Content in Some Common Foods

Food/Portion	Potassium Content (mg)	Food/Portion	Potassium Content (mg)
Fruits		**Juices**	
Apricots, 2–3	281	Grapefruit, 1 cup	420
Avocados, ¼	240	Orange, 1 cup	500
Banana, medium–large		Tomato, 1 cup	550
size	500	Prune, 1 cup	600
Cantaloupe, ¼	250	**Dairy**	
Dates, 10	500		
Orange, medium size	300	Milk, 1 cup	350
Raisins, 3 T	210	Cheese, 1 oz	23
Watermelon, 5-inch by		Egg, 1	60
8-inch wedge	450	**Meat, Fish, Poultry**	
Vegetables			
		Beef, 3 oz	300
Artichoke, 1	300	Veal, 3 oz	400
Asparagus, ½ cup	120	Pork, 3 oz	280
Bamboo shoots, ½ cup	335	Lamb, 3 oz	315
Broccoli, ½ cup	207	Chicken, 3 oz	370
Carrot, 1 small	170	Tuna, 3 oz	240
Celery, ⅓ cup	170	Salmon, ½ cup	430
Cauliflower, ½ cup	129	Sardines, 8	560
Lima beans, ½ cup	255	Halibut, 3 oz	500
Lentils, ½ cup	250	**Grains**	
Mushrooms, ½ cup	145		
Potato w/skin, medium		White bread, 1 slice	29
size	550	Whole-wheat bread, 1 slice	68
Sweet potato, large size	350	Oatmeal, ½ cup	70
Winter squash, ½ cup	470	Brown rice, ½ cup	69
		White rice, ½ cup	29
		Spaghetti, ½ cup	50
		Wheat germ, 1 T	57

Source: "Potassium—Keeping a Delicate Balance." FDA Consumer, 1983. U.S. Department of Health and Human Services, Rockville, MD.

The average daily potassium intake is 2 g to 6 g. Possibly a few extra grams may be needed by individuals who sweat profusely, as in sports activities or in physical labor in hot places. Generally, the kidneys conserve potassium in these conditions so it is debatable as to whether there is an increased need.

Deficiency is very rarely caused by dietary factors, except in starvation. Health problems such as diarrhea, vomiting, burns, injury, and surgery are more likely than diet to create potassium losses. Diuretic medications can carry large amounts of potassium out through the urine. Doctors routinely give potassium supplements to patients on diuretics or instruct patients to take high-potassium foods, usually juices.

Concentrated potassium supplements can injure the intestinal lining unless taken with adequate fluid. Excessive potassium in the blood can lead to death. When the heart is sick and doesn't pump the body fluid or if the kidneys are sick and do not excrete, potassium may need to be limited in the diet. A dietitian can plan a low-potassium diet.

The treatment for high blood pressure (hypertension) usually involves decreasing dietary sodium. It is less well-known that increasing potassium intake also helps control hypertension. The foods with the least sodium and the most potassium are fresh fruits and vegetables that do not have preservatives and added salt. Potatoes, oranges, bananas, tomatoes, cantaloupes, and broccoli, eaten in quantity, and used to replace higher-calorie foods, will result in weight loss that will also improve high blood pressure.

Cooking potassium-containing foods in large amounts of water incurs potassium loss. Minimal amounts of water should be used to retain nutrients. This is true for other minerals.

Iodine

Iodine is needed to produce thyroxine, a hormone made in the thyroid gland. Nearly all of the body's iodine is located in this gland. Thyroxine regulates body heat, influences protein synthesis, keeps connective tissues healthy, and promotes physical and mental development.

Iodine is found in the ocean, and saltwater fish are excellent sources of iodine. Iodine reaches the soil from rain that came from evaporated ocean water. Land near the ocean and land once covered by it are rich in iodine. Foods grown in iodine-rich soil and products such as milk from animals feeding on this land will be natural sources of iodine.

The American diet has extra iodine due to the use of iodine sanitizers on utensils and processing equipment. Certain food colors and dough conditioners also contain iodine. The innovation of iodized salt in 1924 was an important health intervention that wiped out goiter, an enlargement of the thyroid gland, in the United States. Today, salt is available with or without iodine.

The requirement for iodine is set at 150 μg per day. Infants and children need less. The average intake is usually well above the requirement, due to the liberal use of salt.

Deficiency of iodine, less than 50 μg, causes the thyroid gland to enlarge itself so that it can use what iodine is available. The enlarged goiter protrudes and is visible in the neck. Goiters are common in Africa, Asia, and South America. In certain areas of Africa where iodine deficiency is epidemic, whole populations have massive goiters that hang onto the chest. Insufficient thyroid hormone, thyroxin, causes one to be sluggish, tired, cold, and prone to easy weight gain. Iodine deficiency during the first three weeks of pregnancy can result in the birth of a child who is a dwarf and mentally deficient. This condition is called cretinism.

Excess amounts of iodine (25 to 70 times the RDA) will lead to high levels of thyroxin, thyroid enlargement, impaired glucose tolerance, and heart failure. Excessive intake can also cause hypothyroidism, which will cause a lowered metabolic rate and listlessness, because the thyroid will stop producing thyroxin.

In the advent of a nuclear accident, in which radioactive iodine could destroy the thyroid gland, the giving of large doses of iodine (100 mg) would block the thyroid's uptake of the radioactive iodine.

Allergy to iodine can produce a rash that appears as a raised sore over the skin, nasal congestion, or asthmatic symptoms. Allergic persons will need to avoid foods such as kelp, dried seaweed, and shellfish.

Sodium

Sodium, found in the fluids outside of the cells, is one of the most important minerals in the body. Along with potassium and chloride, it is known as an electrolyte. It helps to regulate the acid/base balance of the body and osmotic pressure, it helps neuromuscular transmission of nerve impulses, and it facilitates intestinal nutrient absorption.

All natural foods contain sodium and extra dietary sodium may come from food additives (Fig. 6-9). Some over-the-counter and some prescription drugs are sources of sodium. The greatest addition of dietary sodium is from table salt. Common table salt is chemically called sodium chloride, and sodium makes up about 40% of salt. Soy sauce also contains a lot of sodium. Monosodium glutamate, a natural flavor enhancer, contains substantial amounts. The leavening agents baking soda and baking powder raise foods' sodium levels as well. The more a food is commercially processed, the more likely the sodium count will be high. Home and restaurant kitchens generally produce lower-sodium menus than factory kitchens, but this is not always true. Individual preferences account for wide ranges of salt use.

Preservatives extend the shelf life of a product by preventing spoilage from microorganisms and by protecting color, texture, and flavor. However, they may contribute significantly to the sodium content of food. Some sodium-containing preservatives include:

Sodium acetate	Sodium nitrate
Sodium alginate	Sodium nitrite
Sodium aluminum sulfate	Sodium propionate
Sodium benzoate	Sodium sorbate
Sodium bicarbonate	Sodium stearyl fumarate
Sodium-calcium-alginate	Dioctyl sodium sulfosuccinate
Sodium citrate	Disodium guanylate
Sodium di-acetate	Disodium inosinate
Sodium erythorbate	MSG (monosodium glutamate)

Canned soups and vegetables, factory puddings, frozen dinners, bouillons, and dehydrated soups can contain hundreds of milligrams of sodium in a serving. In general, canned fruits, except for maraschino cherries and certain dried fruits, can be expected to be one of the few processed foods low in sodium.

Food	Sodium content (w/o added salt)
Fresh meat, poultry, fish	30 mg/oz
Milk	120 mg/cup
Natural (hard) cheeses	300 mg/oz
Vegetables	9 mg/one-half cup
Fruits	2 mg/one-half cup
Grains and bread	5 mg/one-half cup or slice
Fats and oils	Trace
Sugar	Trace
Cold cuts and hot dogs	500 mg/oz
Processed cheeses	500 – 600 mg/oz
Sauerkraut	1000 mg/cup
Some processed cereals	over 200 mg/oz
Potato chips	1000 mg/0.3 oz
Some commercial breads	over 100 mg/oz
Some commercial salad dressings and con-diments	over 200 mg/T
Salted butter	50 mg/tsp

Each teaspoon of salt adds 2300 mg of sodium.
Each teaspoon of soy sauce adds 1000 mg of sodium.
Each teaspoon of monosodium glutamate adds 500 mg of sodium.
Each teaspoon of baking powder adds 500 mg of sodium.
Each teasppoon of baking soda adds 1000 mg of sodium.

Fig. 6–9. *Average sodium content of foods prepared without added salt, and the effects of food additives.*

Average daily sodium intake in the United States ranges from about 6000 mg to 10,000 mg. For good health, only 2500 mg is necessary, unless heat or exercise leads to a 5-to-10-lb loss of body water. Circulatory air and low humidity cause more water losses. Salt tablets are dangerous. Sodium for a 5-to-10-lb water loss can be safely replaced with a quart of water to which $\frac{1}{3}$ tsp of salt is added. Body water loss can only be measured by weighing oneself before and after sweating. A pickle or a few potato chips with a refreshing beverage probably will be the most practical way to recoup sweat losses if one works in a very hot kitchen.

Deficiency will cause cardiac arrest, convulsions, collapse, and salt-depleted heart exhaustion. In humans without kidney or heart disorders, 90% of sodium is excreted through the kidneys. Vomiting and diarrhea, especially in children and in the frail and elderly, can cause huge sodium losses which must be attended to medically, as dehydration and disturbance of the body's acid/base balance possibly can lead to death.

Toxicity from sodium happens only if large amounts of sodium and insufficient fluid are taken or if a person has medical problems that create fluid retention so that sodium is not excreted.

The most common health problem linked with sodium is hypertension. High blood pressure has no symptoms at first, and then, years later, a person can become short of breath, develop heart irregularities, or suffer a stroke or a heart attack. Epidemiological evidence shows that in cultures that have a low salt intake, hypertension is rare; in cultures with a high salt intake, hypertension is common. There is a genetic component that predisposes a person to hypertension, and not everyone with a high salt intake will get hypertension. The events leading to high blood pressure include:

- high salt intake, which results in
- high concentration of salt in the blood, which results in
- increased fluid in the blood (brought in by the salt), which causes
- higher demand on the kidneys to excrete the salt and the excess fluid, and
- if the kidney can't handle the load . . .
- the heart works harder to pump the extra fluid.

Sulfur

Sulfur is important as a constituent of many body tissues and enzyme systems. Most sulfur in the diet comes from organic sources. Excessive intake of inorganic sulfur may result in toxic reactions.

Sulfur is found in all flesh foods, milk, eggs, and vegetables of the cabbage family (cabbage, cauliflower, broccoli, and brussels sprouts), as well as in legumes and nuts. There is no RDA for sulfur. The sulfur from sulfur dioxide, which is used to keep color in foods such as dried fruit, is unavailable to the body.

Chlorine

Chlorine's main function involves the acid/base balance of the body and osmotic pressure. Chlorine is one of the body's three mineral electrolytes. The other two are sodium and potassium. Chlorine binds with both of these and also becomes part of hydrochloric acid in the stomach.

The largest dietary source of chlorine is table salt. Flesh foods, milk, and eggs also contain chlorine.

Although sodium is known as the mineral that has a relationship to high blood pressure, one study on hospitalized patients showed that sodium citrate salt did not raise blood pressure the same as sodium chloride salt.* Therefore, it seems that the chloride component of table salt has a role in hypertension, too. This information is supported by previous studies on rats.

Boron

Boron may be helpful in preventing osteoporosis, as it aids the body in retaining calcium, magnesium, and phosphorus in bone. Recent research supports the ideas that boron is involved in brain function and that low intakes of this mineral affect alertness. Boron is found in plant foods, especially beet greens, broccoli, nuts, and all noncitrus fruits.

* Kurtz, Theodore and associates at the University of California, San Francisco, *New England Journal of Medicine*, 1987, pp. 317-1043.

7

Weight control

Proper nutrition also takes into account the necessary amounts of foods to support normal bodily functions. People who consume more food than is needed, especially on a regular basis, are overburdening their bodies with excess weight and fat. These excesses can cause difficulties in breathing, bodily movement, and the proper functioning of many internal organs. Prolonged obesity can contribute to disease, disabilities, and even death.

There are ways to determine the proper food amounts necessary to maintain proper health. Many "fad" diets have problems and careful monitoring of daily menus is absolutely necessary whenever drastic dietary changes are being considered. Anyone considering going on a diet should check with a doctor or physican before starting.

It is important to maintain ideal body weight at all times. Obesity is an unhealthy factor affecting millions of Americans and other peoples. The suggested body weights given in height and weight charts are produced by insurance companies who do not take into account that death from cancer is often preceded by weight loss before the disease's diagnosis. With this method, excess mortality associated with obesity is underestimated. In general, overweight people, especially those who are overweight during their younger adult years, die sooner than individuals of average weight.

Excess poundage creates a burden on the body that can lead to disease. Obesity can lead to heart disease and to hypertension, which, itself, can damage the coronary vessels and cause heart disease. High blood pressure can also cause stroke and kidney disease. Obesity can create the onset of diabetes in those who are genetically prone, which, in turn, can lead to heart disease, blindness, and neuropathies. Arthritis and gout are also seen more often in the obese population. Heart disease and diabetes are associated with obesity characterized by fat over the abdominal area. Fat over the hips and thighs apparently is a normal female attribute that does not correlate with the incidence of these diseases.

THREE WEIGHT FORMULAS FOR ADULTS

1. Height in inches $\times$ wrist in inches = _____ $\div$ 3 = _____
   (Note: wrist and ankle measurements are not influenced by body fat and are accurate sites for measuring frame size.)

2. Men: 106 lbs 1st 60 inches + 6 lbs each inch over 60 inches.
   Women: 100 lbs 1st 60 inches + 5 lbs each inch over 60 inches.
   For both sexes — add 10 lbs for large frame
                          subtract 10 lbs for small frame
                          subtract 1 lb for each year under 25

3. Body Mass Index
   1. $2.2 \overline{)\text{lbs}} = \text{kg}$
   2. ht. in inches
      $\times .0254$
      = ht in meters
   3. Square ht in meters
   4. Divide weight in kg by the square of your height in meters.
   5. Desirable 22.4
      24.8 = 10% overweight
      27.2 = 20% overweight (obese)

Formula #1 developed by Dr. Roger Sherwin, Department of Epidemiology and Preventive Medicine, University of Maryland School of Medicine. Used with permission.

Nondiet approaches

Weight-control programs abound everywhere and diet books are best sellers. Frequently, the person who succeeds in losing fat does so only temporarily. Failure to stay lean leads to guilt and repeated efforts at dieting.

Restrictive diets are unreasonable programs and they spell failure in the long run. We live in a society where food surrounds us. Even if the temptations presented at holidays, birthdays, office parties, and advertisements are overcome, the diet effort is often a disappointment. This is not the fault of the dieter. The body, fearing starvation and death, lowers its metabolism and the dieter now gains weight. Even four years after the weight loss, basal metabolic rate can be down 28%. Possible ways to keep the metabolic rate up include exercise and changing the time and frequency of eating. Exercising the body so that the metabolism increases is based on the premise that a toned body burns more calories than a flabby one. (Table 7-1 lists the approximate calorie expenditures associated with various activities.)

Recommendations to change the time and frequency of eating come from the science known as *chronobiology*. One of the theories of this science is that medicines work best at certain hours of the day. This area of research is not totally developed in regard to eating, but some studies show that changing the day's food intake so that heavier meals are eaten earlier in the day and lighter meals later results in weight loss. Circadian rhythms (biological rhythms in a 24-hour period), such as those of insulin, glucagen, and growth hormone, respond to a

TABLE 7-1.

Approximate Energy Expenditure by a Healthy Adult (about 150 lb)

Activity	Calories Expended per hour
Lying quietly	80–100
Sitting quietly	85–105
Standing quietly	100–120
Walking slowly (2½ mph)	210–230
Walking quickly (4 mph)	315–345
Light work, such as ballroom dancing, cleaning house, office work, shopping	125–310
Moderate work, such as cycling (9 mph), jogging (6 mph), tennis, scrubbing floors, weeding garden	315–480
Hard work, such as aerobic dancing, basketball, chopping wood, cross-country skiing, running (7 mph), shoveling snow, spading the garden, swimming (the "crawl")	480–625

Source: *Nutrition and Your Health: Dietary Guideline for Americans — Home and Garden Bulletin No. 232,* 2nd Ed., U.S. Department of Agriculture/U.S. Department of Health and Human Services, Rockville, MD, 1985.

change from breakfast only to dinner only. Subjects who eat all of their calories in the morning lose weight, whereas those eating the same number of calories at the evening meal gain weight.

Another idea is that food intake spread out into frequent, small meals helps promote weight loss. There are studies to support and refute this. Scientists who conducted a recent study reported that it did not matter whether calories were divided across the day into four meals or taken in two large meals. The total daily energy expended (thermic effect of food) for digestion was the same for both. The results of another study were different—a person's metabolic rate was found to rise after each meal and much of what was eaten was burned off, but this effect was reduced after three meals. Eating less than three meals will burn less calories, but eating more than three meals does not increase metabolism.

Most of the studies were done on small numbers of subjects for short periods of time. Because the rearranging of meal times and sizes is easier to do than placing people on restrictive diets, this author feels that it merits a try; it has worked for some of the author's patients. As for exercise, it is always recommended for emotional and physical health, when it has the approval of the patient's physician and when it is done in a supervised setting with a knowledgeable trainer. A self-prescribed program could lead to injury, especially in those who are obese.

Another nondiet approach to losing weight is behavior modification, which involves careful analysis of the activities that lead to eating and a plan of action to change those patterns that trigger overindulgence. The help of a professional such as a dietitian or psychologist may be necessary. After keeping careful records of when and what is eaten, the obese person will disrupt the activity that leads to eating or will substitute another activity. Eating will be done more slowly, with the patient chewing longer or counting bites of food so that the total intake will be less. Celebrations and social situations involving food will be thought out before the person attends them so that binging will not occur. This method works with those who were not aware of their habits. There are, however, those people who are obsessive-compulsive eaters for whom this method triggers even greater degrees of overeating. These people have deep psychological problems and simple techniques do not work.

Nutrition and weight control

The quality of the diet, along with the exercise program and the timing of meals, is important. The diet's quality is very important when behavior modification is selected as the weight-loss program, because food intake must be nutritious. It is not advisable to follow any program that emphasizes or de-emphasizes a particular food or group of foods. The diet should contain 55% carbohydrates, 15% protein, and 30% fat. Saturated fat should comprise 10% of the total calories, polyunsaturated fat, 7%, and monounsaturated fat, 14%. Cholesterol intake should be no more than 300 mg daily. These are the recommendations of the Committee of Diet and Health of the National Research Council's Food and Nutrition Board.

The number of calories in a diet should be individualized. Each of us eats an amount of food to which our body has become accustomed. By keeping an accurate record of daily intake for a week, one can find the calorie level that supports the present weight. It is very easy to slice off some of these calories but care must be taken. A very-low-calorie diet (500 kilocalories) over a period of two months has been shown to cause gallstones. On the other hand, obesity, especially in women, is also a positive risk for gallstones.

It seems that reducing weight with a sensible diet is the safest program. Fasting is worse than the low-calorie diets, because it results in muscle loss. If a person normally eats 4000 calories and goes on a 1200-calorie diet, he or she will be miserable and the diet will surely be dropped. If, on the other hand, this person cuts back to 3500 calories, the pain of dieting is minimized and weight loss progresses slowly, but successfully. There are formulas that can be used, but none is as accurate as keeping an individual record. The dieter doesn't have to hibernate while losing. Even desserts can be included.

Keeping a diet record is easy if one learns a few basic calorie counts (see Fig. 7-1). Records should be kept for at least three days and each record should be done on a separate page. Eating a variety of foods will balance out the differences between foods within the group. The diet should always be nutritious. Eating according to the Basic Four Plan is one way to get a nutritious diet. A minimum of two servings of milk or cheese, two servings of meats, poultry, fish, eggs, nuts, or legumes, and four servings each of fruits and vegetables and grains meets the Basic Four Food Plan recommendations. Desserts and sweet beverages have many calories because of the large amounts of fat and sugar they contain. Many types of food preparation also add lots of fat and/or sugar. If not eaten too frequently, and in moderation, desserts and special dishes can be a part of the diet. The use of skim milk, for example, can lower the calories in foods such as custards and puddings.

There are those who feel guilty after eating sweets or salty snacks. In some, this failure to restrain one's self causes binge eating and abandonment of a restrictive diet program. Conditioning starts in childhood, when reward and punishment are meted out as food. There is never any wrong done in eating desserts if eaten in moderation; they will not cause any disease or obesity by themselves. Unless desserts replace all nutritious foods, they are not "bad." Desserts, in fact, can be made nutritious if fruits, nuts, whole grains, or molasses, milk, and other valuable foods are used. (Fig. 7-2 shows examples of two desserts with ingredients from the four food groups.) Probably, a small portion of dessert will give the dieter the satisfaction of eating something delicious while still being able to continue a weight program successfully.

A diet should have enough variety and flexibility so that one can follow it for the rest of his or her life. Obesity is mostly due to bad habits: eating too much food and too many foods with fat and sugar.

For those who prefer to use formulas to determine ideal body weight and calorie requirements, Figure 7-3 presents four that could be used. Each of them gives a different answer.

Some of the health spas use a machine that, somewhat like the electrocardiograph machine, has electrodes that are applied to the ankles and arms. The electrical activity relates to body water, which reflects fat-free mass. A computer printout tells the individual his or her body proportions of lean, fat, and water. These machines are reliable indicators of body composition for healthy persons. For those who suffer from conditions that are accompanied

DIET RECORD

Time	*Food Eaten*	*Portion Size*	*Calories*
6 a.m.	Orange juice	6 oz	60
8 a.m.	Coffee	8 oz	0
	Cream (half & half)	1 tsp	15
	Sugar	1 tsp	20
	Bagel	One half	70
	Jelly	1 tsp	20
12 noon	Sandwich:		
	bread	2 slices	140
	mayonnaise	1 T	135
	meat (lean roast)	3 oz	210
	Milk (2% fat)	8 oz	130
	Apple	1 (medium size)	60
	Ice cream	1 cup	300
5 p.m.	Fried fish:		
	fish	2 oz	110
	flour	2 T	70
	oil	2 tsp	90
	Vegetable	One half cup	25
	Margarine	1 tsp	45
	Salad	1 cup	50
	Dressing	2 T	270
		Total:	1820

Fig 7 – 1.   A sample diet record. By keeping an accurate record of daily calorie intake for a week, one can find the calorie level that supports one's present weight.

by abnormal water fluctuations, other equipment, such as skin-fold calipers, may be more appropriate. A skin-fold caliper is a sort of pincher that measures fat in millimeters.

The causes of chronic obesity

Whereas a simple case of being overweight begins with overeating, chronic obesity is an enigma for health professionals. Many theories have been proposed. Among them are the following:

1. Set Point Theory. The set point theory maintains that the hypothalamus in the lower portion of the brain programs a set point for body weight. This hypothesis explains the plateau phase in dieting (when weight loss stops). It also explains why the dieter returns to his former weight after the initial weight loss.

2. Enzyme Theory. According to this theory, the obese person has 15% to 25% less ATPase enzymes. These enzymes exist in all cells and help to burn off calories not used during physical activity.

3. Thermogenesis Theory. This theory is related to body temperature. The hypothalamic area regulates body temperature, and heat production influences food intake. Cold induces more eating. Anorexia nervosa patients are also found to have abnormal responses to heat and cold.

4. Brown Fat Theory. Brown fat, a special type of fat that has extensive blood vessels and lobes, is found in babies and hibernating animals. Adults have only insignificant amounts, in particular, around the neck and chest. Brown fat burns calories, rather than storing them, as regular fat tissue does. There are theories that obese persons have less brown fat than those who are thin.

5. Insulin Theory. Insulin in the brain's cerebrospinal fluid suppresses appetite, whereas insulin in the blood stimulates it. According to this theory, the obese person may have alterations in insulin function. Large fat cells have diminished insulin receptors.

Pumpkin Pie

Pumpkin	(fruit and vegetable group)
Milk	(milk group)
Egg	(meat group)
Flour	(grain group)
Sugar	(extra calories)
Fat	(extra calories)

Ice Cream Sundae

Ice cream	(milk group)
Banana	(fruit and vegetable group)
Nuts	(meat group)
Wheat-germ topping	(grain group)
Syrup	(extra calories)

Fig. 7–2. Examples of two desserts with ingredients from the four food groups. Desserts, when eaten in moderation, are not necessarily "bad" for one's diet.

CALORIE REQUIREMENT FORMULAS FOR ADULTS

Formula #1:

For men, 18 calories/lb
For women, 16 calories/lb

Formula #2:

The "Harris Benedict Equation"
For men, 66.47 + 13.75 (weight in kg) + 5.0 (height in cm)
    − 6.76 (age)

For women, 655.10 + 9.56 (weight in kg) + 1.85 (height in cm)
    − 4.68 (age)

(This formula is for basal calories. Add 5% to 20% for activity, or multiply by 1.3.)

Formula #3:

For sedentary individuals, 25 to 30 calories/kg
For moderately active individuals, 30 to 35 calories/kg
For very active individuals, 35 to 40 calories/kg

Formula #4:

Body weight × 10 = basal calories
    + body weight × activity calories = total calories

$$\left(\begin{array}{l} \text{where activity calories} = \ \ 3 \text{ for sedentary activity} \\ \qquad\qquad\qquad\qquad\ = \ \ 5 \text{ for moderate activity} \\ \qquad\qquad\qquad\qquad\ = 10 \text{ for strenuous activity} \end{array} \right)$$

To this total, one may add additional calories for sports or exercise — for women, 6 calories/min and for men, 10 calories/min.

Adjustments for age are needed for methods 1, 3, and 4:

For individuals aged 35 to 45, 94% of calories
For individuals aged 45 to 55, 92% of calories
For individuals over age 55, 89% of calories

Fig. 7–3. Four examples of formulas that can be used to determine daily calorie requirements on the basis of body weight, age, and activity level.

6. Hormone Theory. This theory is based on the fact that hormones are known to affect fat-cell growth. This is seen during pregnancy. Appetite also is enhanced in many women in the days before each menstruation. At this time, there are heightened cravings for carbohydrates. Around the time of ovulation, when estrogen levels surge, women eat less. Estrogen causes fat to accumulate on the hip. Glucocortical hormone causes fat over the back and trunk.

7. Genetic Theory. A study of adults who were adopted showed that genetic influences have an important role in determining human fatness in adults.

8. Medications. Many medications cause weight or appetite changes. Some antidepressants cause a craving for carbohydrates. Literature on food/drug relationships is usually supplied by the pharmacist upon request.

9. Compulsions and Obsessions. There are those who do have an obsession with leanness and/or compulsions to eat. The resulting eating disorders, anorexia nervosa and bulimia are being treated as psychological problems. Investigation also is being done into the appetite-regulating neurotransmitters that may play a role in these disorders. Experimental studies in animals have provided information to the effect that damage to the hypothalamic area results in overeating. Psychiatrists and psychologists do not treat eating disorders as having to do with food, weight, or appearance. Instead, they believe that thinking about food and dieting blocks thinking about other problems in their patients. Depression, fear, guilt for not being in control, and low self-esteem are characteristics of a patient with an eating disorder. The ritualistic behaviors about food are only one of the sets of symptoms of the anorexic, bulimic sufferer. Antidepressant and psychotherapeutic drugs are being tried. Eating disorders do not exist in countries that do not have the constant food supply available to most of us.

CALORIES IN FOOD

Starchy foods	70 calories	1/2 cup
Fruit and juices	60 calories	1/2 cup
Vegetables	25 calories	1/2 cup
Meats (lean)	55 calories	Per ounce
(medium fat)	70 calories	Per ounce
(fatty)	110 calories	Per ounce
Milk (whole)	170 calories	1 cup
Plain yogurt (whole milk)	170 calories	1 cup
2% Low-fat milk	130 calories	1 cup
Skim milk	80 calories	1 cup
Cheese	110 calories	1 ounce
Pudding	150 calories	1/2 cup
Custard	150 calories	1/2 cup
Ice cream	150 calories	1/2 cup
Flour	400 calories	1 cup
Cake	350 calories	1 slice
Pie	400 calories	1 slice
Cookies	77 calories	Each
Alcoholic beverages	$0.8 \times$ oz. $\times$ proof = calories (double alcohol to get proof)	
Sweet beverages	10 calories	Each ounce
Chocolate	180 calories	1 ounce
Fats and oils	2000 calories	1 cup
	1000 calories	1/2 cup
	500 calories	1/4 cup
	135 calories	1 T
	45 calories	1 tsp
Sugars, syrups, honey, and jelly	1000 calories	1 cup
	20 calories	1 tsp

Based on *Exchange Lists for Weight Management* © 1989 American Diabetes Association, Inc. and the American Dietitic Association.

8

Breakfast foods

Breakfast is perhaps the most important meal for the average person, for it supplies necessary energy to the body to get started on the day. Most of the previous day's food supply has already been used up or stored for later use, and the body needs new fuel.

For some, farmers in particular, the breakfast meal is similar to luncheon in size and variety (fried chicken, biscuits and gravy, mashed potatoes and lima beans, for example). This is because they do most of their work in the morning and need the most energy during that period. For most of us, work is spread out over several hours, and several meals are needed to adequately supply energy.

Breakfasts traditionally have consisted of high-cholesterol foods such as bacon and sausage, and low-fiber foods such as white-flour pancakes and waffles. Many of these traditional recipes can be altered slightly to supply more nutritional value than previously expected. Whole grains can be substituted for part or all of the plain white flours in most pancake and waffle recipes, slightly beaten egg whites, instead of whole eggs, can give volume and texture, and fruit purees and syrups substituted for maple or corn syrups can add flavor and moisture to grain breakfast items.

Sunflower Pancakes with Roasted Figs

✓ *Makes 10 large pancakes.*

2 cups dried figs
2 cups water
1 tsp cardamom, ground
6 egg whites
2 cups oat flour
2½ cups rolled oats
½ cup sunflower seeds

½ cup white raisins
1 T cinnamon
4 cups water
2 tsp vanilla
¼ cup vegetable oil
¼ cup molasses

1. Mix figs, water, and cardamom in a baking dish and bake at 350°F for 40 minutes.
2. Whip egg whites to soft peaks.
3. Mix all dry ingredients together.
4. Whip all wet ingredients together.
5. Blend wet ingredients into dry ingredients and stir well.
6. Fold in whipped egg whites, but do not overmix.
7. Cook pancakes on a lightly oiled griddle at 325°F.
8. When pancakes are done, pour roasted figs on top and serve immediately.

Notes: This is a very interesting variation on a popular breakfast food. It is so full of flavor guests will not even miss the heavy syrups to which they have grown accustomed. The figs make their own syrup as they plump up during roasting.

Vanilla Bran Pancakes with Strawberry Yogurt

✓ *Makes 10 large pancakes.*

2½ cups all-purpose flour
2 T baking powder
½ tsp salt
3 cups bran cereal
1 T cinnamon
4 egg whites
2½ cups skim milk

¼ cup vegetable oil
2 tsp vanilla
¼ cup sugar
½ cup water
1 pint frozen strawberries
½ pint whole strawberries
1 pint plain, low-fat yogurt

1. Sift together flour, baking powder, and salt.
2. Add bran cereal and cinnamon; stir well.
3. Whip egg whites to soft peaks.
4. Whip together milk, oil, and vanilla and add to flour mixture; stir well.
5. Fold in whipped egg whites, but do not overmix.
6. Add sugar and water to frozen strawberries.
7. Heat the frozen strawberries on top of the stove and let them simmer for about 2 minutes.
8. Add whole strawberries and remove from heat.
9. When strawberries are cooled slightly, fold in yogurt.
10. Cook pancakes on lightly oiled griddle and top with strawberry yogurt; serve immediately.

Note: Any fruit can be substituted for the strawberries, giving many variations to this very nutritious breakfast.

Gingerbread Pancakes with Applesauce and Yogurt

✓ *Makes 10 servings.*

½ cup dark molasses
½ cup boiling water
¼ cup oil
¼ tsp salt
2 tsp ginger, ground
1 tsp baking soda

2 cups all-purpose flour
½ tsp cinnamon, ground, for garnish
½ cup plain yogurt
½ cup applesauce

1. Place molasses in mixing bowl and add the boiling water and oil.
2. Stir until well mixed.
3. Add salt, ginger, and baking soda; stir well.
4. Add flour, a little at a time, while stirring lightly; add only enough flour for a pouring-batter consistency.
5. Cook gingerbread pancakes on lightly oiled griddle until lightly browned on both sides.
6. Top each serving with applesauce, yogurt, and cinnamon.

Spanish Pancakes

✓ *Makes 10 servings.*

2 oz onions, small dice
2 oz green bell peppers, small dice
4 oz celery, peeled, small dice
1 oz olive oil
2 cups fresh tomatoes, peeled, seeded, small dice
¼ cup tomato puree
1 tsp cumin, ground
1 tsp black pepper, medium-ground
¼ tsp red pepper, crushed

1 T fresh parsley, chopped
1 cup all-purpose flour
4 tsp baking powder
¼ tsp salt
1 cup yellow cornmeal
1 T sugar
4 egg whites, slightly beaten
1 cup skim milk
¼ cup corn oil
8 oz cheddar cheese, shredded

1. Sauté onions, bell peppers, and celery in olive oil until onions are tender.
2. Add tomatoes, tomato puree, and spices and bring to a quick boil.
3. Reduce sauce to a simmer and cook slowly for 1 hour.
4. Sift flour, baking powder, and salt together.
5. Add cornmeal and sugar; mix well.
6. Mix together eggs, milk, and corn oil, and add to cornmeal mixture.
7. Cook corn-bread pancakes on lightly oiled griddle until golden-brown on both sides.
8. Ladle 2 oz of Spanish sauce on top of each stack of cooked pancakes; top with shredded cheddar cheese before serving.

Country Waffles with Hazelnut Yogurt

✓ *Makes 10 large waffles.*

½ cup all-purpose flour
½ cup whole-wheat flour
1 T baking powder
2 cups rolled oats
1 cup white cornmeal
1 tsp cardamom, ground
1 tsp coriander, ground
½ cup raisins

½ cup dates, chopped, pitted
2 cups skim milk
2 tsp vanilla
¼ cup molasses
¼ cup vegetable oil
2 oz frangelica liqueur
½ cup hazelnuts, sliced
1 pint plain, low-fat yogurt

1. Sift together all-purpose flour, whole-wheat flour, and baking powder.
2. Stir in oats, cornmeal, spices, raisins, and dates.
3. Add milk, vanilla, molasses, and vegetable oil and stir well.
4. Make sure waffle iron is hot and lightly oiled before adding batter.
5. Add frangelica to sliced hazelnuts in small saucepan and cook until liqueur is almost gone.
6. Allow hazelnuts to cool and fold in yogurt.
7. When waffles are done, top with hazelnut yogurt and serve immediately.

Whole-Wheat and Almond Waffles

✓ *Makes 10 waffles.*

1½ cups all-purpose flour
1½ cups whole-wheat flour
1 T baking powder
¼ cup almond slivers

4 egg whites
¼ cup vegetable oil
2 cups skim milk
1 tsp almond extract

1. Sift all dry ingredients together except almonds.
2. Stir almonds into dry mix.
3. Whip egg whites to soft peaks.
4. Mix together oil, milk and almond extract.
5. Add liquid ingredients to dry and stir well.
6. Fold whipped egg whites in batter, but do not overmix.
7. Make sure waffle pan is very hot and lightly oiled before adding batter.
8. Serve fruit syrup (see following recipes) with waffles, serve immediately.

Apple Syrup

✔ *Makes 1 quart.*

4 T cornstarch
1½ cups water
2 cups sliced apples, Macintosh or Wine
   Sap

½ cup apple juice concentrate
2 tsp cinnamon
½ tsp nutmeg

1. Dissolve cornstarch in water and add to the rest of the ingredients in a small saucepan.
2. Bring to a boil and simmer for 10 minutes.
3. Serve hot or cold on any pancakes, waffles, biscuits, or toast.

Peach Syrup

✔ *Makes 1 quart.*

4 T cornstarch
1 cup water
2 cups peaches, sliced

1 cup peach nectar
2 tsp allspice, ground

1. Dissolve cornstarch in water and add to the other ingredients in a small saucepan.
2. Bring to a boil and simmer for 10 minutes.

    Notes: The two syrup recipes can be adapted to any fruit desired. Blueberries, raspberries, strawberries, even melons make a wonderful syrup for breakfast meals. In some cases, you may need to add a little sugar or corn syrup to sweeten the syrup to your specific taste, but try to rely on the natural sweetness found in ripe fruit.

Blueberry Oatmeal Crunch

✔ *Makes 10 servings.*

3 cups rolled oats
1 cup buckwheat flour
1 cup light-brown sugar
½ cup raisins

¼ cup honey
¼ cup butter
1 T cinnamon, ground
1 qt blueberries

1. Mix all ingredients together except the blueberries.
2. Place blueberries in the bottom of a shallow baking pan, or individual dishes, and spread oatmeal topping on top, making sure to cover the berries as evenly as possible.
3. Bake in 350°F oven for 20 minutes.
4. Can be served hot or cold, with or without yogurt or light ice cream.

   Note: Any other seasonal berries or cut fruit can be substituted for the blueberries.

Peach Granola

✔ *Makes 10 servings.*

¾ cup honey
1 tsp vanilla
4 cups rolled oats
2 cups pecans, chopped

1½ cups fresh peaches, sliced
1 cup raisins
1 T cinnamon, ground

1. Mix honey and vanilla together.
2. Stir together all other ingredients in a separate bowl; be careful not to break up the peach slices.
3. Pour honey and vanilla mixture over granola and stir gently.

   Notes: This very simple recipe creates a healthy topping for pies, coffee cakes, light ice cream, and yogurt. With the addition of skim milk and orange juice, fruit granola makes a complete morning meal by itself. Again, the simple substitution of fruits and nuts offers variety.

Strawberry Granola Parfait

✔ *Makes 10 servings.*

2 cups rolled oats
1 cup walnuts, chopped
½ cup raisins
⅓ cup honey
1½ tsp cinnamon, ground

½ tsp vanilla
1 pint fresh strawberries, sliced; reserve 5
   large berries for garnish
2 pints plain, low-fat yogurt

1. Mix together oats, walnuts, raisins, honey, cinnamon, and vanilla.
2. In parfait glasses, layer first some sliced strawberries, then yogurt, and finally, granola.
3. Continue with two more layers, finishing with granola on the top and a half of a strawberry, fanned, for garnish.

Blintzes with Egg and Rice Filling

✓ *Makes approximately 20 blintzes, or 10 portions.*

1 cup water	1 cup flour
2 eggs	1 tsp coarse salt

Filling:

10 eggs	1 tsp white pepper, ground
1 cup brown rice	½ lb unsalted butter
3 cups white vegetable stock	1 pint plain, low-fat yogurt

1. To make blintzes, mix water and eggs with flour and salt and beat together well.
2. Pour ½ oz. batter on lightly oiled crêpe pans and cook until lightly browned; turn blintze over and cook on second side until lightly browned.
3. To make the filling, simmer eggs in water until hard-cooked, about 12 minutes; cool quickly in cold water.
4. Cook rice in vegetable stock in a covered pot on top of the stove; when most of the liquid is absorbed, remove rice from stove and refrigerate.
5. Chop cooked eggs and add to cool, cooked rice.
6. Add white pepper and stir gently.
7. Place some filling on each blintze sheet and roll in envelope form.
8. Heat whole butter in a sauté pan and cook each blintze in butter until lightly browned on both sides.
9. Top with yogurt.

Notes: Many studies have been done on the health benefits of eggs. It has been shown that eggs raise less cholesterol than saturated fats such as palm oil and coconut oil. The egg does contain perfect protein, iron, and vitamins A, D, and B_2.

The butter used to brown the blintzes imparts a superior flavor to that of other fats. As a choice, butter is just as healthy as margarine. The trans-fatty acids in margarine have been shown to raise cholesterol more than naturally occurring saturated fats in natural butter (study was published by the Egg Nutrition Center, "Hydrogenated Vegetable Fats Shown to Increase Serum Cholesterol," vol. 7, no. 3, pp 1, 2 (Nov. 1990).

Apple Blintzes

✓ *Makes 10 portions.*

Use previous blintze recipe for blintze shells

Filling:

2 oz unsalted butter	1 tsp vanilla
8 cooking apples, peeled, small dice, Macintosh or Wine Sap	½ cup raisins
¼ cup apple juice concentrate	½ cup walnuts, chopped
¼ cup water	1 pint plain, low-fat yogurt
	2 T cinnamon, ground

1. Place all ingredients except walnuts in small saucepan and bring to a boil; remove from the heat immediately.
2. Place apples in refrigerator overnight.
3. Add walnuts to apple mixture and fill blintze sheets.
4. Roll blintze sheets in envelope shapes and heat in melted, whole butter until browned on both sides.
5. Serve with plain, low-fat yogurt and ground cinnamon.

Ham and Cheese Grits

✓ *Makes 10 portions.*

2 oz green bell peppers, small dice	¾ cup skim milk
1 lb baked ham, small dice	¾ cup water
¼ tsp cloves, ground	1 tsp white pepper, fine ground
1 T vegetable oil	1 lb American cheese, shredded
1½ cups corn grits	

1. Sauté bell peppers and ham together with ground cloves in vegetable oil for 1 minute.
2. Add grits, milk, and water, and bring to a boil.
3. Reduce to a simmer and allow to cook until most of the water is absorbed.
4. Add pepper and cheese and stir well.

Notes: Instead of an entire portion of ham or bacon, this recipe gives you the taste of ham without supplying a large portion. The entire dish represents a complete meal when accompanied with a good breakfast juice such as tomato or orange juice.

Turkey Breakfast Sausage

✓ *Makes 20 servings.*

1 whole turkey, 11–12 lb, skinned and deboned, or 4 lb ground turkey
6 cloves garlic
1 T celery seed
2 T sage

2 tsp white pepper, fine-ground
¼ tsp red pepper, crushed
1 tsp salt
12 egg whites

1. Grind turkey, spices, and egg whites together.

2. Make a small patty of the mixture and sauté in a small amount of oil to test the seasoning.

3. Add more spice, if desired, make links or patties, and refrigerate overnight.

4. Sauté links or patties in small amount of vegetable oil, browning completely on all sides.

   Note: The casings may be stuffed or left in bulk form, depending on needs.

9

Stews and casseroles

Stews and casseroles are perfect examples of dishes with integrated flavors that are blended together to create an overall taste impression. Because of this, it is easy to reduce the amounts of salt and fats without interfering with the desired taste. Stews and casseroles also supply complete meals-in-one. Everything is there for a healthy diet in every single dish.

Calamari and Eggplant Stew

✓ *Makes 10 portions.*

2 large eggplants, peeled, diced in ½-inch
  cubes
½ cup enriched, unbleached flour
3 oz virgin olive oil (for richer olive flavor)
8 oz Spanish onions, small dice
8 oz green bell peppers, small dice
1 T garlic, chopped
2 tsp black pepper, coarse-ground
½ tsp white pepper, ground
⅛ tsp red pepper, crushed

2 T basil leaves, chopped
1 T marjoram leaves, chopped
2 T parsley, chopped
2 bay leaves
4 oz dry red wine
2 cups tomatoes, peeled, seeded, diced
3 lb cleaned squid, cut in ½-inch slices
½ lb shell macaroni, cooked
2 oz romano cheese, grated

1. Dredge eggplant in flour and sauté in hot oil until golden-brown; remove eggplant and hold.
2. Add onions, bell peppers, garlic, and other spices to the pan and cook until onions are lightly browned.
3. Deglaze pan with red wine.
4. Add tomatoes and eggplant to pan and simmer for 45 minutes.
5. Add squid and simmer for an additional 5 minutes.
6. Stir in cooked macaroni.
7. Sprinkle with grated romano cheese after plating the stew. (Be sure to remove bay leaves before serving.)

Notes: This recipe is a fine example of how a combination of flavors can create an overall impression of taste, rather than a contrast of dominant flavors. Eggplant and squid (calamari) both have distinct flavors, yet in combination with the pronounced flavors of the tomatoes, the wine, and the cheese, these become less dominant and there is more contrast in the final taste impressions. Squid is a good source of fluorine, which has been shown to inhibit tooth decay in humans.

Corn Bread Oyster Florentine

✓ *Makes 5 portions.*

1 cup yellow cornmeal	4 oz Spanish onions, fine dice
1 cup corn flour	2 T garlic, chopped
2 tsp baking powder	1 T oregano leaves, chopped
1 tsp white pepper, ground	2 lb fresh spinach
⅛ tsp red pepper, crushed	30 select whole oysters
2½ oz canola oil	1 lb Swiss cheese, shredded
2 egg whites	

1. Place cornmeal, corn flour, baking powder, white and red pepper, 2 oz canola oil, and egg whites in a bowl and mix thoroughly; set aside.
2. Sauté onion, garlic, oregano, and spinach with ½ oz of oil until spinach is tender.
3. In lightly oiled casserole dish, layer spinach, oysters, then cheese; repeat the process until all the ingredients are used.
4. Pour corn bread mix over entire casserole and bake in 375°F oven until corn bread is done.
5. Cut and serve like a pie.

Note: Some customers may like to melt whole butter over the pie before eating it, but it is perfectly good without butter. The old wives' tale about sex and oysters may stem from the fact that oysters are the best natural source of zinc. The main function of zinc is in sperm production in human males. Perhaps an overconsumption of oysters does speed up this production system, causing other related senses to be heightened.

Zinc is also important to the ability to taste and smell. Therefore, diets that are rich in oysters can help overall in the reduction of a dependency on chemical flavor enhancers and excessive salts. Four oysters will fulfill the daily zinc requirement. In addition, oysters supply iron, iodine, and copper.

Scallops and Pineapple Shell Macaroni

✓ *Makes 20 portions.*

1 lb dry shell macaroni
8 oz leeks, white only, sliced thin
8 oz celery, peeled, small dice
3 lb sea scallops
2 oz corn oil
1 T allspice, ground
1 tsp orange zest, grated

1 tsp lemon zest, grated
1 cup pimientos, small dice
1 medium pineapple, fully ripe
4 oz concentrated pineapple juice
2 cups water
½ cup pine nuts
2 T fresh mint, fine chopped

1. Precook macaroni in plain, unsalted water until just tender, cool quickly to stop further cooking.
2. In large, straight-sided pot, sauté leeks and celery together in hot corn oil until leeks are barely tender.
3. Add allspice, orange zest, lemon zest, scallops, and pimientos and heat thoroughly.
4. Add diced pineapple meat, pineapple juice, and cooked macaroni.
5. Add 2 cups of water and stir well.
6. Cover pan and bake in 375°F oven for 20 minutes.
7. Toast pine nuts in hot oil until lightly browned.
8. Garnish each serving of scallops with ½ tsp toasted pine nuts and fresh, chopped mint.

Notes: Adding the toasted pine nuts and mint at the end is more than just garnish; each one of these ingredients adds a uniquely exciting taste. The pine nuts are toasted to bring out their deepest flavors. Fresh mint can take the place of chopped parsley in many garnish techniques, giving color and flavor to the final dish.

Veal and Shrimp Country Gumbo

✓ *Makes 10 portions.*

1½ lb fresh veal chuck, medium dice
2 oz peanut oil
4 oz onions, small dice
4 oz red bell peppers, small dice
2 tsp garlic, fine chopped
2 bay leaves
1 T fresh thyme, chopped fine
2 tsp black pepper, coarse-ground
½ tsp white pepper, coarse-ground

⅛ tsp red pepper, crushed
8 oz fresh okra, sliced
1 pint brown rice
6 oz white button mushrooms, whole
1 qt tomatoes, peeled, seeded, and diced
8 oz fresh sweet peas
1 lb yellow turnips, peeled, medium dice
1 qt red vegetable stock
1½ lb large shrimp, peeled and deveined

1. Sear veal cubes in hot oil until lightly browned.
2. Add onion and bell pepper, sauté together for 2 minutes.
3. Add garlic, bay leaves, thyme, peppers, okra, rice, and mushrooms and stir well.
4. Add tomatoes, peas, turnips, and vegetable stock and bring entire mixture to a boil.
5. Add shrimp and stir.
6. Cover and bake in 350°F oven for 20 minutes. (Be sure to remove bay leaves before serving.)

Note: To create the most exciting tastes possible in these recipes, the chef needs a variety of flavoring ingredients. Once the preparation is completed, the amount of cooking time is minimal.

Beef Sirloin and Rigatoni Stew

✔ *Makes 10 portions.*

2 lbs lean beef (well-trimmed top or bottom sirloin), cubed
1 pint pearl onions, peeled
2 oz peanut oil
1 T shallots, chopped
1 T garlic, chopped
$\frac{1}{2}$ cup white turnips, small dice
$\frac{1}{2}$ cup Spanish paprika
$\frac{1}{4}$ cup all-purpose flour
2 tsp black pepper, cracked

$\frac{1}{2}$ tsp white pepper, ground
$\frac{1}{8}$ tsp red pepper, crushed
1 qt lean beef stock
$\frac{1}{4}$ cup tomato paste
2 bay leaves
2 T marjoram
6 oz celery, peeled and cut on bias
8 oz carrots, medium dice
1 lb rigatoni noodles, cooked in plain water

1. In a heavy saucepan, sear cubed beef and pearl onions in hot oil until well-browned.
2. Add shallots, garlic, turnips, and paprika and continue to cook for 30 seconds.
3. Add flour and black, white, and red peppers, and cook for an additional 2 to 3 minutes.
4. Add beef stock, tomato paste, bay leaves, marjoram, celery, and carrots and stir well.
5. Bring to a quick boil and reduce to a simmer; cook slowly for $1\frac{1}{2}$ hours.
6. When the meat is tender, add the cooked rigatoni and stir well. (Be sure to remove bay leaves before serving.)

Notes: This recipe contains a variety of highly flavored ingredients, for example, the garlic, shallots, turnips and peppers, which completely awaken the taste sensation. There also is a variety of blending flavors, as in the marjoram, celery, pearl onions, and carrots, which create subtle contrast. These flavors are bound together by the tomato paste and the beef stock. The noodles are added to make this a full meal through the use of vegetables, meat, and grains (complex carbohydrates).

Beef Noodle Barbecue

✓ *Makes 10 portions.*

6 oz onions, small dice
4 oz green bell peppers, small dice
2 oz oil (your choice)
2 tsp garlic, fine chopped
1 tsp cumin, ground
1 tsp celery seed, freshly ground
1 tsp mustard seed, crushed
2 tsp black pepper, coarse-ground

½ tsp white pepper, coarse-ground
⅛ tsp red pepper, crushed
3 lb chuck roast, medium dice
1 lb dry noodles any variety
2 cups tomato sauce
1 qt red vegetable stock
½ cup dried currants
1 T fresh lemon juice

1. Sauté onions and bell peppers in hot oil until tender.

2. Add garlic, cumin, celery seed, mustard seed, and peppers; stir well.

3. Add beef and sauté until it is well-seared.

4. Add the tomato sauce, vegetable stock, currants, and lemon juice; bring to a full boil.

5. Reduce to a low simmer and cook for 1 hour; sauce should reduce to a coating consistency.

6. Cook the noodles separately in plain water.

7. Lightly oil a large oven pan.

8. Place a thick layer of noodles on bottom of pan (should fill about half the pan).

9. Cover noodles with beef and sauce, cover and bake in hot oven (450°F) for 20 minutes for total blending.

Cholent (Braised Beef and Dumplings)

✓ *Makes 10 portions.*

4 oz onions, small dice
8 oz carrots, small dice
2 oz canola oil
3 lb chuck roast, medium dice
2 tsp garlic, finely chopped
½ cup barley
2 oz all-purpose flour

2 oz tomato paste
2 oz molasses
½ tsp salt
3 pints defatted beef stock
1 cup cooked lima beans
1 lb white potatoes, peeled, medium dice,
    blanched

Dumplings:
1 whole egg
2 egg whites
1 T canola oil

2 T water
½ cup matzo meal

1. Sauté onion and carrots in hot oil until onion is tender.

2. Add beef cubes and cook until well seared.

3. Add garlic and barley; mix well.

4. Add flour and cook over low flame for 5 minutes, stirring regularly.

5. Add tomato paste, molasses, salt, beef stock, lima beans, and potatoes.

6. Bring to a quick boil, cover pan, and bake in 325°F oven for 1 hour.

7. Return pot to top of stove and keep at a simmer while making dumpling mixture.

8. Beat together egg, egg whites, oil, and water.

9. Stir in matzo meal to a thick consistency.

10. Form dumplings on the inside of a large spoon, and drop on top of simmering stew.

11. When dumplings are done, serve immediately. Test dumplings by removing one from the pot and tasting it. The dumpling should be dry but moist inside.

Chili Macaroni

✓ *Makes 10 portions.*

3 lb chuck roast, small dice

2 oz corn oil

8 oz onions, small dice

4 oz red bell peppers, small dice

2 tsp black pepper, coarse-ground

½ tsp white pepper, coarse-ground

⅛ tsp red pepper, crushed

1 T paprika

2 tsp cumin, ground

2 T chili powder

1 T basil, freshly chopped

¼ cup jalapeño peppers, sliced, (optional) as garnish

3 pints tomatoes, peeled, seeded, and diced

2 oz tomato paste

1 lb whole-kernel corn

2 cups red beans, cooked

4 oz water

1½ lb elbow macaroni

12 oz cheddar cheese, shredded

5 oz shredded iceberg lettuce

2 oz sliced ripe olives

10 oz low-fat sour cream

1½ cup diced fresh tomatoes

1. Sear beef cubes in hot oil until well-browned on all sides.

2. Add onions and bell peppers and cook until onions are tender.

3. Add all spices and stir well.

4. Add 3 pints tomatoes, tomato paste, corn, red beans, and water.

5. Bring to a boil and reduce to a simmer for 1 hour.

6. Cook the macaroni separately in plain, unsalted water.

7. When chili is done, add macaroni and stir well.

8. Pour into shallow baking pans and cover with shredded cheddar cheese.

9. Bake in 375°F oven for 20 minutes.

Note: This dish may be garnished with many different items, including shredded lettuce, low-fat sour cream, sliced black olives, freshly diced tomatoes, and sliced jalapeño peppers.

Farmer's Chicken Marsala and Rice

✓ *Makes 10 portions.*

2 whole frying chickens; remove all
   bones, skin, and excess fat, dice into
   large pieces
2 oz olive oil
8 oz onions, diced
1 T garlic, chopped
8 oz red bell peppers, diced
½ cup wild rice
1½ cup long-grain rice

2 T thyme leaves
2 T Spanish paprika
2 tsp black pepper, coarse-ground
½ tsp white pepper, ground
⅛ tsp red pepper, crushed
4 cups lean chicken stock
1 lb tomatoes, peeled, diced
1 cup dry marsala wine

1. Brown chicken in hot oil and remove from pan.
2. Stir in onions, garlic, and bell peppers and cook very quickly for a few seconds.
3. Stir in rice, making sure to coat each grain with the remaining oil.
4. Add half of the marsala wine, thyme, paprika, and black, white, and red peppers to rice and stir well.
5. Add boiling stock and diced tomatoes; bring mixture to a full boil.
6. Remove from heat, add chicken pieces, cover pot, and cook in 375°F oven for 20 minutes, or until all the liquid is absorbed.
7. Add the remaining marsala to the pan and stir gently.
8. Allow chicken and rice to rest slightly before spooning onto hot plate.

Notes: Adding the marsala at the last minute will offer good use of its unique flavor. If added too early, the wine would lose most of its flavor through the cooking process. All fortified wines should be treated in this manner because of their high alcohol content, which burns away quickly.

Chicken is an excellent source of vitamin B_6; white-meat chicken has nearly twice the amount of B_6 as dark-meat chicken. Although deficiency of B_6 is not common, when it does occur, it causes lesions around the mouth, nose, and eyes.

Maryland's Chicken Succotash

✓ *Makes 10 portions.*

2 whole frying chickens, skinned, deboned, cut in 2-oz portions
2 oz corn oil
6 oz onions, small dice
2 T fresh lemon thyme

2 tsp white pepper, coarse-ground
3 pints white vegetable stock
1 lb new potatoes, peeled, medium dice
1¼ lb whole-kernel corn
1 lb baby lima beans

1. Brown chicken pieces in hot corn oil.

2. Add onion, lemon thyme, and white pepper, and cook until onion is tender.

3. Add stock, potatoes, corn, and lima beans.

4. Bring to a quick boil.

5. Cover pan and cook at 325°F for 1 hour; when potatoes are fully cooked, dish is done.

Sicilian Chicken Stew

✓ *Makes 20 portions.*

2 T fresh marjoram, finely chopped
2 tsp sage
½ cup flour
2 whole chickens, skinned, deboned,
   large dice
3 oz virgin olive oil
8 oz onions, small dice
8 oz fresh fennel, peeled and diced
1 T garlic, finely chopped

2 lb zucchini, medium dice
4 oz white dry Sicilian wine (Etna bianco
   is one type)
1 qt lean chicken stock
8 oz white mushrooms, halved
1 qt tomatoes, peeled, seeded, and diced
10 artichoke hearts, cut into halves
1 T black pepper, coarse-ground
1 lb dry pasta, any shape

1. Mix marjoram and sage with flour.

2. Dredge chicken pieces in seasoned flour.

3. Heat oil in large, straight-sided pot.

4. Cook chicken in hot oil until well-browned on all sides.

5. Remove chicken from pot.

6. Sauté onions and fennel in same pot until tender.

7. Add garlic and zucchini and sauté together for 2 to 3 minutes.

8. Add white wine and cook together until wine is reduced by half.

9. Return chicken to pot, along with mushrooms, tomatoes, chicken stock, and artichoke hearts; add pepper.

10. Cover and bake in 350°F oven for 45 minutes.

11. In the meantime, cook the pasta in plain, unsalted water until just tender.

12. Strain pasta and add to hot chicken stew before serving.

Chicken Piedmont

✔ *Makes 20 portions.*

2 whole chickens, skinned, deboned, large dice
8 oz fresh fennel, peeled, sliced thin
3 oz virgin olive oil
2 T shallots, finely chopped
2 T fresh basil, finely chopped
2 T coriander leaves, finely chopped
1 T black pepper, coarse-ground

8 oz dry white wine (perhaps a nebbiolo d'Alba, or pinot grigio)
½ tsp salt
1 qt lean chicken stock
2 lb new potatoes, peeled, sliced thin
1 cup black olives, sliced
1 lb spinach, chopped

1. Sauté chicken and fennel together in hot olive oil.

2. Add shallots, basil, and coriander leaves and stir together.

3. Add white wine and cook until wine is reduced by half.

4. Add black pepper, salt, and chicken stock; bring to a boil.

5. Add potatoes, olives, and spinach and stir well.

6. Cover pot and bake in 325°F oven for 1½ hours.

Note: This northern Italian recipe illustrates beautifully how basic preparation can produce delicious and healthy dishes. The small amount of salt called for in this recipe is just enough to help blend the delicate flavors of the other ingredients. The recipe still meets low-salt-diet standards.

Tzimmes (Jewish Chicken Stew)

✓ *Makes 20 portions.*

6 oz leeks, white only, sliced thin
8 oz celery, peeled, medium dice
8 oz carrots, peeled, medium dice
3 oz olive oil
2 whole chickens, skinned, deboned,
   large dice
1 T cinnamon, ground

2 tsp white pepper, ground
2 oz all-purpose flour
2 qt defatted chicken stock
1 lb sweet potatoes, peeled, medium dice
1 lb red bliss potatoes, peeled, medium dice
1½ cups dried, pitted prunes

1. In large, straight-sided pot, sauté leeks, celery, and carrots in hot oil until leeks are tender.
2. Add chicken, cinnamon, and white pepper; stir well.
3. Cook until chicken is firm but not brown.
4. Add flour and stir.
5. Reduce flame and cook for 5 minutes, stirring frequently.
6. Add chicken stock and stir well.
7. Add potatoes and dried prunes and simmer for 1½ hours, or until potatoes are tender.

    Note: Prunes are a refreshing change in this poultry dish. They are a good source of iron and vitamin A, and are known for their function in digestive tract regulation. Prunes and other dried fruits add extraordinary flavors to many stews and sauces.

Raspberry Duck and Pinto Beans

✓ *Makes 10 portions.*

12 oz pinto beans, dried
2 qt white vegetable stock
6 oz onions, small dice
4 oz celery, peeled, small dice
1 T rosemary leaves, fresh
2 tsp sage

2 tsp black pepper, coarse-ground
½ tsp white pepper, coarse-ground
½ pint fresh raspberries
4 ducklings, skinned, deboned, diced
1½ lb dry noodles, any style
2 oz chambord liqueur

1. Soak pinto beans in cold water overnight.
2. Drain beans and cook in vegetable stock until tender (about 2 hours).
3. Add onion, celery, and spices and cook together for 15 more minutes.
4. Puree raspberries and add strained pulp and juice to beans.
5. Add diced duck meat and simmer together for 15 more minutes.
6. Cook noodles separately in plain, unsalted water.
7. Add noodles and chambord to duck and beans.
8. Simmer together for 5 minutes.

Note: Although duck is considered a fatty bird, the removal of the skin and fat before cooking makes it a nutritious choice. The raspberries and chambord blend nicely with the duck and the beans, making a truly great casserole.

Sweet-and-Sour Pork with Rice

✓ *Makes 10 portions.*

6 oz celery, peeled, small dice	2 tsp white pepper, coarse-ground
4 oz red bell peppers, small dice	½ tsp mace, ground
2 oz peanut oil	1 pint white vegetable stock
3 lb lean pork roast, small dice	¼ cup wine vinegar
1 pint brown rice	¾ cup concentrated pineapple juice
1 T ginger, freshly chopped	1 cup pineapple, fresh, diced

1. Sauté celery and bell peppers in hot oil until peppers are tender.
2. Add pork meat and sauté for 2 minutes together.
3. Add rice and spices and stir well.
4. Add stock, vinegar, pineapple juice, and pineapple; stir well.
5. Cover and bake in 350°F oven for 20 minutes.

Black-eyed Peas and Pasta

✓ *Makes 10 portions.*

2 lb black-eyed peas, cooked
2 cups crushed tomatoes
2 T rosemary leaves
2 T thyme leaves
1 T black pepper, coarse-ground

2 tsp white pepper, ground
1 tsp red pepper, crushed
1½ qt vegetable stock
½ lb dried pasta, any variety

1. Mix all ingredients, except the pasta, together in a single pot.
2. Bring this mix to a full boil and then add the pasta.
3. As the pasta cooks, it will also absorb the cooking liquid; you may need to add a little more vegetable stock to give the final product a flowing consistency.

Notes: The starches from the pasta and the breakdown of the peas will produce a sauce with the absorbed stock and tomatoes. Dried beans and peas, which are also called legumes, are an excellent source of protein, vitamins, and minerals. They also contain less than 1 g of fat per serving. A very simple application — the combination of grains, nuts, or seeds with beans — helps to supply the diet with all of the essential amino acids needed for regular body functions and growth. Beans are easy to cook and lend themselves to many variations in recipe themes and tastes.

To cook dried beans, follow these simple steps:

1. Cover beans with cold water and soak overnight for best results. This softening process may be quickened by bringing the beans first to a quick boil and allowing them to rest for at least 1 hour.
2. Pour off the soaking liquid, discarding any foreign substances found in the liquid. Cover beans a second time with fresh cold water, about 1 inch above the beans.
3. Slowly simmer the beans with bay leaves and pepper.
4. Cook until the beans are tender, but still whole; at this stage they are ready for use in various recipes.

10

Meat entrées

The one key thing to remember about choosing a cut of meat or a meat recipe in order to prepare a healthy meal is the amount of fat present. Most meat cuts can be trimmed of their exterior fat and marinated in vegetable oils to return some of the lubricating properties of fat in cooking. Naturally lean cuts — the shank, brisket, and chuck — can be tenderized through various methods to make them more palatable and exciting.

Meat contains many vitamins and minerals needed for proper nutrition, as well as all eight of the essential amino acids. Some of those vitamins, as well as the essential amino acids, are not easily found in other natural food sources. Vegetarians and people who greatly reduce their meat consumption must make sure they get these vitamins and amino acids through other sources. People who eat moderate amounts of lean meat will have a less difficult time meeting their daily nutritional needs.

A variety of types of meat, beef, pork, lamb, and venison, are used in these recipes. Each recipe concentrates on a different theme: the type of meat, the marination process, the slow-cooking methods, and the use of natural flavors to create flavorful, nutritious entrées.

Caraway Beef with Pearl Onions

✔ *Makes 10 portions.*

4 lb lean beef, cubed
3 oz olive oil
2 T garlic, chopped
2 T shallots, chopped
3 bay leaves
2 T caraway seeds
4 oz all-purpose flour

1 T whole black peppercorns, coarse ground
4 oz tomato paste
1 qt lean beef stock
1 cup dry red wine
1 pint pearl onions, peeled

1. Sear the beef cubes with 2 oz of olive oil.
2. Add the garlic, shallots, bay leaves, and caraway and cook quickly for 2 minutes.
3. Add the flour and cracked peppercorns; cook another 2 minutes.
4. Add the tomato paste and cook slowly for an additional 2 minutes.
5. Add the beef stock and stir completely.
6. Reduce the heat and simmer for about 45 minutes (may be finished in a covered pot in a 350°F oven).
7. Stir in the red wine.
8. Sauté the pearl onions with another ounce of olive oil until golden-brown; add these to the caraway beef just before service. (Be sure to remove bay leaves before serving.)

Notes: Meat contains saturated fat. Although studies on stearic acid, one of the saturated fats in meat, have shown that stearic acid reduces total plasma cholesterol 14% when fed as the sole fat in a liquid formula, the fact is that fatty acids do not occur alone in food. Stearic and palmitic fatty acids seem to be together in many foods. The saturated fatty acids that raise serum cholesterol are palmitic, myristic, and lauric.

Meat does not need to be eliminated from menus, but we do need to eat it in moderate portions and well-trimmed of visible fat, whenever possible.

Braised Beef Eye Round

✓ *Make 10 portions.*

3 to 4 lb beef eye round, trimmed, cut into ½-inch steaks

Marinade:

¼ cup peanut oil	2 tsps ginger, chopped
4 oz onions, small diced	4 oz fresh tomatoes, diced
8 oz celery, small diced	1 T black peppercorns, cracked
2 whole cloves	½ cup red wine

Braising liquid:

4 oz whole-wheat flour	1 qt lean beef stock
3 oz peanut oil	8 oz tomatoes, peeled, seeded, and diced

1. Mix all marinade ingredients together and bring to a quick boil.
2. Immediately remove from the heat and allow to cool before adding steaks.
3. Marinate steaks for a minimum of 12 to 24 hours.
4. Remove steaks from marinade and pat dry.
5. Drain half the liquid from the marinade and discard, reserving the other half, vegetables, and spices to add to the seared beef steaks.
6. Dredge steaks in whole-wheat flour and sear in hot peanut oil in heavy pan until well-browned.
7. Add vegetables from marinade, beef stock, and tomatoes to the pan.
8. Make sure steaks do not stick to the pan bottom.
9. Cover the pan and cook in a 400°F oven for 45 minutes.
10. Remove the steaks, and strain the sauce through a fine chinois.
11. Serve over steaks with a braised bouquetière of vegetables.

Notes: Beef eye round is a muscle with little internal fat. Much like the tenderloin, the outer layer of fat can be easily removed, leaving behind a relatively lean piece of meat. The difference between the two is in the degree of tenderness. Whereas tenderloin is very tender, the eye round is much more tough. This muscle comes from the bottom round of the steer (the inner thigh muscle), which supports a great deal of the animal's weight. Braising is the proper cooking method to use to transform a tougher meat cut into a delicate steak.

Several nutritional cooking tips are included in this recipe. The use of whole-wheat flour instead of white flour to coat the steaks before browning adds extra vitamins, minerals, and fiber. Using peanut oil to sear the steaks and make the roux for the sauce (roux, which is half fat and half starch, is used as a thickening agent for sauces and usually calls for clarified butter as the fat) reduces the amount of saturated fats that would normally be found in this preparation. The use of wine as a flavor enhancer reduces the need for salts. And finally, using herbs, spices, and other natural flavorings creates a full-tasting product.

Braised Beef Bottom Round in Ginger-Orange Sauce

✓ *Makes 10 portions.*

3 lb beef bottom round, trimmed, diced
    into 1-inch cubes
2 oz whole-wheat flour
2 oz corn oil
2 T garlic, finely chopped
6 oz leeks, white only, sliced
2 T ginger, finely chopped

2 cinnamon sticks
10 whole cloves, freshly ground
1 T black pepper, coarse-ground
⅛ tsp red pepper, crushed
4 oz curaçao
4 T orange zest
1 qt defatted beef stock

1. Dredge beef cubes in flour and sear in hot oil until well-browned.
2. Add garlic, leeks, ginger, cinnamon, cloves, and peppers to sauté pan and cook for another 2 minutes.
3. Add curaçao and orange zest and allow a slight flaming of the alcohol.
4. Add beef stock and bring to a quick boil.
5. Cover pan and finish in 350°F oven for 45 minutes.

Beef Tenderloin Tips in Cherry-Mushroom Sauce

✓ *Makes 10 portions.*

3 lb beef tenderloin, trimmed, cut into 1-
    inch cubes
3 oz peanut oil
2 T shallots, finely chopped
2 T garlic, finely chopped
1 lb button mushrooms, halved
2 cups dark, pitted cherries

3 oz cherry brandy
1 T black pepper, coarse-ground
⅛ tsp red pepper, crushed
¼ cup fresh thyme, chopped
1 qt lean beef stock
1 oz arrowroot

1. Sauté tenderloin tips in peanut oil to slightly under desired degree of doneness; remove from pan.
2. To the same pan add the shallots, garlic, and mushrooms and cook until mushrooms are almost done.
3. Add cherries and cherry brandy and cook until brandy is reduced by half.
4. Add spices and thyme, toss quickly.
5. Add beef stock, mixed with the arrowroot, and bring to a full boil.
6. Reduce sauce to a simmer and return beef tips to pan.
7. Heat through and serve.

Peppered Flank Steak with Sherry-Ginger Sauce

✔ *Makes 10 portions.*

3 lb beef flank steak, trimmed, sliced on bias

Marinade:
2 oz peanut oil   8 cloves garlic, crushed
3 T black pepper, coarse-ground   8 oz onion, rough-cut
4 oz dry sherry

Sauce:
4 T ginger, freshly chopped   4 oz dry sherry
8 oz white mushrooms, sliced   1 qt lean beef stock
1 T orange zest   2 T arrowroot

1. Marinate the steak for at least 24 hours.
2. Sauté flank steak quickly in a small amount of peanut oil. Remove from pan.
3. In the same pan, add ginger and mushrooms; cook until mushrooms are tender (about 2 minutes).
4. Add orange zest and sherry; cook until wine is reduced by half.
5. Mix arrowroot with beef stock and add to sautéed mushrooms.
6. Bring the sauce to a complete boil and reduce to a simmer.
7. Add flank steak back to sauce and heat through.

Roast Leg of Lamb with Honey-Berry Sauce

✓ *Makes 10 to 12 portions.*

1 boneless leg of lamb, approximately 5
   to 6 lb
4 oz olive oil
4 oz dry sherry

½ cup fresh mint, chopped
1 T black pepper, coarse-ground
¼ tsp red pepper, crushed

Sauce:
2 pints fresh strawberries
1 pint fresh raspberries
1 pint fresh blueberries

4 oz honey
2 T fresh lemon juice

1. Mix oil, sherry, mint, and peppers together and rub completely over boned lamb leg before tieing for roasting.
2. Roast lamb in a 275°F oven until desired doneness: rare, medium-rare, etc.
3. Reserve ½ pint strawberries, ½ pint raspberries, and all of the blueberries to add to the sauce at the last stage.
4. Puree 1½ pints strawberries and ½ pint raspberries and heat slowly with the honey and the lemon juice.
5. When thoroughly warmed, add the remaining whole berries.
6. Slice lamb thinly and serve over berry sauce.

Notes: Lamb is usually ready for slaughter at a very young age, between six and nine months. Therefore, lamb meat is very lean. The excess fat that accompanies lamb is mostly exterior fat that can be easily removed before cooking. Lamb is known as a very flavorful meat; even with all the excess fat removed, there is still plenty of flavor.

The simple sauce preparation preserves the full-bodied flavor of the fresh berries. The honey is just enough to add a fresh sweetness, and the lemon juice is added for a slight contrast. The end result is a type of sweet-and-sour berry sauce that marries with the full flavor of the roasted lamb extremely well.

Lamb Stew with Cranberries and Madeira

✓ *Makes 10 portions.*

3 to 4 lb leg of lamb, well-trimmed, in 1-inch cubes
4 oz whole-wheat flour
4 oz peanut oil
2 pints pearl onions, peeled
2 T garlic, finely chopped
1 cup cranberries

1½ cups madeira wine
2 qt lamb stock
¼ cup fresh parsley, chopped
2 bay leaves
1 T black pepper, coarse-ground
⅛ tsp red pepper, crushed

1. Dredge lamb cubes in flour and sear in hot oil until lightly browned.
2. Add pearl onions and continue to cook until onions are browned; lamb will continue to brown.
3. Add garlic, cranberries, and madeira.
4. Cook over low heat for 10 minutes.
5. Add stock and the rest of the spices.
6. Bring to a boil; reduce to a simmer for 1½ hours, or until lamb is tender. (Be sure to remove bay leaves before serving.)

Grilled Leg of Lamb with Golden Raisins and Port Wine

✓ *Makes 10 portions.*

3 lb boneless leg of lamb, trimmed, in 1-inch slices

Marinade:
1 T garlic, finely chopped
2 T shallots, finely chopped

1 T coarse-prepared mustard
2 oz peanut oil

Sauce:
8 oz golden raisins
2 oz tawny port
2 cups white vegetable stock

1 T lemon zest
1 T cornstarch

1. Marinate lamb steaks for a minimum of 24 hours.
2. Remove from marinade and broil until desired doneness.
3. Put raisins, port, vegetable stock, lemon zest, and dissolved cornstarch in saucepan and bring to a full boil.
4. Reduce sauce to a simmer and cook for 15 minutes.
5. Ladle sauce over lamb steaks and serve.

Pork Pot Roast and Cider

✓ *Makes 10 portions.*

4 lb well-trimmed pork loin
4 oz corn oil
2 T whole cloves
1 T white pepper, coarse-ground
1 T ginger, freshly chopped
1 T garlic, freshly chopped
8 oz onions, medium dice
4 oz whole-wheat flour

2 qt white vegetable stock
2 cinnamon sticks
2 cups hard cider
1 lb white turnips, medium dice
1 lb yellow turnips, medium dice
1 lb carrots, sliced
1 lb red bliss potatoes, medium dice

1. Sear pork loin in hot oil until well-browned on all sides; remove from pan.
2. Stick whole cloves in loin.
3. Add garlic, pepper, ginger, and onions to pan and cook until onions are soft and slightly browned.
4. Add flour to make a roux and cook over medium heat for 5 minutes.
5. Add vegetable stock, cinnamon sticks, and cider.
6. Bring to a boil.
7. Return pork roast to pan, cover, and bake in 350°F oven for 1 hour.
8. Blanch turnips, carrots, and potatoes separately and add to pot for last 15 minutes.
9. Slice the roast thin and serve with sauce and vegetables. (Remove cinnamon stick before serving.)

Notes: Although pork is normally considered to be a fatty food, the pork loin is a very lean muscle. Trimmed of all excess fat, pork loin is a very healthy meat. To replace some of the flavor lost by the fat removal use the braising technique to help the flavors of the cloves, cinnamon, and cider to penetrate into the meat's flesh. The vegetables are blanched separately to retain their natural color and flavor.

Fresh Ham Ragoût with Liebfraumilch, Currants, and Plums

✓ *Makes 10 portions.*

3 lb fresh, ham, in 1-inch cubes
3 oz whole-wheat flour
3 oz corn oil
6 oz onion, finely diced
2 T garlic, finely chopped
1 T white pepper, coarse-ground
1 tsp mace, ground

1 qt white vegetable stock
8 oz liebfraumilch
1 cup dried currants
2 cups red plums, sliced
2 T fresh rosemary leaves

1. Dredge the ham cubes in flour.
2. Sauté ham in hot oil until well-browned.
3. Add onions, garlic, mace, and white pepper to pan.
4. Sauté 2 additional minutes.
5. Add vegetable stock, liebfraumilch, currants, and plums.
6. Simmer together on top of the stove for 15 minutes.
7. Add rosemary leaves and simmer an additional 15 minutes, or until ham is tender.

Braised Pork Loin with Cabbage and White Beans

✓ *Makes 10 portions.*

3½ lb pork loin, well-trimmed, in ½-inch slices
3 oz corn oil
2 lb cabbage, shredded
8 oz onions, sliced thin
1 lb white beans (cooked in white vegetable stock)

1 T dill seed
1 T white pepper, coarse-ground
⅛ tsp red pepper, crushed
1 cup German dry white wine

1. Sear pork slices on both sides in hot oil; remove from pan.
2. Add cabbage, onions, beans, dill seed, and white and red peppers to sauté pan; toss together.
3. Add wine with the vegetables to deglaze pan.
4. Return pork to pan, cover, and bake in 350°F oven for 45 minutes.
5. Serve pork slices with cabbage and beans.

Broiled, Rolled Pork Loin with Turkey Sausage

✓ *Makes 20 portions.*

1 boneless, well-trimmed pork loin, approximately 6 lbs

1 cup sesame seeds (toasted in olive oil)

Filling:
2 lbs turkey, fine-ground
8 oz onion, finely chopped
1 T garlic, finely chopped
1 T black pepper, coarse-ground

½ tsp red pepper, coarse-ground
½ T fennel seeds
1 T sage
2 T parsley, fresh chopped

Deglazing liquids:
2 oz brandy

2 oz lean (defatted) pork stock

1. Trim the pork loin by cutting into the flesh 1 inch from the bottom side of the loin and rolling the loin, continuing to cut until the entire loin is flat.

2. Mix together all ingredients for filling except sesame seeds. Take a small piece of the sausage and cook it under a broiler or in a quick pan (sauté) to test the seasonings.

3. Spread sesame seeds over flat loin and place turkey sausage in the center, making sure the sausage reaches the loin's two outer edges.

4. Roll the loin over the sausage; the two ends should just overlap slightly.

5. Roll the loin in cheesecloth and shape as round as possible.

6. Refrigerate wrapped loin for up to 1 hour, to firm up the shape.

7. Remove from the cheesecloth and slice into ½-inch slices, use a toothpick to hold the ends together while broiling.

8. Broil slices until well-marked; finish cooking in a hot oven.

9. Pour off any fat extracted during cooking; deglaze pan with brandy and lean stock.

10. Spoon liquid from pan over loin slices.

Notes: The vitamin niacin is found in great amounts in pork products, peanuts, fruits, and some vegetables. Although niacin deficiency is rare in the industrial world, it can be quite destructive where these foods are not part of the average diet. Signs of such a deficiency include disorientation, confusion, and other psychosomatic symptoms.

The use of the turkey sausage as a filling in this recipe actually reduces the amount of fat consumed in an average portion. Where a normal portion might be 3 oz to 6 oz of roast pork, when pork is the main entrée, this procedure reduces that serving to 1½ oz to 3 oz.

Venison Pie with Corn Bread Topping

✔ *Makes 10 portions.*

3 lb venison, in 1-inch dice
2 oz corn oil
1 pint shallots, peeled and halved
¼ cup fresh rosemary leaves
2 T garlic, chopped
2 T black peppercorns, cracked
½ tsp salt
2 T allspice, freshly grated
2 oz whole-wheat flour

1 qt venison stock (use red vegetable
    stock if venison stock is not available)
4 oz tomato paste
1 lb yellow turnips (rutabagas), peeled
    and tournéed
1 lb butternut squash, peeled, seeded,
    and tournéed
1 lb red bliss potatoes, tournéed

Corn Bread Topping:
4 oz cornmeal
3 oz flour
1 T sugar
1 T baking powder

¼ tsp salt
½ cup low-fat milk
1 egg white, beaten
2 tsp oil

1. Sear venison in hot oil until lightly browned.
2. Add shallots and cook until tender.
3. Add rosemary, garlic, pepper, ½ tsp salt, and allspice and heat thoroughly.
4. Add flour to make a light roux.
5. Add stock and bring to a simmer.
6. Stir in tomato paste.
7. Add turnips, butternut squash, and potatoes; cook for 20 minutes.
8. When vegetables are tender, adjust the seasoning and ladle the stew into oven crocks.
9. To make the topping, sift dry ingredients together.
10. Add milk, egg white, and oil, mixing well.
11. Spoon topping over each portion and bake at 400°F for about 30 minutes.

Notes: This recipe reflects the use of a combination of different culinary techniques to nutritionally enhance an otherwise simple meat pie.

Substituting venison for beef gives the dish a much leaner and more flavorful meat while still contributing the all important B vitamins and iron.

Corn oil is one of the richest sources of linoleic fatty acid, an essential fatty acid the human body cannot make, which, therefore, must be a part of the daily diet. Only the necessary amount of oil is used for the searing of the meat and vegetables; calories are thus properly maintained.

The whole-wheat flour used in the making of the roux provides a nuttier flavor than would the more traditional white flour, but also adds a great deal more nutritionally. Whole-wheat flour contains the bran germ, which has valuable fiber, minerals, and vitamins.

The squash, tomatoes, and potatoes are laden with potassium, which helps control high blood pressure. Even though the recipe uses salt, which also may affect high blood pressure, it is an extremely small amount, considering the entire volume of the finished dish.

Venison and Cabbage Stir-Fry

✓ *Makes 10 portions.*

2½ lb venison steak, cut into finger-length strips
2 oz peanut oil
2 T garlic, chopped
2 T ginger, freshly grated
1 T black pepper, coarse-ground
¼ tsp red pepper, crushed

2 lb cabbage (pascal, savory, or Chinese), shredded
1½ lb carrots, cut on the bias
1½ lb celery, peeled, cut on the bias
1 lb red bliss potatoes, cut into thin slices
2 bunches spring onions, sliced thin
4 oz sherry, dry sack

1. Sear venison strips in hot oil until lightly browned; remove from pan.
2. Heat garlic, ginger, and peppers in pan for a few seconds.
3. Add cabbage, carrots, celery, and potatoes; cook until almost tender (should still have a slight "bite").
4. Return venison to pan with sliced onions.
5. Add sherry and cover pan for 5 minutes to finish cooking.

Notes: Cabbage makes this dish a very nutritious choice. Cabbage is one of the cruciferous vegetables recommended for the prevention of cancer (American Cancer Society). Cabbage also contains an unusually high amount of vitamin C for a vegetable. If cooked quickly with little or no water, as in this recipe, and if not shredded too soon before cooking, cabbage can provide between 33 mg and 48 mg of vitamin C per cup. This goes a long way toward supplying the daily allowance of 60 mg.

11

Poultry entrées

Poultry is gaining in popularity in American meals, partly because of its lower cost per pound than other meats, but also because of its relatively low fat content. Most birds, with the exception of geese and ducks, have very lean flesh, with most of the meat in the breast portions.

It is important to find new ways to prepare poultry so that customers and friends do not tire of eating it. Favorite recipes can be given a little twist (roasted sage chicken, for example, can be prepared a little differently than usual, and served with a special sour-cream-flavored sauce), or new recipes can be created to take advantage of poultry's ability to blend extremely well with almost any flavor combination.

Broiled Sesame Chicken Breast with Basil Marinade

✔ *Makes 10 portions.*

10 skinless, boneless chicken breasts, approximately 3 to 4 oz each

Marinade:

1 cup peanut oil	1 tsp lemon juice
4 T sesame oil	1 tsp black pepper, coarse-ground
2 oz onions, finely chopped	1 T fresh basil leaves
1 tsp garlic, chopped	

Sauce:

1 qt lean chicken stock	¼ cup sesame seeds, toasted, for garnish
2 T cornstarch	

1. Whisk all marinade ingredients together thoroughly.
2. Place chicken in marinade and refrigerate for a minimum of 1 hour.
3. Chicken breasts will broil very quickly; do not overcook.
4. Serve with lean chicken stock thickened slightly with cornstarch or arrowroot.
5. Garnish with sesame seeds.

   Notes: Sesame oil has been used in this recipe much like a seasoning added to enhance the taste. If sesame oil were the only oil in the marinade, the taste of the basil would have been lost, and the chicken disguised. The desired end result is an awakening of taste, not its overpowering.

Roasted Sage Chicken

✔ *Makes 5 to 6 portions.*

1 whole roasting chicken, approximately 3 to 4 lb

Filling:

2 oz olive oil	1 tsp white pepper, coarse-ground
4 oz celery, peeled, fine dice	1 tsp black pepper, coarse-ground
2 oz onions, fine dice	2 cups corn bread, crumbled
1 tsp garlic, chopped	¼ cup lean chicken stock
1 T rubbed sage	

Sauce:

2 oz olive oil	4 oz low-fat sour cream
2 oz all-purpose flour	2 tsp white pepper, fine-ground
1 qt lean chicken stock including the drippings from the roasting pan	

1. To make the filling, sauté onion and celery in oil until tender.
2. Add garlic, sage and peppers; sauté for an additional minute.
3. Remove from the heat and stir in corn bread and chicken stock.
4. To make the sauce, mix oil and flour together in a heavy saucepan; cook over low heat for 2 minutes.
5. Add cool stock and stir well.
6. When sauce thickens, reduce to a simmer for an additional 20 minutes.
7. Add white pepper and stir.
8. Stir in sour cream just before serving.
9. Completely debone the chicken (reserving the skin for wrapping; it will be removed for service); remove all excess fat.
10. Once the chicken has been deboned, reserve the bones for stock.
11. Lay the skin flat on the table, and layer the flesh back onto the skin, covering as much area as possible.
12. Spoon the filling onto the center of the flesh, so that when the skin and flesh are rolled together, the ends meet without overlapping.
13. Roast, seam-side down, on a rack in a roasting pan at 375°F for approximately 45 minutes. (Rolled chicken may be tied first to preserve its shape.)
14. Cool slightly to remove the skin, and slice into 10 to 12 even slices approximately 2 oz each.
15. Spoon 3 oz of sauce onto hot plate; layer two slices of chicken on top.

Notes: The addition of garlic to this recipe may enhance the healthfulness of the dish, as well as the flavor of the filling. Garlic is known to include the chemicals allium, diallyl sulfide, and ajoene. Allium is responsible for garlic's odor and kills the bacteria *staphylococcus, salmonella,* and *mycobacteria.* It also kills fungi and yeast. Diallyl sulfide inhibits colon, lung, and esophageal cancer in mice, and may have similar results in humans. Ajoene causes blood platelets to become less sticky and slows clotting in test-tube experiments. Rabbits fed garlic oil on a regular basis have actually showed a reversal of arterial cholesterol deposits. Unfortunately, research is still needed to determine garlic's healthful benefits for humans. Researchers still do not know how much garlic would be needed for any direct effect, or even if the active parts can withstand cooking temperatures or the body's digestive process. Nevertheless, the possibilities seem too great to ignore, and garlic does contribute a great amount of flavor to a wide variety of recipes.

Chicken Paprika

✓ *Makes 4 portions.*

1 whole chicken, quartered	$\frac{1}{2}$ cup dry white wine
2 oz peanut oil	4 oz tomatoes, peeled, seeded and diced
2 tsp garlic, chopped	2 tsp black pepper, coarse-ground
2 oz onions, chopped	$\frac{1}{8}$ tsp red pepper, crushed
4 oz red bell peppers, or canned pimientos, if not available	1 bay leaf
	2 T Spanish paprika

1. Sear the chicken in hot oil until well-browned.
2. Remove chicken from pan and sauté garlic, onion, and bell peppers in same pan for 2 minutes.
3. Add white wine to pan and reduce until almost dry.
4. Add tomatoes, black and red peppers, bay leaf, and paprika to pan; heat through.
5. Return chicken to pan and cover.
6. Cook in hot oven (375°F) for 35 minutes.
7. Remove chicken from pan and place on hot plates for service.
8. Puree vegetables in blender to form a smooth sauce. (Remove the bay leaf first.)
9. Strain and pour over chicken.

Cajun Chicken Burgers with Jack Cheese Pockets

✓ *Makes 10 portions.*

3 lb chicken meat (taken from 2 whole chickens), ground

12 oz onions, fine dice

¼ cup prepared mustard, coarse-prepared (or dijon mustard)

2 T Cajun spice

1 T cumin, ground

1½ T black pepper, coarse-ground

2 tsp white pepper, coarse-ground

⅛ tsp cayenne pepper, crushed

½ cup dry bread crumbs

1 lb Jack cheese, shredded

1. Mix all ingredients together except cheese.
2. Form cheese into 1½-oz balls.
3. Form 6 oz of ground chicken mixture over each cheese ball and press into patty shape.
4. Cook burgers on broiler grates until well-marked on both sides (about 4 minutes each side).
5. Finish cooking burgers in hot oven (400°F) until cheese seeps out from center and burgers are cooked through.

Notes: Chicken is a perfect meat for making specialty burgers. A plain chicken-meat burger may seem a poor substitute for beef burgers; yet, when seasoned properly, it provides a special taste.

Chicken's generally mild flavor blends well with various spices and herbs. Tarragon, thyme, basil, garlic, cumin, and even cinnamon can be added to create an entire menu of low-fat, delicious burgers.

Chicken Indienne

✓ *Makes 10 portions.*

2 whole chickens, deboned and skinned,
  in 1-inch cubes
½ cup corn flour
2 oz corn oil
8 oz celery, fine dice
4 oz leeks, white only, fine dice

1 T garlic, chopped
¼ cup curry powder
1 T white pepper, coarse-ground
1 cup whole-kernel corn
1 qt lean chicken stock (hot)
½ cup almonds, toasted

1. Dredge chicken in corn flour.
2. Sauté chicken in hot oil until well-browned.
3. Remove from pan.
4. Sauté celery, leeks, and garlic in pan until tender.
5. Add curry powder and white pepper, stir well.
6. Return chicken to pan, add corn, and stir.
7. Add hot chicken stock and stir again.
8. Cover pan and finish cooking over low flame for 20 minutes, stirring occasionally.
9. Garnish with almonds before serving.

Smothered Chicken and Onions

✓ *Makes 8 portions.*

2 whole chickens, quartered
3 oz virgin olive oil
1 lb Spanish onions, sliced thin
1 lb leeks, white parts only, sliced thin
  (reserve a few green rings for garnish)

2 T garlic, chopped
1 T white pepper, coarse-ground
2 T fresh marjoram
2 bay leaves
4 oz dry white wine

1. Sear chicken pieces in hot oil until well-browned; remove from pan.
2. Add onions to pan and sauté until just beginning to brown (about 10 minutes).
3. Add leeks, garlic, bay leaves, and white pepper and sauté for another 5 minutes.
4. Return chicken to pan and cover partly with cooked onions.
5. Add white wine and marjoram.
6. Cover the pan and bake in 350°F oven for 1 hour.

Note: Because chicken has such a delicate taste, a simple application using these flavoring vegetables and liquids — the onions, leeks, garlic, and white wine — helps to create a very exciting taste. The chicken is served with the cooked onions; the pan drippings are a healthy sauce.

Baked Chicken in Cucumber-Lime Sauce

✓ *Makes 8 portions.*

1 T garlic, chopped
8 oz leeks, white only, sliced
2 oz olive oil
2 whole chickens, quartered
2 T fresh lemon thyme, chopped
1 qt lean chicken stock
4 cucumbers, peeled, seeded, and sliced
  (about 2 cups)

½ cup plain, low-fat yogurt
juice from 2 limes
1 T cilantro, fresh chopped
1 T mint, fresh chopped
1 T parsley, fresh chopped

1. In a large roasting pan, sauté garlic and leeks in olive oil, until leeks are tender.
2. Add chicken, lemon thyme, and stock.
3. Cover and bake in 350°F oven for 1 hour.
4. Remove chicken and return to oven to keep hot.
5. Add cucumbers to stock and simmer together until cucumbers are tender (about 10 minutes).
6. Puree stock with cucumbers and leeks in a blender at high speed.
7. Add yogurt and lime juice and blend for another 30 seconds.
8. Pour sauce over chicken and garnish with blend of chopped fresh cilantro, mint, and parsley.

Georgia Chicken

✓ *Makes 5 portions.*

1 egg white	5 chicken breasts, boned
¼ cup corn flour	2 oz peanut oil
1 T water	3 oz peach wine
⅓ cup raw peanuts, chopped	½ cup fresh peaches, skins removed, sliced
1 tsp white pepper, ground	1 tsp lemon juice

1. Mix egg white, water, and corn flour together to make a thin batter.
2. Add chopped peanuts and white pepper.
3. Dip chicken breasts in batter and sauté in hot peanut oil until well-browned and cooked through.
4. Remove excess oil from pan and add peach wine, lemon juice, and sliced peaches.
5. Simmer together for 1 minute and serve.

Note: The flavors of the peaches, peach wine, lemon juice, and the peanuts give great character to an otherwise simple dish.

Italian Peasant Chicken

✓ *Makes 10 portions.*

2½ whole chickens, cut into quarters	2 tsp rubbed sage
2 oz virgin olive oil	2 T fresh rosemary leaves
1 T garlic, chopped	1 qt Italian plum tomatoes, peeled, seeded, and diced
4 oz onions, small dice	
4 oz bell peppers (red preferably), small dice	1 T white pepper, coarse-ground
1 cup dry white wine (soave)	4 bay leaves
	1 lb mushrooms, sliced

1. Sear chicken quarters in hot oil until well-browned on both sides; remove from pan.
2. Add garlic, onions, and bell peppers, and cook for 2 minutes.
3. Add wine, sage, and rosemary and simmer until wine is reduced by half.
4. Add tomatoes, pepper, bay leaves, and mushrooms and cook for 2 additional minutes.
5. Return chicken to pan, cover, and bake in 350°F oven for 45 minutes. (Be sure to remove bay leaves before serving.)

Notes: The very simple, "peasant"-style recipes perfectly use local ingredients in creating very exciting and nutritional menus. Salt and butter may not have been readily available for use in the peasant kitchen, so cooks had to rely on a combination of flavoring vegetables and fresh herbs to supply taste to their family meals. Wine, usually a table variety, is used in large quantities to add richness and gourmet quality to the simplest of preparations.

Turkey Breast with Bulgur-Clam Stuffing

✔ *Makes 10 portions.*

4 oz celery, peeled, small dice
2 oz olive oil
1 T garlic, chopped
4 oz shallots, small dice
4 oz pimientos, small dice
1½ cups bulgur
4 dozen littleneck clams, removed from the shells, chopped
2 T marjoram leaves, freshly chopped
2 T thyme leaves, freshly chopped

2 T white pepper, ground
3 qt turkey stock
1 whole turkey breast, deboned, skin removed
1 cup flour
4 egg whites
2 cups fine bread crumbs
2 tsp mace, ground
1 cup low-fat sour cream

1. Sauté celery in 2 T olive oil until tender.
2. Add garlic, shallots, and pimientos and cook an additional 2 minutes.
3. Add the bulgur and chopped clams and stir completely.
4. Add herbs, 1 T white pepper, and 3 cups boiling turkey stock and cook in a covered pan until liquid is completely absorbed.
5. Cool cooked bulgur and clam stuffing for easier handling.
6. Slice turkey breast into ½-inch slices and pound thinly.
7. Place ¼ cup stuffing on each piece of turkey and roll the turkey like a cigar.
8. Dredge turkey roll in flour, egg whites (whipped with 2 T water), and then dried bread crumbs.
9. Roast turkey rolls in hot oven (375°F) until golden-brown and stuffing has reached internal temperature of 160°F.
10. Mix rest of the olive oil with remaining flour and cook for 5 minutes to form a roux.
11. Stir in remaining turkey stock and cook until thickened.
12. Stir in ground mace, the other tablespoon of white pepper, and sour cream.
13. Serve turkey rolls, sliced, over the sauce.

Notes: This recipe, a lean, complete protein choice, is enhanced by the rich minerals of the clams. Clams are an important source of iodine, which is necessary for the proper functioning of the thyroid gland. Without iodine, the thyroid gland cannot produce thyroxen, a hormone that directly affects the body's metabolism, causing sluggishness and easy weight gain. Severe iodine deficiencies can cause a great swelling of the thyroid gland as the result of goiter, which causes the gland to malfunction. **Important:** People who have reduced the amount of salt in their diets also reduce the amount of iodine, which is part of iodized table salt. Clams and oysters become even more important, in these instances, for their natural iodine content.

Bulgur is whole wheat that has been parboiled to crack the germ and then redried. In this form, it can be used much like rice in many recipes.

Turkey Breast Parmigiana

✓ *Makes 10 portions.*

10, 4-oz slices of boneless turkey breast
2 egg whites
2 oz low-fat skim milk
½ cup flour

2 cups fresh bread crumbs
2 oz virgin olive oil
5 T parmesan cheese

Sauce:
4 oz onions, fine dice
2 oz green bell peppers, fine dice
1 T garlic, chopped
1 oz virgin olive oil
3 cups plum tomatoes, peeled, seeded, and diced

2 T tomato paste
2 T fresh basil, chopped
1 T fresh parsley, chopped
2 tsp black pepper, coarse-ground
4 oz barolo wine (or any complementary wine substitute)

1. To make sauce, sauté onions, bell peppers, and garlic in olive oil until onions are soft.
2. Add the rest of the sauce ingredients and bring to a boil.
3. Reduce sauce to a simmer and cook for 1 hour.
4. Pound turkey slices very thin.
5. Mix egg white and skim milk together for a low-fat, cholesterol-free egg wash.
6. Dredge turkey slices in flour, then egg wash, and finally in bread crumbs, making sure to evenly coat each slice.
7. Sauté breaded turkey slices in olive oil until well-browned on both sides.
8. Place turkey on roasting sheet pan and spoon 2 oz of tomato sauce on each.
9. Sprinkle about ½ T parmesan cheese on each slice.
10. Bake in 400°F oven for 10 minutes.

Notes: Breaded turkey breast is an excellent substitute for breaded veal, which is traditionally used in a parmigiana dish. It is low in fat and cholesterol and a great buy economically. The use of virgin olive oil for cooking gives the breading an excellent olive flavor that can complement the powerful flavor of the tomato sauce and parmesan cheese. It is not necessary to use virgin olive oil for the sauce, because the flavor will be wasted. A more economical type of oil can be used instead.

Turkey and Tomato Stir-Fry

✔ *Makes 10 portions.*

3 lb boneless turkey, trimmed and cut
   into strips
2 oz sesame oil
1 T ginger, chopped
1 T garlic, chopped
½ lemon, for its juice
1 lime, for its juice
1 T black pepper, coarse-ground

⅛ tsp red pepper, crushed
10 oz celery, peeled and cut on bias
8 oz green onions, diced (reserve the
   green parts for garnish)
2 cups tomatoes, peeled, seeded, and cut
   into julienne strips
1 cup lean turkey or chicken stock
2 T cornstarch

1. Using a wok or large sauté pan, sear turkey strips in hot oil.
2. Remove turkey and hold. Add ginger, garlic, peppers, celery, and whites from onions and stir together quickly in the remaining oil.
3. Return turkey strips and add tomatoes.
4. Cook quickly to heat everything through.
5. Dissolve cornstarch in stock and add to mix.
6. Add green onion garnish and stir well.
7. Add lemon and lime juice.

Notes: Stir-frying is a technique that is gaining great renewed popularity in consumers' fight to reduce saturated fats in the cooking process. It is a high-heat, quick-cooking method that needs very little fat, as the ingredients are tossed quickly around a well-seasoned pan, preventing them from sticking and scorching. Vegetables and meats are cooked so quickly they retain most of their natural nutrients, which then contribute to the overall nutritional worth of the recipe.

All foods contain phosphorus. Poultry has an unusually generous amount, about 95 mg in a 3-oz serving. Phosphorus is needed by all body cells. Most of the phosphorus is found in the body with magnesium and calcium to make strong bones and teeth. Phosphorus also combines with sugars, fats, and vitamins to perform many essential body functions. In general, protein foods supply most of the phosphorus. Turkey is a high-quality protein, and with the skin removed, is leaner than all red meats. Turkey is also a good source of vitamins B_{12}, B_1, B_3, and heme iron.

Braised Game Hens with Zucchini-Tomato Sauce and Chianti

✓ *Makes 5 portions.*

5 Cornish game hens, cut in halves	2 T tomato paste
2 oz virgin olive oil	6 oz Chianti classico riserva
4 oz onions, sliced thin	1 lb zucchini, sliced thin
1 T garlic, chopped	2 tsp black pepper, coarse-ground
2 cups fresh tomatoes, peeled, seeded, and diced	2 T fresh basil, chopped

1. In large sautoir (straight-sided sauté pan), sear game hens in hot oil until well-browned on both sides.
2. Remove hens from pan.
3. Sauté onions and garlic until onions are soft.
4. Add tomatoes, tomato paste, and wine.
5. Bring to a boil and add zucchini and spices.
6. Stir well.
7. Return game hens to pan, cover, and bake in 350°F oven for 40 minutes.

   Notes: Game hens can be substituted for the other forms of poultry in all the recipes of this chapter; however, they lend themselves particularly well to this braised-style preparation. Combining the hens with the tomatoes, garlic, onion, and zucchini in the same cooking pan allows those distinct flavors to intertwine, forming a delicate balance.

Broiled Game Hens with Pineapple-Barbecue Sauce

✓ *Makes 10 portions.*

10 Cornish game hens, cut in halves

Sauce:

1½ cups pineapple juice concentrate	2 oz fresh lemon juice
2 tsp fresh ginger, grated	2 oz peanut oil

1. Mix all sauce ingredients together in a pot and bring to a boil.
2. Pour hot sauce over game hens and place in refrigerator.
3. Marinate game hens overnight.
4. Remove hens from marinade to cook.
5. Cook game hens slowly on an open-flame broiler for best results. (Do not cook too quickly, or sauce will burn before the hens are done.)
6. Baste game hens with sauce during cooking, and serve with heated sauce for dipping when done.

12

Seafood entrées

Seafood is proving to be one of the healthiest food choices. Its low fat content and omega 3 fatty acids, which appear to aid in the prevention of some coronary heart disease, make it a good option for a variety of menus.

The delicate flesh, although highly perishable, is the perfect medium for many different taste combinations and cooking methods. Most varieties of seafood can be poached, steamed, broiled, grilled, fried, or baked, making seafood very versatile.

Poached Salmon with Leek and Fennel Sauce

✓ *Makes 10 portions.*

Fresh salmon fillets, cut into 4- to 6-oz portions

Court bouillon:
1 qt. lean fish stock, preferably salmon
1 tsp white pepper, coarse-ground
½ tsp lemon juice

1 bay leaf
1 tsp cardamom seed
½ cup dry white wine

Sauce:
1 oz olive oil
1½ lb leek, white only, diced
1 lb fresh fennel, diced
1 T shallots, chopped

1 oz all-purpose flour
3 cups salmon stock
1 T orange juice

1. Mix all ingredients for the court bouillon and bring to a simmer.
2. Poach salmon fillets until they flake apart.
3. To make sauce, sweat leeks, fennel, and shallots in oil until tender.
4. Add flour and stir well for 2 to 3 minutes.
5. Add stock; continue to cook for 15 to 20 minutes.
6. Puree sauce in blender, adding orange juice last.
7. Spoon on hot plate and place poached salmon steak on top.

Salmon Fricassee with Tomatoes and Artichoke Hearts

✓ *Makes 10 portions.*

1 T shallots, finely chopped
3 oz virgin olive oil
3-lb salmon fillet, skinless, in 1-inch strips
4 T cynar (aromatized wine flavored with
    artichokes)

2 cups tomatoes, seeded, peeled, and diced
2 tsp white pepper, coarse-ground
10 artichoke hearts, sliced in quarters
¼ cup fresh basil, chopped
1 tsp fresh lemon juice

1. Sauté shallots in olive oil.
2. Add salmon strips and cook quickly, turning on both sides.
3. Remove salmon and reserve on side.
4. Add cynar and reduce liquid by half.
5. Add tomatoes, pepper, artichoke hearts, and basil.

6. Cook together for 15 minutes.

7. Add lemon juice and stir.

8. Return salmon to pan and heat through. Serve immediately.

Notes: Salmon is a cold-water fish, and therefore has a higher than average amount of omega 3 fatty acids in its flesh. Omega 3 fatty acids prevent clumping of the blood cells and the formation of blood clots. Eskimos, who consume large amounts of these types of fish, do not suffer, in general, from heart disease.

Broiled Tuna with Chili-Garlic Sauce

✓ *Makes 10 portions.*

10, 6-oz fresh tuna steaks

Marinade:

1 oz canola oil	2 tsp white pepper, coarse-ground
1 fresh lemon, for its juice	1 T paprika

Sauce:

1 whole garlic bulb, broken into cloves	1 T cumin, ground
1 oz canola oil	2 tsp celery seed
8 oz celery, peeled, small dice	1 T black pepper, coarse-ground
8 oz Spanish onions, small dice	⅛ tsp red pepper, crushed
8 oz bell peppers, small dice	3 cups fresh tomatoes, seeded and diced
2 T chili powder	2 T lemon juice

1. To make the sauce, place garlic cloves in small roasting pan with oil.

2. Roast in hot oven until dark-brown.

3. Place pan on top of the stove and remove the garlic.

4. Add celery to the pan and cook until tender.

5. Add onions, bell peppers, and spices; cook until tender.

6. Add tomatoes and cook for 30 minutes.

7. Add lemon juice and adjust seasonings to taste.

8. After tuna has marinated for 20–30 minutes, remove from the marinade and broil until flaky.

9. Serve with sauce.

Notes: The Western diet is rich in saturated fat and omega 6 polyunsaturated fatty acids. Much of the omega 6 polyunsaturated fat comes from grains, nuts, and seeds. Too much omega 6 fatty acid converts to an overload of thromboxane, the prostaglandin that causes platelet aggregation in the blood and vasoconstriction, which can lead to blood clots and decreased blood flow to the heart. Omega 3 fatty acid competes with omega 6 fatty acid in the cell membrane and produces a prostaglandin that decreases platelet aggregation and increases vasodilation. Fish is the best source of this valuable omega 3 fatty acid.

Broiled Cajun Catfish

✔ *Makes 1 portion.*

1, 6-oz catfish fillet or small, whole catfish
2 oz peanut oil
1 tsp thyme leaves
1 tsp marjoram leaves
½ tsp black pepper, coarse-ground

¼ tsp white pepper, coarse-ground
⅛ tsp red pepper, crushed
½ tsp garlic, chopped
1 tsp lemon juice

1. Mix all the ingredients together and use as a marinade for the catfish.
2. Marinate the catfish for 3 to 4 hours.
3. Place the catfish on a hot broiling rack and cook about halfway through.
4. Turn the fillet carefully and finish cooking; the catfish should not be turned more than once, or it may break apart.

   Notes: Fresh-water catfish supplies magnesium, phosphorus, iron, and copper. Catfish should be stored in the coolest part of the refrigerator and used within 1 to 2 days to maintain their nutritive qualities. Bacteria that cause food-borne illness grow more rapidly in fresh-water fish than in salt-water fish. Room temperature aids in the growth of these bacteria, so it is vitally important to keep the fish refrigerated until cooking.

   Magnesium, along with calcium, produces strong teeth and bones and proper functioning of muscles and nerves. Magnesium also works as a co-enzyme in energy production.

Hazelnut Sea Trout

✔ *Makes 10 portions, preferably done in single orders.*

1 T white pepper, coarse-ground
½ cup corn flour
10, 6-oz fillets of sea trout
2 oz canola oil
2 oz hazelnut oil

1 lemon, for its juice
4 oz frangelica liqueur
2 cups fish stock, preferably sea trout
3 T cornstarch
½ cup hazelnuts, sliced, toasted

1. Mix white pepper with corn flour.
2. Dredge fish in flour and sauté in the combined oils.
3. Deglaze pan first with lemon juice, then with frangelica.
4. Mix the stock with the cornstarch and add to pan.
5. Garnish with hazelnuts.

Notes: The mild flavor of canola oil makes it a versatile cooking medium. The benefits of canola oil are close to those of olive oil, without the pronounced olive taste. Canola oil comes from the rapeseed plant. However, one of the fats in rapeseed is euric acid, which has a toxic substance. The FDA did not allow rapeseed to be used in this country until recently, when the euric acid levels were lowered.

Canola oil also contains monounsaturated oleic acid, the same acid that makes olive oil such a great substitute for other saturated oils and fats. Studies show that oleic acid actually lowers the LDL cholesterol in humans while leaving alone the HDL (good) cholesterol.

Flounder Hawaii

✓ *Makes 1 portion.*

2 T flour
$\frac{1}{8}$ tsp white pepper, coarse-ground
1, 6-oz flounder fillet
$\frac{1}{2}$ oz walnut oil
$\frac{1}{2}$ oz peanut oil
$\frac{1}{2}$ mango, medium-ripe
1 T walnuts, chopped, toasted

$\frac{1}{4}$ tsp allspice, freshly ground
$\frac{1}{4}$ lemon, for its juice
1 tsp lemon zest
3 oz fish stock, preferably made from
    flounder bones
1 T cornstarch

1. Season flour with white pepper, and dredge fillet in flour.
2. Heat both oils together in sauté pan until quite hot.
3. Sauté fillet until golden-brown on both sides.
4. Remove flounder from pan and keep hot.
5. Add mango and walnuts to pan with the allspice.
6. Deglaze pan with lemon juice and add the zest.
7. Dissolve the cornstarch in the stock and add to the pan.
8. When the stock thickens, spoon lightly over flounder and serve.

Notes: A very interesting experiment was done in which the fatty acid composition of eggs was changed. The chickens in the experiment were fed fish oil, which is thought to have beneficial effects on the heart and brain. Of course, it is more practical to eat fish than to feed fish oil to chickens. What is not well-known is that we would do just as well by eating walnuts. The body changes the linolenic fatty acid in walnuts to the same fatty acid obtained from fatty fish.

Grouper Florentine with Yogurt-Sesame Topping

✓ *Makes 5 portions.*

1 T garlic, finely chopped
2 oz virgin olive oil
2½ lb spinach, cooked and chopped
¼ tsp nutmeg
2 tsp white pepper, coarse-ground
5 grouper fillets, 6 oz each
1½ cups plain, low-fat yogurt

6 oz green onions, sliced thinly (include some of the tender greens)
¼ tsp red pepper, crushed
½ tsp sesame oil
¾ cup dry bread crumbs
¼ cup sesame seeds, toasted

1. Sauté garlic in olive oil for a few seconds.
2. Add spinach, nutmeg, and half of the white pepper.
3. Sauté together for 1 minute.
4. Place spinach mixture on baking tray and lay fillets on top.
5. Mix together yogurt, onions, the remaining white pepper, red pepper, and sesame oil.
6. Divide yogurt mixture evenly over each fillet.
7. Cover the pan and bake in 400°F oven for 20 to 25 minutes, or until fish flakes apart.
8. Combine bread crumbs and sesame seeds and sprinkle on top of cooked fish.
9. Place pan under salamander (overhead broiler) until bread crumbs become slightly toasted.

Note: Any fish can be substituted for the grouper in this recipe; even oysters, clams, and crab can be treated this way. It is not only a very tasty recipe, but is also one of the most attractive plate presentations.

Tarragon Trout

✓ *Makes 1 portion.*

1 pan-size trout or 6-oz fillet
1 piece of parchment paper
1 oz dry white wine
1 tsp shallots, chopped
¼ tsp fresh ginger, chopped
1 tsp fresh tarragon, chopped

¼ tsp white pepper, coarse-ground
3 oz fish stock, preferably made from the same type of trout
1 tsp cornstarch
few drops of lemon juice

1. Lay fillet on paper, and pour wine directly on top.
2. Add shallots, ginger, half of the tarragon, and white pepper.
3. Fold paper over the fish and fold the edges tightly to seal in the steam.
4. Place fish in hot oven (400°F).
5. Fish is completely cooked 2 minutes after the paper bag inflates with steam.
6. Thicken fish stock with cornstarch and add rest of the tarragon.
7. Add lemon juice to finish the sauce.
8. Place fish on hot plate still wrapped in paper and serve sauce on the side.

Notes: Steaming has long been known to help lock in vitamins and minerals rather than letting them leach out, as happens when poaching or baking. However, steaming fish is not an easy task using conventional methods. The procedure used in this recipe does replicate the steaming process on an individual scale for the wrapped trout. The wine and juices trapped inside the paper pouch generate steam during the cooking process. The pouch will expand like a balloon, letting the chef know that the steam is working.

Baked Snapper with Pecan-Corn Bread Topping

✓ *Makes 10 portions.*

2 oz olive oil	1 T coriander, ground
10, 4-oz snapper fillets, boneless	1 T white pepper, coarse-ground
4 oz bell peppers, small dice, preferably red	2 T paprika
4 oz onions, small dice	½ cup pecans, chopped
¼ cup fresh parsley, chopped	2 T fresh lemon juice
2 cups corn bread crumbs	4 oz skim milk

1. Rub 1 oz of oil on baking dish large enough to hold the fillets without touching.
2. Place fillets in pan.
3. Mix together all other ingredients, except milk and lemon juice, and divide evenly on top each fillet.
4. Pour milk in pan, without getting the corn bread topping wet.
5. Bake in hot oven (about 375°F) for 45 to 50 min until fillets begin to flake.
6. Drizzle lemon juice over fillets just before serving.

Maryland Bluefish Cakes

✓ *Makes 10 portions.*

2 lb bluefish fillets, dark fat strip removed

Dressing:

6 oz onions, fine dice

6 oz red bell peppers, fine dice

¼ cup mustard coarse-prepared

4 egg whites

1 T garlic, chopped

4 T Old Bay sasoning (a Baltimore Spice Co. seasoning blend)

1 T black pepper, coarse-ground

¼ tsp red pepper, ground

2 cups dry bread crumbs

Poaching liquid:

1 qt water

1 lemon

4 ribs of celery

2 bay leaves

1. Combine all ingredients for the poaching liquid and bring to a simmer for 5 minutes.
2. Poach the fillets in the poaching liquid until they easily flake apart.
3. Mix well all other ingredients except the bread crumbs.
4. When the bluefish is finished cooking, allow it to cool completely and, using a fork, break it into large flakes.
5. Mix the broken fillets with the dressing.
6. Add bread crumbs, a little at a time, until the mix holds together when pressed (the actual amount of bread crumbs needed may vary each time).
7. Form 2-oz patties; shape them tight and flat.
8. Pan-fry in large pan with any vegetable oil (virgin olive oil gives the best results).

Notes: Bluefish is a relatively inexpensive fish. Many people are not accustomed to the pronounced fishy taste that bluefish has, and shy away from using this very versatile seafood. The strong taste is primarily associated with the fatty vein, almost black in color, that runs along the back of each fillet. Removing this vein makes the flavor more acceptable.

This recipe takes into account the fish's stronger flavor by combining it with other pronounced flavors such as those of onion, mustard, and the spices. Made into fish patties, bluefish can serve as an inexpensive menu choice, either as an appetizer or main entrée.

Ocean Perch Sambucca

✓ *Makes 5 portions.*

1 T anise seeds, crushed	1 T ginger, freshly chopped
2 tsp white pepper, coarse-ground	6 oz white mushrooms, sliced
1½ cups corn flour	6 oz fresh fennel, julienne
2 oz corn oil	3 oz sambucca liqueur
2 lb ocean perch fillets	

1. Mix crushed anise seeds and pepper with corn flour.
2. Heat oil in sauté pan.
3. Dredge fillets in flour and pan-fry quickly in hot oil.
4. Remove fish from pan and place on hot plate to keep warm.
5. Pour off most of the remaining oil and add ginger, mushrooms, and fennel to sauté pan; cook quickly while stirring constantly.
6. Add sambucca and allow this to reduce by half.
7. Spoon mushroom and fennel mixture over fillets.

Notes: The use of sambucca, or any other flavored liqueur, adds a lot of character to this otherwise simple preparation. Because of the liqueur's sweetness, it must be used sparingly. As it reduces, it takes on a syrupy consistency that binds together the other ingredients in a very healthful sauce.

The fresh fennel gives an interesting taste combination with the ginger and sambucca. Sambucca, which is made from the elderbush, has a licorice flavor that is a good complement to the fennel.

Sautéed Oysters and Leeks in Toasted Whole-Wheat Saucers

✔ *Makes 5 portions.*

5, 1-inch slices of whole-wheat bread
2 T butter, melted
1 T garlic, finely chopped
8 oz leeks, sliced white only
1 tsp white pepper, coarse-ground

⅛ tsp red pepper, crushed
2 oz olive oil
40 select oysters, with their liquid
2 oz dry vermouth
2 T fresh tarragon, chopped

1. Trim bread slices around the edges, shaping them into round circles.
2. With a spoon, press down on the centers of each slice, leaving a ¼-inch rim in place.
3. Brush on melted butter and toast under broiler.
4. Sauté garlic, leeks, and white and red peppers in oil.
5. Add oysters and oyster liquid and toss gently.
6. Add vermouth and tarragon and cook until wine is reduced by half.
7. Spoon oysters into whole-wheat saucers and garnish with chopped fresh tarragon.

Maryland Crabmeat with Mushrooms and Leeks

✔ *Makes 5 portions.*

4 oz leeks, white only, sliced thin
2 tsp garlic, chopped
2 oz virgin olive oil
5 oz mushrooms, sliced
2 T fresh tarragon, chopped
½ cup dry sherry

2 tsp white pepper, coarse-ground
⅛ tsp red pepper, crushed
1½ lb lump Maryland crabmeat
½ cup low-fat sour cream
5 slices whole-wheat toast, unbuttered
1 T fresh parsley, chopped

1. Sauté leeks and garlic in olive oil until leeks are soft, but not brown.
2. Add mushrooms and 1 T tarragon; sauté until mushrooms are tender.
3. Add sherry and white and red peppers; reduce wine by half.
4. Add crabmeat and sour cream and heat together.
5. When heated through, serve on toast points and sprinkle with chopped parsley.

Notes: This recipe uses the virgin olive oil for its flavor as well as its nutritional benefits. Substituting a lesser-grade olive oil will not produce the same effect. Because the crabmeat is already cooked, it only needs to warm up in the sauce. A lot of cooks make the mistake of overcooking crabmeat.

Stir-Fry Shrimp and Scallops with Oriental Mushrooms

✓ *Makes 10 portions.*

2 oz peanut oil

1 T sesame oil

2 T ginger, freshly chopped

2 T garlic, freshly chopped

1½ lb large shrimp, peeled and deveined

1½ lb sea scallops, cut in half-inch circles

1 lb spring onions (scallions), sliced thin
  (keep the green for garnish)

4 oz shiitake mushrooms, sliced

8 oz straw mushrooms, sliced

4 oz water chestnuts

2 T white pepper, coarse-ground

¼ tsp red pepper, crushed

4 oz dry sherry

½ cup sesame seeds, toasted

1. In a large sauté pan or wok, heat the peanut and sesame oils together.

2. Add ginger and garlic and cook for 5 seconds.

3. Add shrimp, scallops, and spring onions and cook quickly for 1 minute, moving the product constantly.

4. Add mushrooms, water chestnuts, and other spices and mix thoroughly.

5. Add sherry and cover pan for a final 30 seconds of cooking.

6. Add sesame seeds and onion greens for garnish before serving.

Notes: For the best results, this dish should be cooked in smaller batches than the 10 portions in the recipe.

This is a typical Oriental-style dish that uses sherry in place of the more traditional soy sauce. Soy sauce is very high in sodium and should be used very sparingly. The sherry adds such a complementary flavor to the seafood and mushrooms that the soy sauce is not missed.

Madeira Shrimp Kabobs

✓ *Makes 10 portions.*

40 jumbo shrimp, peeled and deveined
20 pearl onions, peeled
4 large tomatoes, peeled, cut into
   wedges, and seeded

20 pieces cucumber, seeded, tournéed

Marinade:
2 oz olive oil
2 T shallots, chopped
1 T garlic, chopped
1 T fresh ginger, chopped

4 oz madeira wine
2 T basil leaves
1 T white pepper
¼ tsp liquid red pepper

1. Put kabobs together, alternating shrimp with vegetables, 4 shrimp per order.

2. Place kabobs in marinade for 1 hour.

3. Broil quickly until done.

4. Serve with cranberry-rice pilaf (see recipe in Vegetables and Starches chapter) or other pilaf.

   Notes: Although fatty fish are a generous source of omega 3 fatty acid, which prevents clotting in the arteries, these fish are also more likely to pick up toxins, which then accumulate in the fat. Therefore, in addition to heeding state health department warnings, it is best to choose lean fish more often. Lean fish will also help to keep the total dietary fat down to the 30%-of-calories level most widely recommended. Shrimp, which are very low in total fat, supply a good amount of protein and the minerals iron and zinc.

13

Vegetarian entrées

Proper vegetarianism requires a good nutritional education. Placing specific restrictions on our diets necessitates supplementing those diets with other foods, or varieties of foods, to supply the essential nutrients.

Beans, peas, nuts, and grains play essential roles in the diets of vegetarians. In combination, they are the only vegetable sources for the eight essential amino acids needed for proper health. Luckily, they also lend themselves to a variety of flavors and styles of cooking. The one thing that is essential to great taste in vegetarian cooking is the cook's creativity.

Vegetable and Wild Rice Stir-Fry with Roasted Cashews

✓ *Makes 10 portions.*

1 lb yellow squash, medium dice
1 lb zucchini squash, medium dice
8 oz red bell peppers, medium dice
8 oz white mushrooms, medium dice
2 bunches spring onions, diced
1 T ginger, freshly grated
3 oz virgin olive oil

2 tsp white pepper, coarse-ground
¼ cup marjoram, freshly chopped
1 qt wild rice (cooked in white vegetable stock)
2 cups tomato concassé (peeled, seeded, and diced)
½ cup cashews, roasted

1. Sauté squash, bell peppers, mushrooms, and onions with ginger in very hot olive oil.
2. Add marjoram, pepper, rice, and tomatoes and heat through, stirring quickly and constantly.
3. Add cashews just before serving.

   Notes: The roasted cashews and wild rice both contribute protein to the vegetarian diet. Diets that lack animal proteins must become dependent on grains and nuts to supply the proteins needed for building and renewing body tissues.
   Although it is not considered necessary to consume grains and nuts in the same meal to retain the benefits of their proteins, it is beneficial because each contributes something the other lacks. When meat is not part of the diet, the essential amino acids can only be obtained through a variety of vegetable foods.

Herbed Black-eyed Peas With Almonds and Raisins

✓ *Makes 10 portions.*

1 lb black-eyed peas
2½ qt white vegetable stock
8 oz onions, medium dice
4 oz bell peppers, medium dice
8 oz celery, peeled and diced
8 oz dried raisins
1 T fresh thyme leaves, chopped

2 tsp garlic, finely chopped
2 tsp cumin, ground
2 tsp rosemary leaves
1 tsp cloves, ground
2 tsp black pepper, coarse-ground
⅛ tsp red pepper, crushed
1½ cups almonds, sliced, toasted

1. Soak peas overnight in cold water.
2. Drain water from peas and cook in vegetable stock until almost tender (about 2 hours).
3. Add onions, bell peppers, celery, raisins, herbs, and spices and cook for an additional 30 minutes. The raisins will plump and the celery will still have a slight crunch.

4. Using a slotted spoon, spoon peas onto the serving plate.

5. Garnish each serving with the almonds.

Notes: Raisins are a concentrated source of all the nutritional elements available in grapes. It was once thought that wine helped kill viruses, but it was later discovered that the grapes contributed those properties.

Raisins' most valuable nutritional feature is iron. There is 5.1 mg of iron in 1 cup of raisins. (The daily requirement for a man is 10 mg.) Black-eyed peas also have a lot of iron — 3.3 mg per 1 cup (cooked).

To get the most iron absorption from the raisins and the peas, it is best to have a food rich in vitamin C also present in the meal. In this recipe, the bell peppers have this function.

Millet Pilaf with Dates, Apples, and Pistachio Nuts

✓ *Makes 10 portions.*

4 cups millet	2 tsp black pepper, coarse-ground
¼ cup olive oil	½ tsp white pepper, coarse-ground
8 oz onions, small diced	8 cups white vegetable stock
2 tsp garlic, finely chopped	4 cups red delicious apples, small dice
2 tsp fresh ginger, grated	2 cups pistachio nuts, roasted (vegetari-
½ T whole allspice, cracked	ans need the fat from nuts)

1. In a large, oven-proof pan, sauté millet, onions, garlic, and ginger in oil until millet begins to brown and gives off a slightly nutty aroma.

2. Add stock and spices and stir well.

3. Bring the stock to a full boil.

4. Cover the pan and bake in a 350°F oven for 20 minutes.

5. Stir in apples and pistachio nuts just before service; apples should stay crunchy.

Notes: Millet is a staple in Africa, China, and Japan. It has a bland taste, but lends itself to a variety of other flavors when cooked together with vegetables and spices. A whole grain, millet contains more iron than many other grains, along with a good supply of magnesium, a nutrient that is removed from processed grains.

The apples, coupled with the olive oil, make this a heart-healthy dish — albeit high in calories because of the dates, oil, and nuts. You should not try to weigh calories at all costs. The concentrated caloric foods often have concentrations of nutrients. This is the case with dates and pistachios.

Dates have five of the B vitamins, including B_6 and folacin, and are a source of potassium, calcium, phosphorous, magnesium, iron, zinc, copper, and manganese (10 dates have 228 calories).

All nuts have protein, but pistachios have one of the highest amounts, exceeded only by black walnuts. Three ounces of pistachio nuts have the same amount of calcium as a whole cup of cottage cheese, and more phosphorus than 3 oz of liver. Pistachio nuts also contain vitamin A, which is usually found in nuts, and vitamins B_1, B_3, and E.

Indian Bean and Cabbage Pie

✓ *Makes 10 portions.*

6 oz pinto beans	2 tsp garlic, finely chopped
6 oz black beans	2 tsp cumin, ground
2 qt white vegetable stock	2 tsp coriander, ground
4 oz celery, peeled, fine dice	2 tsp turmeric, ground
4 oz leeks, white only, fine dice	2 tsp ginger, freshly grated
8 oz green cabbage, finely shredded	

Topping:

2 cups white cornmeal	2 oz peanut oil
4 egg whites, slightly beaten	1 cup water
1 T baking powder	

1. Soak beans in cold water overnight.
2. Drain the beans and simmer them in the vegetable stock until tender, about 2 to 3 hours.
3. Add celery, cabbage, leeks, garlic, and spices to the beans and stock; cook together for 30 minutes.
4. Mix together the cornmeal and the baking powder in a separate bowl, then add the egg whites, oil, and water.
5. Stir the corn-bread ingredients to the consistency of a heavy batter; if too thick, add a little more water.
6. Ladle bean mixture into individual, portion-size oven crockery, or a similar type of dish or terrine.
7. Spoon corn-bread mixture on top and smooth evenly up to the rim.
8. Bake at 375°F for 20 to 25 minutes, or until corn bread is lightly browned.

Vegetable Creole with Aromatic Rice

✓ *Makes 10 portions.*

6 oz onions, small dice
4 oz bell peppers, small dice
4 oz celery, peeled, fine dice
2 oz peanut oil
2 tsp garlic, finely chopped
2 oz tomato paste
1 tsp black pepper, coarse-ground
¼ tsp cayenne pepper
½ cup dry sherry
2 cups tomatoes, peeled, seeded, and
    diced, concassé

12 oz yellow squash, thinly sliced
1 T fresh lemon juice
8 oz button mushrooms, whole
12 oz green beans, French-cut
1½ cups aromatic rice
3 cups white vegetable stock
1 T fresh thyme leaves, chopped
2 T fresh parsley
8 oz okra, sliced

1. Sauté onions, bell peppers, and celery in oil until tender.
2. Add garlic, tomato paste, and peppers and cook for 2 minutes.
3. Add sherry; reduce liquid by half.
4. Add tomatoes, squash, okra, and lemon juice and simmer for 1 hour.
5. Add mushrooms and green beans for last 15 minutes of cooking.
6. Cook scented rice in vegetable stock with thyme and parsley.
7. Serve the creole over the rice.

Note: Aromatic rice is a special variety grown in the southeastern United States, especially in Louisiana, Georgia, and Mississippi. It is a long-grain rice with a natural aromatic taste. If aromatic rice is not available, use brown rice and increase the amounts of herbs during cooking.

Spaghetti Squash with Red Bean Goulash

✓ *Makes 10 portions.*

1 lb dry red beans	2 tsp fresh thyme, chopped
2½ qt red vegetable stock	2 tsp black pepper, coarse-ground
4 oz celery, peeled, fine dice	2 T Hungarian paprika
4 oz onions, small dice	2 bay leaves
2 oz virgin olive oil	4 oz tomato paste
1 T garlic, finely chopped	1½ lb boiling potatoes, peeled, medium dice
2 tsp caraway seeds	2 large spaghetti squash

1. Soak dry beans in cold water overnight.
2. Cook drained beans in vegetable stock until tender.
3. In the meantime, sauté celery and onion in oil until onions are tender but not brown.
4. Add garlic, caraway seeds, thyme, pepper, paprika, and bay leaves to sauté pan and toss together quickly.
5. Stir in tomato paste and reduce heat to low for an additional 10 minutes.
6. Cook potatoes separately in plain water.
7. When the beans are tender, drain most of the liquid off and save.
8. Add tomatoes and spices to the beans and stir in well.
9. To the same pot, add potatoes and just enough of the bean juices to make a light sauce.
10. Simmer together for 20 minutes before serving.
11. Cut squash in halves.
12. Place flesh side down in a pan with ¼ inch of water and bake in 375°F oven for 45 minutes.
13. When squash is tender, remove from the pans and scoop the flesh right onto the serving plate (will resemble strings of spaghetti).
14. Serve bean goulash over squash. (Make sure to remove the bay leaves first.)

Fennel-Seed Noodles with Cabbage and Yellow Split Peas

✓ *Makes 10 portions.*

2 lb green cabbage, shredded	2 T fresh basil, chopped
1 cup yellow split peas, dry	1 lb dry fettuccine noodles
4 oz leeks, white only, sliced	1 T fennel seeds
2 tsp garlic, finely chopped	2 oz olive oil
2 tsp white pepper, fine-ground	2 oz pernod (optional)
⅛ tsp cayenne pepper	2 T fresh parsley, finely chopped
4 cups white vegetable stock	2 oz parmesan cheese

1. Place peas, leeks, garlic, peppers, and stock in saucepan and cook until peas are tender.

2. Add cabbage and basil and simmer for an additional 20 minutes.

3. In the meantime, cook the fettuccine noodles in plain boiling water until tender.

4. In a sauté pan, heat the oil with the fennel seeds (grind half the seeds in a pepper mill before adding).

5. Add drained noodles to sauté pan, then the pernod, and toss all ingredients together.

6. Plate noodles and spoon cabbage and split-pea sauce on top.

7. Sprinkle each serving with parmesan cheese, then parsley.

Eggplant Lasagne

✓ *Makes 10 portions.*

1 large eggplant, peeled, in ½-inch cubes
3 oz virgin olive oil
4 oz onions, small dice
2 oz green bell peppers, small dice
1 T garlic, finely chopped
2 T fresh basil, chopped
1 T fresh oregano, chopped
2 T fresh parsley, chopped

2 tsp black pepper, coarse-ground
⅛ tsp cayenne pepper, fine-ground
4 cups plum tomatoes, peeled, seeded,
   and diced, concassé
1½ lb dry lasagne noodles
4 oz mozzarella cheese, grated
2 oz parmesan cheese, grated
6 oz ricotta cheese

1. Sauté eggplant in oil until tender and lightly browned.
2. Add onions, bell peppers, and garlic and cook for 2 minutes.
3. Add spices, herbs, and tomatoes; cook for 1 hour.
4. Cook lasagne noodles in plain water until tender.
5. Mix together mozzarella and parmesan cheese and reserve for topping.
6. In large baking pan, spoon enough eggplant sauce to cover the bottom.
7. Lay in lasagne noodles to cover sauce (all noodles should be laid in one direction).
8. Spoon on more sauce to cover noodles.
9. Divide ricotta cheese into 4 portions and drop first portion in ½-tsp dots over the sauce.
10. Repeat procedure with noodles (layered in the opposite direction from the previous layers), sauce, and cheese four times.
11. Cover the last layer of sauce and cheese with a final layer of noodles and sauce.
12. Cover entire dish with the parmesan and mozzarella mixture.
13. Bake in 350°F oven for 45 minutes.

Notes: In layered dishes such as a lasagne, the overall flavor comes from the taste combinations in each layer. It is extremely important to make each layer as evenly distributed with ingredients as possible. The lasagne noodles will absorb some of the excess moisture in the sauce and vegetables, making the final product firm and easy to cut into portions.

The eggplant gives the sauce a unique flavor without overpowering the total taste. The addition of any other vegetables in the layered sections would also give excellent results.

Vegetable Pizza

✓ *Makes 10 portions.*

Dough:
2 cups warm water (about 80°F)
2 tsp dry yeast
1 tsp sugar
¼ tsp salt

3 oz virgin olive oil
1½ cups oat flour
1½ cups whole-wheat flour
1½ cups bread flour

Sauce:
4 oz onions, small dice
2 oz bell peppers, small dice
6 oz zucchini squash, small dice
2 oz virgin olive oil
1 T garlic, finely chopped
2 T fresh basil, chopped

2 T fresh oregano, chopped
2 T fresh parsley, chopped
2 tsp black pepper, coarse-ground
4 cups tomatoes, peeled, seeded, and
  diced, concassé

Topping:
4 oz onions, sliced thin
4 oz zucchini, sliced thin
4 oz mushrooms, sliced thin
4 oz fresh tomatoes, peeled, seeded, and
  diced, concassé

1 T olive oil
12 oz mozzarella cheese, coarse-grated
1 T fresh basil, chopped

1. To make the dough, add sugar, yeast, and salt to warm water and mix thoroughly.
2. Allow yeast and water to set for a few minutes until a foam-like substance begins to form on the top.
3. Add oil, oat flour, and whole-wheat flour and mix until smooth; if using a mixing machine, run at first speed for only a few seconds.
4. Add bread flour, a little at a time, until a good dough consistency is reached. The finished dough should roll freely on a lightly floured table without sticking to the fingers.
5. Cover dough with plastic wrap and place in refrigerator for at least 2 hours.
6. Make the sauce by sautéing vegetables and garlic in olive oil, add herbs, spices, and tomatoes and cook for 1 hour.
7. Sauté vegetable toppings in olive oil until tender, but not brown.
8. After dough has rested for 2 hours, divide it into 2 portions.
9. Roll out dough to ¼-inch thickness and place in shallow pan (the shape is unimportant).
10. Cover the dough generously with the sauce and spread evenly.
11. Cover entire pizza with cheese and distribute vegetable toppings on top.
12. Sprinkle basil over entire pie.
13. Bake in 500°F oven for 20 minutes, or until crust is well-browned.

Notes: This complete meal demonstrates how a few ingredient substitutions can transform a traditionally high-calorie, high-fat dish into a nutritionally balanced vegetarian meal. Substituting oat and whole-wheat flours for the normal amounts of plain white flour in the dough actually increases the flavor of the crust and adds bran for nutrition and fiber. Substituting fresh flavoring vegetables for the high-fat meat toppings of other pizzas keeps the percentage of fat in line with recommended levels.

The important thing to remember in reproducing recipes that rely so heavily on taste and appearance is always to use the freshest ingredients.

Portuguese Beans and Pasta with Madeira

✓ *Makes 10 portions.*

4 oz red kidney beans, dry
4 oz baby lima beans, dry
1½ qt red vegetable stock
12 oz tomatoes, crushed
1 T rosemary leaves
2 T thyme leaves

1 T black pepper, coarse-ground
⅛ tsp red pepper, crushed
6 oz madeira wine
1 lb green beans, cut in half-inch pieces
4 oz red bell peppers, julienne
1 lb dry pasta, any shape

1. Soak kidney and lima beans in cold water overnight.
2. Drain the beans and add vegetable stock, tomatoes, and spices; cook together until beans are tender.
3. Add madeira, green beans, and bell peppers to cooked beans and allow to cook for 20 more minutes.
4. Cook pasta in separate pot with plain water (unsalted).
5. Add cooked pasta to beans and serve.

Notes: This recipe is simple to prepare. It allows the cook to use any variety of beans, spices, and vegetables to prepare a host of similar recipes.

14

Salads

A salad can be part of a meal or a whole meal in itself. The significant difference between a salad and other types of dishes usually is the inclusion of lettuce greens and a highly seasoned dressing.

Salads can be served cold or hot, or even as a combination of cold and hot, as in "Grilled Chicken Salad." It is important always to use the freshest produce possible and to serve cold salads very cold and hot salads very hot.

Marinated Pinto Bean Salad

✔ *Makes 10 portions.*

2½ lb pinto beans, cooked
¼ cup red wine vinegar
⅔ cup virgin olive oil
2 cups green bell peppers, small dice
1 cup dried dates, chopped
1 cup almonds, sliced and roasted

2 T cumin, ground
2 T basil, dried leaf, or ¼ cup fresh,
   chopped (preferred)
2 T black pepper, coarse-ground
¼ tsp red pepper, crushed

1. Mix all ingredients together, except for the almonds, which are added just before service, and allow them to rest for at least 12 hours.
2. Serve with any mix of lettuce, carrots, radishes, etc.

   Notes: This salad is a good example of the total concept of nutritional cooking. The olive oil contains 75% monounsaturated fat, which is known to help reduce LDL (bad cholesterol) in the diet without affecting the HDL (good cholesterol). When eaten raw, bell peppers are one of the best sources of vitamin C, a water-soluble vitamin that needs daily replenishing. Dried dates are very rich in iron, which is needed to form hemoglobin, and natural sugars, which add a sweetness to the finished salad. The almonds contain a better-quality protein than that found in almost any other plant. The beans also contain protein and a high amount of calcium. The peppers, beans, dates, and nuts are also good nutritional choices because of their fiber. When this salad is served on a bed of green lettuce, such as romaine, it becomes a complete meal. The combination of beans and nuts contains complete protein and could substitute for meat.

Cajun Bean Salad

✔ *Makes 10 portions.*

4 oz dry pinto beans
4 oz dry black-eyed peas
4 oz dry lima beans
4 pints white vegetable stock
2 tsp garlic, finely chopped
2 oz shallots, finely chopped
1 T thyme, freshly chopped
2 tsp black pepper, coarse-ground

1 tsp white pepper, coarse-ground
½ tsp red pepper, crushed
4 oz corn oil
2 T white vinegar
1 T lemon juice, freshly squeezed
1 lb mustard greens, cooked, chopped
½ cup pecan halves

1. Soak all three beans together in cold water overnight.
2. Cook beans in vegetable stock until tender, about 2 hours.
3. Drain beans and cool.
4. Mix garlic, shallots, spices, and oil together; stir well.
5. Add vinegar and lemon juice and stir.
6. Add cold beans to dressing and marinate for at least 1 hour.
7. Drain beans again and serve on a bed of mustard greens.
8. Drizzle some of the dressing on the greens and garnish with pecan halves.

Curried Rice Salad

✓ *Makes 10 portions.*

6 oz celery, peeled, small dice
2 oz peanut oil
1½ pints brown rice
2 tsp ginger, freshly grated
1 tsp cumin, ground
1 tsp white pepper, coarse-ground
1 T curry powder

1½ cups raisins, plumped in hot water and strained
1 cup pitted dates, chopped
3 pints white vegetable stock
2 T lemon juice, freshly squeezed
2 oz peanut oil
½ cup almonds, toasted, sliced

1. Sauté celery in 2 oz of hot oil until tender.
2. Add rice and spices and stir well.
3. Add raisins, dates, and vegetable stock and bring to a full boil.
4. Cover pan and bake in 350°F oven for 20 minutes.
5. Refrigerate cooked rice overnight.
6. Mix lemon juice with 2 oz of peanut oil and stir into cold rice.
7. Serve on bed of lettuce greens with appropriate salad vegetables; garnish with almonds.

Note: This type of marinated rice salad is always better if prepared one day, allowed to sit to give the flavors a chance to mingle, and finished and served the second, or even third, day. The addition of diced apples, orange sections, or any other fruit could further enhance the overall appearance and taste.

Barley Salad with Sweet Yellow and Red Peppers

✔ *Makes 10 portions.*

2 cups barley
6 cups white vegetable stock
2 bunches spring onions, small dice
6 oz celery, peeled, fine dice
2 tsp garlic, finely chopped
½ cup virgin olive oil

2 oz red wine vinegar
2 T lemon juice, freshly squeezed
2 tsp black pepper, coarse-ground
4 oz yellow bell peppers, julienne
4 oz red bell peppers, julienne

1. Cook barley in vegetable stock until tender.

2. Mix all other ingredients together except the bell peppers.

3. While the barley is still hot, stir in the dressing; refrigerate overnight.

4. Stir in bell peppers and serve on a bed of lettuce greens.

Asparagus with Port-Wine Vinaigrette

✔ *Makes 10 portions.*

2½ lb fresh asparagus, peeled and blanched
8 oz olive oil
2 bunches spring onions, whites and tender greens, sliced thinly

2 oz tawny port
2 oz red wine vinegar
½ tsp black pepper, finely ground

1. Cook the asparagus, placing it in boiling, unsalted water for only 1 to 2 minutes. Remove it quickly and place in an ice bath to stop the cooking process. (The asparagus should be bright green and still a little crunchy.)

2. Whisk all other ingredients together and pour over asparagus.

3. Allow asparagus to marinate for at least 1 hour.

4. Pull asparagus from marinade, strain out spring onion, and save some for garnish.

Notes: Tawny port gives an interesting accent to this simple vinaigrette, showing clearly how a simple ingredient substitution can transform a basic dressing into a classic sauce.

Asparagus salad should be garnished appropriately with tomato wedges, cucumber slices, or carrot shavings to add color and taste.

Broccoli-Pasta Salad with Fresh Tuna

✔ *Makes 10 portions.*

1 qt white vegetable stock
2 lb fresh tuna steaks, boneless and skinless
1 lb dry pasta, any shape
1 large bunch broccoli, cut in 2-inch spears
8 oz virgin olive oil
2 T lemon juice, freshly squeezed
2 oz red wine vinegar

2 bunches spring onions, thin sliced
4 oz red bell peppers, small dice
2 T fresh basil, chopped
2 T fresh parsley, chopped
2 tsp white pepper, coarse-ground
⅛ tsp red pepper, crushed

1. In a shallow pan, bring vegetable stock to a simmer.
2. Poach tuna steaks until the flesh can be easily flaked apart with a fork.
3. Remove tuna and cool quickly.
4. Cook pasta separately in plain, unsalted water.
5. Cool pasta quickly to prevent overcooking.
6. Blanch broccoli in boiling, plain water until just tender; cool it quickly to prevent overcooking.
7. Mix all other ingredients together and stir well.
8. Cut cooked tuna into small pieces.
9. Gently mix all ingredients together.
10. Allow salad to marinate for at least 1 hour.

Note: Tuna is not a newcomer to American salads, but fresh tuna gives this salad an interesting twist. The salad is better when allowed to marinate for 24 hours or more. Add the tuna at the last minute to retain its distinctive taste and delicate texture.

Smoked Turkey and Ziti

✓ *Makes 10 portions.*

1 lb ziti
1 lb fresh asparagus, peeled, in 2-inch pieces
1 cup red kidney beans, cooked
4 oz celery, peeled, small dice
2 bunches spring onions, whites and tender greens, thinly sliced
2 tsp garlic, finely chopped

6 oz corn oil
1 T thyme, freshly chopped
1 T parsley, freshly chopped
2 tsp white pepper, coarse-ground
2 oz red wine vinegar
2 T lemon juice, freshly squeezed
2 lb smoked turkey breast, cooked, julienne

1. Cook ziti in plain, unsalted water.

2. Blanch asparagus in boiling water for 2 minutes.

3. Remove asparagus from water and place in an ice bath to stop the cooking process.

4. Mix together all other ingredients, except turkey, and stir well.

5. Pour dressing over the pasta and gently stir in the asparagus.

6. Allow the salad to marinate for at least 1 hour.

7. Garnish with turkey breast.

   Note: Smoked products are usually avoided in the preparation of nutritious meals because of their generally high percentage of salt or natural fats. Smoked turkey breast, however, does not contain a lot of salt because it is not a preserved meat; nor does it contain a lot of fat. There may be some concern that the smoke that flavors these foods is carcinogenic, yet the quantity of smoke that the average person would have to consume to stimulate cancer growth could never be ingested through food. Like everything else, moderation is the best course.

Avocados with Almond-Raspberry Vinaigrette

✓ *Makes 10 portions.*

2 oz raspberry vinegar
6 oz peanut oil
2 tsp orange zest, shavings
5 ripe avocados, sliced thinly
5 small heads bibb lettuce, cleaned, cut in halves

1 pint fresh raspberries
1 T fresh mint, chopped
½ cup almonds, toasted, sliced

1. Mix together raspberry vinegar with oil and orange zest.

2. Layer avocado slices on bed of lettuce and garnish with fresh raspberries.

3. Pour dressing over avocados and raspberries; garnish with almonds and mint.

Note: Avocados are a great, nutritious food. Although fairly high in calories (about 350 each), they are full of vitamins and minerals and very low in saturated fats. Their fat content is made up mostly of oleic fatty acid, with a trace amount of linoleic fatty acid.

Eggplant Salsa Salad

✔ *Makes 10 portions.*

1 medium eggplant, peeled, small dice
2 oz virgin olive oil
4 oz onions, small dice
4 oz celery, peeled, small dice
1 T garlic, finely chopped
2 tsp black pepper, coarse-ground
½ tsp white pepper, coarse-ground
⅛ tsp red pepper, crushed

2 tsp cumin, ground
1 T marjoram, freshly chopped
4 oz green bell peppers, small dice
5 cucumbers, peeled, seeded, and small dice
1 qt tomatoes, peeled, seeded, and small dice
2 T lemon juice, freshly squeezed

1. Sauté eggplant in hot oil until lightly browned.

2. Add onions, celery, garlic, and spices and cook for 3 additional minutes.

3. Add all other ingredients and remove from fire.

4. Refrigerate salad overnight before serving.

5. Serve on a bed of mixed salad greens.

Broccoli and Cauliflower Coleslaw

✓ *Makes 10 portions.*

1 bunch broccoli, finely chopped	2 tsp white pepper, ground
1 head cauliflower, finely chopped	¼ tsp liquid red pepper
½ cup carrots, shredded	1 tsp celery seed
½ cup plump raisins	4 oz cider vinegar
4 oz onions, finely chopped	1 pint corn oil

1. Mix all ingredients together and allow to marinate overnight for best results.

2. Drain salad and serve on crisp salad greens.

   Notes: This recipe illustrates how a traditional coleslaw can be made more exciting by substituting other cruciferous vegetables for the commonly used cabbage. Broccoli and cauliflower both add taste and dimension to a simple dish.

   The use of the cider vinegar also makes this slaw a little different by adding a natural sweetness to the dressing. Together with the carrots and the raisins, it gives this recipe full-bodied flavor.

Country Slaw

✓ *Makes 10 portions.*

2 lb green cabbage, finely shredded	1 T mustard, coarse-prepared
8 oz leafy kale, finely shredded	1 tsp celery seed
4 oz green bell peppers, fine julienne	2 tsp black pepper, coarse-ground
4 oz radishes, sliced thin	3 T cider vinegar
4 oz onions, sliced thinly	2 T lemon juice, freshly squeezed
2 T sugar	1 cup corn oil

1. Mix together cabbage, kale, bell peppers, radishes, and onions.

2. In a saucepan, mix sugar, mustard, celery seed, pepper, oil, vinegar and lemon juice; bring to a boil.

3. Pour hot dressing over vegetables and refrigerate overnight.

Italian Vegetables with Tomato-Basil Vinaigrette

✓ *Makes 10 portions.*

1 cup virgin olive oil
2 oz tomato paste
2 oz red wine vinegar
2 tsp black pepper, coarse-ground
2 tsp garlic, finely chopped
2 T basil, freshly chopped
8 oz fresh fennel, julienned
8 oz zucchini, sliced thinly
8 oz artichoke hearts, sliced

5 cucumbers, peeled, seeded, and sliced
4 oz onions, sliced thinly
4 oz green bell peppers, sliced thinly
2 lb plum tomatoes, $\frac{1}{2}$-inch slices
8 oz curly spinach, cleaned, in bite-size
    pieces
1 head curly endive, cleaned, in bite-size
    pieces

1. Mix oil, tomato paste, vinegar, pepper, garlic, and basil together for the dressing.

2. Mix fennel with other vegetables except spinach and endive.

3. Pour dressing over vegetables and allow to marinate for at least 1 hour.

4. Mix spinach and endive together and use as bed for marinated vegetables and dressing.

Sweet Potato Salad with Pecan-Honey Dressing

✓ *Makes 10 portions.*

3 lb sweet potatoes
8 oz celery, peeled, small dice
8 oz carrots, peeled, small dice
4 oz bell peppers, small dice

2 oz peanut oil
2 T lemon juice, freshly squeezed
2 oz honey
1 cup pecans, chopped

1. Cook sweet potatoes in their jackets in hot, not boiling, water.

2. When potatoes can easily be pierced with a fork, they are done.

3. Cool potatoes and peel; cut into medium dice.

4. Mix all other ingredients together and stir well.

5. Stir sweet potatoes into mix gently so they don't break up too much.

Note: This Southern recipe transforms another simple dish, potato salad, into an exciting taste sensation. Because of the vegetable choices, only a small amount of honey is needed to give it a signature taste.

International Greens and Walnut Vinaigrette

✓ *Makes 20 portions and 1 qt of dressing.*

1 head curly endive, cleaned, in bite-size pieces

1 head romaine lettuce, cleaned, in bite-size pieces

1 head radicchio, cleaned, in bite-size pieces

6 Belgian endive, cleaned, in bite-size pieces

5 ripe tomatoes, cut in wedges

3 bunches spring onions, white part only, cut in strips

Dressing:

6 oz walnut oil

12 oz canola oil

6 oz red wine vinegar

2 T lemon juice, freshly squeezed

1 T black pepper, coarse-ground

6 oz walnuts, broken

1. Toss together romaine, curly endive, and radicchio.

2. Mix together all dressing ingredients except the walnuts. (They will be used as a garnish.)

3. Place salad greens on cold plates and put a few Belgian endive leaves on each; decorate with tomatoes and spring onions.

4. Spoon dressing over salad just before service; garnish with walnuts.

Notes: To make a salad exciting, it is important to choose ingredients that in themselves give excitement. The tendency is to use only mild-flavored greens and vegetables and spice them up with an overpowering dressing. Instead, greens should be selected to give as much character to the salad as a wine does to a meal; the dressing should complement the salad ingredients, not overpower them.

In this simple salad, the curly and Belgian endives add character through their mild bitterness. Tossed with the sweet romaine lettuce and the vibrantly colored radicchio, they give punch to an otherwise average salad.

The walnut oil is only a portion of the total oil used because it is so strongly flavored. It is used more as a seasoning for the dressing than as a main ingredient. Canola oil is used as an accompanying oil because of its bland flavor. It produces the desired effects for a salad dressing (shine, appeal, even distribution of seasonings and vinegars on the main salad ingredients), yet does not conflict with the walnut oil's taste. Using another flavored oil with the walnut oil (olive oil, for example) would confuse the palate.

Grilled Chicken Salad

✓ *Makes 10 portions.*

2 oz onions, finely chopped
1 tsp garlic, finely chopped
¼ cup lime juice, fresh
¼ cup olive oil
10 chicken breasts, boneless, skinless
1 head iceberg lettuce

1 head romaine lettuce
½ head curly endive
4 oz radishes, sliced thinly
2 cucumbers, peeled and sliced thinly
5 tomatoes, cut in 6 wedges each
½ cup pine nuts, toasted

Dressing:
½ cup olive oil
¼ cup lime juice, fresh

1 T mint, freshly chopped
2 tsp black pepper, coarse-ground

1. Mix onions, garlic, ¼ cup of lime juice, and ¼ cup olive oil and stir well.
2. Pour over chicken breasts and marinate overnight.
3. Remove chicken from marinade and broil slowly until done.
4. In the meantime, clean the salad greens.
5. Cut the lettuces in bite-size pieces and mix with radishes and cucumbers.
6. When chicken is cooked, cut into long strips and place on top of a bed of the salad mixture.
7. Mix dressing ingredients together.
8. Garnish with 3 wedges of tomatoes on each salad and drizzle some dressing over entire dish.
9. Garnish entire salad with pine nuts.

Note: The mixture of different salad greens gives any salad a new taste dimension. The proportion of endive to the sweeter lettuces is low because of its slightly bitter taste.

Fruit Salad with Honey-Orange Dressing

✓ *Makes 10 portions.*

5 red delicious apples, cored and diced
5 Bartlett pears, cored and diced
2 cups red seedless grapes, cut in halves
2 cups fresh peaches, sliced

½ cup honey
¼ cup orange juice, freshly squeezed
¼ cup walnuts, chopped
¼ cup raisins

1. Place diced apples in small amount of lemon water to prevent them from discoloring.
2. Place all fruit, except raisins, in a bowl.
3. Mix honey and orange juice and pour over fruit.
4. Garnish with walnuts and raisins.

Note: The interesting twist to this otherwise simple salad is the orange juice-honey dressing.

15

Soups

The second oldest cooking method known to humans (the first was roasting) also provides the most nutrition in a single dish. Placing a hollow, bowl-shaped object on a hot rock near a fire (gourds probably were the first soup pots), the ancient cook added a variety of meats, vegetables, roots, flowers, and seeds, along with some water, and prepared a tasty dish.

Later, the popularity of soups grew because dried and other types of preserved foods could be rehydrated when fresh meats and vegetables were not available. In many early homes, a cauldron of soup was continuously cooking over open flames, and anything hunted, harvested, or raised was thrown in the simmering liquid for the regular meals, day after day. Accompanied by a piece of crusty bread, this became a very healthy meal.

Soups can be made in such a way as to supply all a healthy meal's essential parts — proteins, carbohydrates, fats (easily kept within the 30% recommended for daily caloric intake), vitamins, and minerals — in a single dish.

White Vegetable Stock

✓ *Makes 1 gallon.*

1 lb leeks (white only), rough-cut
1 lb onions, rough-cut
2 lb celeriac (or hearts of celery only), rough-cut
1 lb white turnips, rough-cut

4 bay leaves
2 T garlic, chopped
¼ cup white peppercorns, cracked
5 qt water

1. Place all ingredients in a large stockpot and simmer for 2 hours.
2. Strain.

   Notes: The ingredient proportions in this recipe are only guidelines. Vegetable stocks can be made from any kitchen vegetables. However, some vegetables, especially in the cruciferous family (cabbage, broccoli, cauliflower, etc.), may create a bitter taste if cooked too long and should be avoided in reduced stocks. Stocks that are made quickly and used right away can utilize these vegetables. For the sake of consistency, it is important to use similar vegetable stocks in similar preparations. For example, if a particular vegetable stock is used for a casserole or soup, the same type of stock should be used each time that dish is made.
   This white vegetable stock has a wider range of applications than red or darker stocks because it will add very little color to the final product.

Red Vegetable Stock

✓ *Makes 1 gallon.*

1 lb leeks, rough-cut
1 lb onions, rough-cut
2 lb celery, rough-cut
2 lb tomatoes, rough-cut
2 lb carrots, rough-cut

4 bay leaves
2 T garlic, chopped
2 T black peppercorns, cracked
2 T white peppercorns, cracked

1. Place all ingredients together into a large stock pot and simmer for 2 hours.
2. Strain.

   Notes: The white and red vegetable stocks have very different flavors, so they will each have their own applications. In this stock, the tomatoes, celery, and carrots add color and taste.

When vegetables are cooked in water, the minerals and some vitamins are leaked into the stock; therefore, these stocks not only add flavor but nutrition to the dishes in which they are used. It is also important to cook the stock in a covered pot because oxygen can rob it of essential vitamins.

Vegetable Barley Soup

✔ *Makes 10, 10-oz portions.*

1 lb carrots, julienned	8 oz white mushrooms, julienned
8 oz onions, julienned	2 T rosemary leaves
8 oz bell peppers, julienned	2 T thyme leaves
2 oz olive oil	2 T celery seed
2 qt red vegetable stock	1 T black pepper, coarse-ground
4 cups tomatoes, peeled, seeded, and diced, concassé	1 tsp white pepper, coarse-ground
1 cup dried barley	¼ tsp red pepper, crushed

1. Sweat carrots, onions, and bell peppers in hot oil until tender but not browned.
2. Add vegetable stock and tomatoes and bring to a quick boil.
3. Add barley and reduce to a simmer.
4. When barley is cooked (about 15 minutes) add spices and mushrooms.
5. Allow soup to simmer for an additional 15 to 20 minutes.

Notes: This excellent soup features two exceptionally nutritious foods: carrots and barley. Carrots are a known source of beta carotene, a precursor for vitamin A. Carotene is converted through the intestinal walls into vitamin A. Some fat is also needed for this process, so raw carrots would not have as high a nutritional benefit if consumed by themselves. Vitamin A is needed for growth, for night vision, and for healthy skin. It also helps the body resist infections of the respiratory tract by keeping the tissues moist. Research says that beta carotene is a factor in preventing the growth of certain types of tumors.

Further research suggests that cholesterol levels can be significantly lowered in cases where carrots become a regular food source. Similar results have been reported with broccoli, cabbage, and onions.

Barley is a good source of dietary fiber. Fibers probably lower cholesterol by binding together the bile acids that contain cholesterol. Usually, the cholesterol from the bile acids are recycled and used again when the liver makes more bile. The soluble fibers are not digested and therefore carry the bile acids and the cholesterol with them when they are excreted from the body.

Mexican Lentil

✔ *Makes 10, 10-oz portions.*

2 T garlic, chopped	½ cup cilantro, chopped
8 oz onions, diced	4 bay leaves
1 lb celery, peeled and diced	2 T celery seed
8 oz red bell peppers, small dice	1 T black pepper, coarse-ground
4 cups tomatoes, diced	1 tsp white pepper, coarse-ground
1 lb yellow turnips, small dice	¼ tsp red pepper, crushed
1 lb whole-kernel corn	2 qt lean chicken stock
1 lb dried lentils	2 oz corn oil
2 T cumin, ground	1 lb lima beans
2 T coriander, ground	juice from 2 limes

1. Sauté garlic, onions, celery, and bell peppers in hot oil until tender but not brown.

2. Add all other ingredients except the lima beans, lime juice, and cilantro.

3. Bring the soup to a full boil; reduce to a simmer for 20 minutes.

4. Add lima beans and cilantro; cook for an additional 10 minutes.

5. Finish with lime juice just before service. (Remove bay leaves before serving.)

Notes: Lentils, which are legumes, are an excellent source of calcium. In many parts of the world, they are the main source of dietary calcium. Although milk is the best source, it is not always available, and some people have trouble drinking milk. In diets where there is less phosphorus, either by reduction or elimination of milk and meat, legumes become an adequate source because the amount of calcium needed in the diet is directly related to the amount of phosphorus. All legumes are also an excellent source of copper, a mineral not readily found in other foods.

Three-Bean Soup with Kale

✔ *Makes 10, 10-oz portions.*

8 oz onions, medium dice	8 oz red kidney beans, cooked
1 lb celery, peeled, small dice	8 oz baby lima beans, cooked
1 T garlic, chopped	8 oz cut green beans
2 oz olive oil	2 T cumin, ground
½ gallon red vegetable stock	2 T coriander, ground
3 bay leaves	1 T black pepper, coarse-ground
1 lb kale, finely shredded	1 T jalapeño peppers, finely chopped, with seeds
2 cups tomatoes, concassé	
2 oz tomato paste	

1. Sweat onions, celery, and garlic in olive oil until tender but not brown.
2. Add vegetable stock, bay leaves, and kale, cook until kale is tender, about 30 minutes at a quick simmer.
3. Add all other remaining ingredients and cook until well-blended, approximately 20 more minutes. (Remove bay leaves before serving.)

Notes: This soup is an excellent representation of a full-flavored food full of proteins, vitamins, and minerals. The kale is an excellent source of calcium and B vitamins; it also has vitamin K, iron, and dietary fiber. When used as a flavoring vegetable for soup, the otherwise strong taste of kale gives body to the overall flavor.

The combination of the three beans is another good example of the way to use variety in guaranteeing good nutrition. All three beans contain water-soluble fibers and protein, along with iron. The lima beans are especially valuable for their folicin, an important B vitamin that comes in 213 forms. In lima beans, folicin has a form that is easily absorbed by the body.

Cabbage and Broccoli Soup with Chick-Peas

✔ *Makes 10, 10-oz portions.*

2 lb broccoli
8 oz red bell peppers, small dice
8 oz leeks, small dice
1 T garlic, chopped
1 T ginger, chopped
2 oz olive oil
2 lb cabbage, medium dice
2 qt vegetable stock

2 cups tomato paste
2 sticks cinnamon
1 T cloves, ground
1 lb chick-peas, cooked
1 T black pepper, coarse-ground
2 tsp white pepper, coarse-ground
⅛ tsp red pepper, crushed

1. Cut florets from the broccoli and reserve for the finished soup. Peel the remaining stems and fine-dice the tender centers.
2. Sweat the bell peppers, leeks, garlic, and ginger in the hot oil until tender but not brown.
3. Stir in the cabbage and broccoli stems and sweat for an additional 2 to 3 minutes.
4. Add the stock, tomato paste, cinnamon, cloves, and chick-peas and allow the soup to simmer for about 30 minutes.
5. Add florets and peppers and cook until broccoli is tender.

Notes: This is a very nutritious soup. Chick-peas are very high in iron, which is the one mineral responsible for the prevention of anemia. Especially for vegetarian diners, whose iron supply cannot come from meat consumption, legumes such as chick-peas become essential. Chick-peas are also high in protein and fiber, and contain no cholesterol.

Cabbage is a good source of vitamin K and fiber. Vitamin K is needed for four protein substances that are involved in blood coagulation (i.e., prothrombin, which converts to thrombin, then to fibrinogen, and finally to fibrin, the key substance). Vitamin K also plays an important part in the immune system. Fifty percent of the needed vitamin K is made through the intestinal tract, the remaining 50% must come from food sources.

Winter Squash Potage

✓ *Makes 10, 10-oz portions.*

2 large butternut squash, peeled, seeded, in 1-inch cubes
2 large acorn squash, peeled, seeded, in 1-inch cubes
1 medium pumpkin, peeled, seeded, in 1-inch cubes
1 lb leeks, white part only
4 cinnamon sticks
2 tsp nutmeg, ground
2 qt white vegetable stock
2 large spaghetti squash
2 T white pepper, coarse-ground
4 oz amaretto
2 cups plain yogurt
fresh mint leaves for garnish

1. In a soup pot, put butternut and acorn squashes, pumpkin, leeks, cinnamon, nutmeg, and vegetable stock and cook for 30 minutes, or until squash is tender.

2. Remove cinnamon sticks and puree soup in a blender at high-speed.

3. In the meantime, cut the spaghetti squash in half and roast, cut side down, on a lightly oiled pan. When the squash is tender, remove the pulp with a spoon. The strands (resembling spaghetti noodles, thus the name) can be rough-cut and added to the pureed soup.

4. Season with the pepper and amaretto.

5. Serve hot or cold, garnished with a spoon of yogurt and mint leaves.

Notes: For centuries, winter squashes have supported the human diet through the very hard and cold winters of the Western continents. Grown with relative ease, especially in the cooler climates, these fruits can be stored in cold and dry areas for as long as nine months. Before the advent of refrigeration, they were a most popular winter vegetable. These varieties are a good source of vitamin A and fiber.

Cream of Pumpkin

✓ *Makes 10, 10-oz portions.*

8 oz onions, small dice	1 T nutmeg
8 oz celery, peeled, small dice	2 tsp kosher salt
2 oz corn oil	2 T white pepper, fine-ground
2½ lb pumpkin, peeled, seeded, and diced	8 cups white vegetable stock
1 T garlic, chopped	1½ cups low-fat sour cream
4 cinnamon sticks	

1. Sauté onions and celery in oil until tender but not brown.
2. Add pumpkin, garlic, and spices and cook together for another 2 minutes.
3. Add stock and simmer for about 30 minutes, or until the squash is very tender.
4. Remove cinnamon sticks.
5. Puree soup in a blender at high speed or in a food mill until very smooth.
6. Float 1 tsp sour cream on top of each portion and sprinkle with ground cinnamon before serving.

   Notes: Pumpkin is a delicious way to get vitamin A. One cup of pumpkin has 15,680 IU of this vitamin. (The recommended daily allowance for a healthy male is 50,000 units.) Vitamin A deficiency results in unhealthy hair, poor night vision, poor growth in children, dry skin, and lowered resistance to colds. A bowl of pumpkin soup is a fresh alternative to the greens that children (and some adults) do not like.

Puree of Cauliflower and Yellow Split Peas

✓ *Makes 10, 10-oz portions.*

1 lb leeks, whites only (reserve some
   green rings for garnish)
2 T garlic, finely chopped
2 oz canola oil
2 lb cauliflower (rough-cut, after reserving
   some florets for garnish)

1 lb dried yellow split peas
3 qt white vegetable stock
1 T white pepper, coarse-ground
1 tsp red pepper sauce (tabasco is one type)
1 cup chablis
1 cup low-fat sour cream

Croutons:
sliced French bread
virgin olive oil

crushed garlic

1. Mix virgin olive oil with garlic and brush on sliced French bread. Lay flat on baking sheet and bake in hot oven (450°F) until well browned for 2 to 3 minutes.
2. Sweat leeks and garlic in canola oil.
3. Add cauliflower, split peas, and vegetable stock.
4. Bring to a boil and simmer for 1 hour.
5. Add spices and chablis and cook for another 15 minutes.
6. Puree in a blender at high speed and strain.
7. Add sour cream and garnish with croutons.

Notes: Puree soups are more nutritious than many other types because there is no need for a thickening agent, such as a roux or cornstarch dilution, other than the pureed vegetables and beans. The yellow split peas make an excellent thickening agent by themselves, and the pureed cauliflower gives a pleasant taste to this soup without overpowering the other flavors.

Forester Chicken Soup

✔ *Makes 10, 10-oz portions.*

1½ lb chicken meat, diced
4 oz olive oil
8 oz onions, small dice
1 lb celery, peeled and diced
2 T garlic, chopped
4 oz whole-wheat flour
2 qt lean chicken stock
4 cups tomatoes, diced

2 T marjoram leaves
3 bay leaves
2 T thyme leaves
2 T black pepper, coarse-ground
1 tsp white pepper, coarse-ground
1 lb white mushrooms, sliced
4 oz dry red wine

1. Sear chicken meat in hot oil until lightly browned; remove from pot and reserve.
2. Add onions and celery to pot and cook until tender.
3. Add garlic and flour; cook for 5 minutes over low flame.
4. Add chicken stock, tomatoes, marjoram, bay leaves, thyme, and peppers.
5. Add chicken meat back to the soup.
6. Bring the soup to a full boil; reduce to a simmer for an additional 20 minutes.
7. Add mushrooms and red wine and cook for 10 additional minutes.
8. Adjust seasonings to taste. (Remove bay leaves before serving.)

Notes: Mushrooms are a very good source of chromium. Other good sources include whole-wheat breads, meats, and vegetables. Chromium is essential for the body's absorption of sugars and fats. It may help prevent diabetes in some cases. Long-term chromium deficiency is associated with cardiovascular disease. Physical stress, such as running, causes a loss of chromium through the urine.

Country Chicken and Shrimp

✓ *Makes 10, 10-oz portions.*

2 T garlic, chopped
1 lb shrimp (medium count), peeled and
   deveined (retain shells for stock)
2 oz peanut oil
2 T white peppercorns, cracked
1 bunch parsley stems
4 bay leaves
1 whole chicken (3 to 4 lb), deboned, in
   1-inch cubes (retain bones for stock)
1 gallon water

8 oz onions, small dice
8 oz celery, peeled, small dice
2 oz all-purpose flour
1 lb yellow turnips, medium dice
4 oz red bell peppers, small dice
1 lb lima beans, cooked
1 lb spinach, cooked, chopped
1 lb button mushrooms, whole
¼ cup basil, freshly chopped
¼ cup oregano, freshly chopped

1. Sauté garlic and shrimp shells together in 1 oz of oil for 2 minutes.
2. Add peppercorns, parsley, and bay leaves.
3. Add chicken bones and water and simmer for 2 hours.
4. Strain the stock through a fine strainer (chinois) or cheesecloth.
5. In the other ounce of oil, sauté onions and celery until tender.
6. Add chicken meat and sear lightly.
7. Add flour to make a light roux.
8. Add stock and stir well.
9. Add turnips and bring soup to a simmer for 30 minutes.
10. Add all other ingredients and heat thoroughly for about 15 minutes.
11. Adjust seasoning to taste. (Remove bay leaves before serving.)

Notes: Soups are by far the easiest way to obtain the greatest nutritional variety in a single meal. This soup is a good example.

Chicken and shrimp have perfect proteins for building body tissue, which needs regular renewal. Peanut oil is a great choice because of its high percentage of monounsaturated fat (47%). The lima beans add more protein and the cholesterol-reducing, water-soluble fibers. All of the vegetables, celery, peppers, turnips, spinach, mushrooms, and even the parsley, combine to lace the soup with a variety of vitamins and minerals needed to regulate bodily processes.

Coriander Turkey Chili

✓ *Makes 10, 10-oz portions.*

2 lb turkey meat, coarse-ground	8 cups tomatoes, diced
1 lb onions, small dice	2 T basil leaves
1 lb green or red bell peppers, diced	$\frac{1}{4}$ cup chili powder
2 T coriander seeds	2 T jalapeño peppers, chopped
2 oz vegetable oil	1 T black pepper, coarse-ground
2 T garlic, chopped	1 tsp white pepper, ground
4 oz tomato paste	2 cups red beans, cooked

1. In a large pot, cook the turkey, onions, bell peppers, garlic, and coriander seeds in the oil until the turkey is well-browned.

2. Add all other ingredients and bring to a quick boil.

3. Reduce to a simmer for 45 minutes.

4. Allow to sit overnight; adjust the seasonings before service. (Chili will have a better flavor.)

Notes: Turkey meat can replace all or part of the beef in more traditional recipes without affecting the overall taste. Using turkey greatly reduces the amount of saturated fats. In this recipe, where traditionally used beef is totally replaced with turkey, coriander has been added to create a new taste.

Red beans are in the legume family. Legumes are a good source of protein and the best source of the mineral molybdenum. Molybdenum is an important part of the enzymes that are involved in body chemical processes called oxidative and reductive reactions. In cases where molybdenum was inadvertently left out of the diets of intravenously fed patients, symptoms of headaches, night blindness, nausea, vomiting, lethargy, disorientation, and even coma developed. Immediate reversal occurred when molybdenum was reintroduced into the diets.

Italian Beef and Tomato Ziti

✓ *Makes 10, 10-oz portions.*

2 lb lean beef, diced
2 oz virgin olive oil
8 oz onions, small dice
8 oz green or red bell peppers, small dice
2 T garlic, chopped
2 T black pepper, coarse-ground
⅛ tsp red pepper, crushed
3 bay leaves

2 qt tomatoes, concassé
4 oz tomato paste
8 oz white mushrooms, sliced
2 T basil leaves, freshly chopped
2 T oregano leaves, freshly chopped
2 T marjoram leaves, freshly chopped
1 cup dry red wine
1 lb dry ziti noodles, cooked in unsalted
    water

1. Sear beef in hot oil with onions and bell peppers.

2. Add garlic, black and red peppers, and bay leaves and cook an additional 2 minutes.

3. Add tomatoes and tomato paste; cook for 1 hour.

4. Add mushrooms and herbs; simmer for 15 minutes.

5. Add wine and cooked noodles for last 5 minutes of cooking. (Remove bay leaves before serving.)

   Notes: Almost every publication today says to avoid red meat because of the concern for cholesterol. However, what these same studies do not point out are red meat's beneficial properties.

   Red meats are one of the best sources for vitamin B_{12}, cobalamin. A deficiency of this vitamin may lead to tingling and numbness in the extremities and may even progress to a lack of muscle coordination and paralysis. Such a deficiency may also lead to memory difficulties that are easily reversed when the deficiency is corrected.

   Red meats are also one of the best sources of iron, necessary for anemia prevention. Iron deficiency is one of the major dietary deficiencies worldwide.

Apple and Pear Calvados

✓ *Makes 10, 10-oz portions.*

3 lb Granny Smith Apples, peeled and
    seeded
3 lb Bartlett pears, peeled and seeded
1½ qt apple juice, unsweetened
1½ qt pineapple juice, unsweetened

4 cinnamon sticks
2 tsp nutmeg, ground
¾ oz cornstarch, dissolved in 2 T water
1 pint plain, low-fat yogurt
4 oz calvados brandy

1. In a large pot, put apples, pears, apple juice, pineapple juice, and cinnamon sticks.
2. Bring mixture to a boil and cook for about 20 minutes, or until fruit is very tender.
3. Remove cinnamon sticks and puree mixture in a blender at high speed.
4. Return cinnamon to pot with pureed fruit and juice.
5. Add nutmeg and dissolved cornstarch.
6. Bring soup back to a boil until thickened.
7. Remove from the heat and allow to cool completely.
8. Before service, stir in yogurt and calvados.

Notes: Fruit soups are gaining in popularity on menus, particularly in the hot summer months. Although they are not as complete a meal as the heartier soups, they are excellent nutritional choices to round out the daily meal.

In this recipe, the calvados is added after the soup is chilled, so the alcohol will still be present. Calvados, made from apple wine, will not leave a strong alcohol taste on the palate.

Cherry and Peach Soup

✓ *Makes 10, 10-oz portions.*

4 lb fresh peaches, peeled, stones removed
2 qt peach nectar or peach juice
1 qt water
1 pint orange juice, unsweetened
4 oz grenadine syrup
1 T allspice, ground
2 tsp white pepper, ground

¾ oz cornstarch, dissolved in 2 T water
10 oz maraschino cherries with the juice, quartered
4 oz peach brandy
2 oz cherry brandy
1 pint plain, low-fat yogurt
fresh mint leaves for garnish

1. Place peaches, peach nectar, water, orange juice, grenadine, allspice, and pepper in large saucepan and cook until peaches are quite soft, about 20 minutes.
2. Place in a blender at high speed and puree until quite smooth.
3. Add dissolved cornstarch and maraschino cherries with juice; return to pot and heat until thickened.
4. Cool in refrigerator.
5. When thoroughly chilled, add peach and cherry brandies and stir well.
6. Garnish with a teaspoon of yogurt and a mint leaf on each serving.

Notes: Using fresh peaches instead of canned ones will make this soup more delicious. But when fresh peaches are not available, it is preferable to use canned peaches in "water," not in "syrup," which would make the soup too sweet. The white pepper gives the soup an interesting bite, which complements its fruitiness.

White Bean and Clam Chowder

✓ *Makes 10, 10-oz portions.*

4 dozen littleneck clams
4 oz dry white wine
1 lb celery, peeled, small dice
8 oz leeks, white part only, small dice
8 oz whole white beans, dried navies or northern
1½ lb boiling potatoes, medium dice
2 qt neutral fish stock, preferably clam stock

8 oz whole-kernel corn
8 oz baby lima beans
2 bay leaves
2 T white pepper, ground
¼ tsp red pepper, ground
½ tsp nutmeg, ground

1. If using fresh clams, steam clams in a large pot with white wine, celery, and leeks. When clams open, remove and discard the shells, chop the clams, and reserve for later.

2. In another pot, cook the white beans in plain water until half done, then add the potatoes.

3. When the potatoes are fork-tender (can be broken easily with a fork), the beans should be completely cooked. Divide the beans and potatoes into two portions.

4. Add the fish stock and half the beans and potatoes to the pot with the celery and leeks. Puree in a blender at high speed.

5. Add the clams, corn, lima beans, the other half of the white bean and potato mix, and spices to the soup; simmer for approximately 30 minutes.

6. Adjust the seasonings to taste. (Remove the bay leaves before serving.)

Note: Clams are one of the best sources of selenium. Dietary selenium comes from the soil and from water taken into food. Selenium has the ability to affect both initiation and promotion stages of chemically induced cancers and tumors.

16

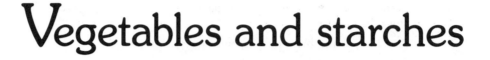

Vegetables and starches

Many chefs tend to take vegetable and starch accompaniments for granted, giving their customers unimaginative, repetitive choices. The professional chef needs to realize that these "side dishes" lend as much to the meal's completeness as the entrée.

Vegetables and starches come in many varieties. It is therefore often possible to make substitutions for specific ingredients in most recipes. A little forethought can translate plain preparations into exciting tastes for the guest's dining pleasure.

Braised Cabbage and Bell Peppers

✓ *Makes 20 portions.*

4 lb green cabbage, finely shredded
1 lb onions, thinly sliced
1 lb green or red bell peppers, fine julienne
½ cup water

2 T basil leaves
1 tsp cloves, ground
1 T black pepper, coarse-ground
2 oz white vinegar

1. In an uncovered pot, place cabbage, onions, bell peppers, and water to cook on top of the stove until tender.
2. Add basil, cloves, black pepper, and vinegar and stir well.
3. Serve immediately using slotted spoon.

    Notes: Cooking the cabbage uncovered will allow the strong sulfuric odor to dissipate with the steam. This is advisable when cooking any of the cruciferous vegetables. These vegetables are thought to reduce cancer risk in almost all cases. Members of this family include cabbage, broccoli, cauliflower, turnips, and brussels sprouts.

    The National Cancer Institute recommends a low-fat diet, with 20 g to 30 g of fiber per day. However, fiber must be added slowly to the diet. When fiber is added too quickly to a low-fat diet, diarrhea, gas, bloating, and cramping may occur. An increased consumption of fruits, vegetables, and whole grains would go a long way toward increasing dietary fiber and micronutrients and reducing fat. Bell peppers are an excellent way of adding fiber and nutrients, along with flavor.

Summer Squash with Ginger and Spring Onions

✓ *Makes 20 portions.*

4 oz peanut oil
¼ cup fresh ginger, finely chopped
8 oz spring onions, whites, washed
   and chopped (reserve the greens
   for garnish)

6 lb yellow squash, zucchini, or any combination of summer squash, washed, cut to desired shape
3 T white pepper, ground
¼ cup lime juice, freshly squeezed

1. In a sauté pan, heat the oil with the ginger and the whites of the spring onions.
2. Add squash and pepper and toss until squash becomes tender.
3. Finish with lime juice and garnish with green onion tops.

Notes: This recipe demonstrates the enhancement of mild-flavored vegetables, in this case summer squash, with highly flavorful natural ingredients such as ginger and spring onions. The flavors so complement each other that the customer does not even miss the taste of salt.

Peanut oil has a high proportion of monounsaturated fat. Although many studies have been done on olive and canola oils, the two highest in monounsaturated fat, very little attention has been given to studies on the uses of peanut oil. Peanut oil is widely used in the Southeastern United States, and is now gaining popularity in other areas.

Glazed Yellow Turnips with Figs

✓ *Makes 10 portions.*

2½ lb yellow turnips (rutabagas), peeled, cut in any uniform shape
2 oz olive oil
1 T anise seed, crushed
2 tsp rosemary leaves

2 cups dried figs, chopped
1 T white pepper, coarse-ground
1 T pink peppercorns, whole
1 pint vegetable stock

1. Cook the turnips in hot oil until lightly browned.
2. Add anise seed and rosemary and cook for an additional 2 to 3 minutes.
3. Add remaining ingredients and bring to a quick boil.
4. Reduce to a slow simmer and continue to cook until all the liquid is absorbed (about 45 minutes).

Notes: Dietary changes can have an impact on high blood pressure. An increase in potassium, a decrease in sodium, and a loss of extra body weight can do the job particularly well. Fruit is the food highest in potassium and lowest in sodium, thus contributing two of the three normalizing blood pressure factors at the same instance.

In this recipe, the dried figs provide a glazing sauce when reconstituted during the cooking process, giving the dish an excellent taste balance.

Fried Kale with Mustard-Honey Sauce

✓ *Makes 10 portions.*

2 lb fresh curly leaf kale, peeled, washed
2 cups buttermilk
2 cups cornmeal
1 tsp white pepper, fine-ground

⅛ tsp red pepper, ground
2 T paprika
peanut oil for deep frying

Sauce:
2 oz honey
4 oz coarse mustard

2 oz lemon juice

1. Soak the kale leaves in buttermilk for 2 minutes before breading.
2. Combine cornmeal, peppers, and paprika.
3. Remove kale from buttermilk, allowing the excess milk to drain off the leaves.
4. Dredge the kale in the seasoned cornmeal.
5. Fry in a deep-fryer, using peanut oil, until crispy.
6. To make the sauce, heat the combined mustard, honey, and lemon juice over a low flame.
7. Drain the kale well, and drizzle sauce over it before serving.
8. This dish may be served with an extra wedge of lemon or a dash of hot sauce.

Notes: Kale is a relative of cabbage, although it does not form a head. It is rich in calcium and B vitamins. Although many people find its taste rather strong and its texture tough, when picked young and cooked, uncovered, until tender, kale blends well with various tastes.

In this recipe, the buttermilk helps tenderize the tough kale leaves, and its sourness contrasts perfectly with kale's strong taste. The cornmeal will help retain the structure of the fried kale leaves, giving the end product a crunchy texture with a sweet aftertaste. The sauce also adds an exciting taste variation to the final dish.

Sesame Carrots and Raisins

✓ *Makes 10 portions.*

3 lb fresh carrots, julienned
2 oz sesame oil
½ cup dried raisins, plumped
2 T peanut butter

2 tsp white pepper, coarse-ground
1 lime, for its juice
¼ cup sesame seeds, toasted

1. Blanch the carrots by cooking in boiling water for 10 minutes or in a steamer for 2 to 3 minutes; drain and cool.
2. At service time, heat the sesame oil in a sauté pan before adding the carrots, raisins, and peanut butter.
3. Add the pepper and lime juice and toss freely.
4. Add the sesame seeds just before plating.

Notes: This recipe has polyunsaturated fat in the form of sesame oil and seeds. The seeds are also an excellent source of vitamin E and magnesium. Fat is especially necessary for women. If a woman loses one-third of her body fat stores, her reproductive functions can be affected. Estrogen metabolism requires fat. On the other hand, obesity also affects hormone function, causing an increase in androgen. Ideal body fat for women is about 26% to 28% of body weight.

Walnut French Beans

✓ *Makes 10 portions.*

$2\frac{1}{2}$ lb French-cut green beans
1 oz peanut oil
2 T walnut oil
1 T honey

2 tsp black pepper, coarse-ground
1 T fresh lemon juice
1 tsp lemon zest
$\frac{3}{4}$ cup walnuts, chopped

1. In a sauté pan, toss green beans in hot peanut and walnut oils until tender.
2. Add honey, black pepper, lemon juice and zest; continue to cook for 2 more minutes.
3. Add walnuts and serve.

Notes: This recipe transforms a usually bland vegetable, green beans, into an exciting dish. The walnut oil is used more as a seasoning than as a frying oil; the 1 oz of peanut oil is sufficient for cooking the beans. The lemon juice and zest and the honey give this almost a sweet-and-sour taste.

Curried Corn and Lima Beans

✓ *Makes 10 portions.*

6 oz onions, small dice
4 oz green bell peppers, small dice
2 oz pimientos, small dice
1 T curry powder
2 tsp white pepper, coarse-ground

2 oz olive oil
1½ lb whole-kernel corn
1 lb baby lima beans
½ cup dried golden raisins
½ cup low-fat sour cream

1. Sauté onions, bell peppers, pimientos, curry powder, and white pepper in olive oil until onions are tender.
2. Add corn, lima beans, and raisins.
3. Cook together for 10 minutes.
4. Add sour cream and stir well.

   Note: Curry powder is a spice blend made to resemble the spices used in Indian curries. It is excellent in transforming any vegetable into an international dish.

Sautéed Mixed Greens with Garlic

✓ *Makes 10 portions.*

1½ lb spinach, washed, trimmed, stems removed
1½ lb escarole, washed, trimmed
1½ lb romaine, washed, trimmed
¼ cup water

2 oz olive oil
2 T garlic, freshly chopped
1 T black pepper, coarse-ground
1 tsp fresh lemon juice

1. Coarsely chop the greens and place in large pan with the water.
2. Cover the pan and cook over medium heat until tender, about 5 minutes.
3. Drain greens in colander.
4. Sauté garlic and black pepper in olive oil.
5. Add drained greens and toss.
6. Sauté for an additional 5 minutes.
7. Add lemon juice and serve.

Notes: It is the mixture of greens that makes the difference in this recipe. Just as in a salad, a mix gives dimension to the overall taste—some sweeter than others, some slightly bitter. The garlic, olive oil, and lemon juice are used as a dressing to hold the tastes together. It is important to cook the greens very quickly so that they do not lose their beautiful dark-green color and vitamins.

Sweet-and-Sour Brussels Sprouts with Raisins

✓ *Makes 10 portions.*

6 oz onions, small dice
2 oz peanut oil
2½ lb fresh brussels sprouts, blanched
½ cup seedless raisins

¼ cup white vegetable stock
3 T fresh lemon juice
4 T honey
2 tsp black pepper, coarse-ground

1. Sauté onions in oil until soft.
2. Add brussels sprouts, raisins, and vegetable stock.
3. Simmer together for 10 minutes, or until most of the stock is absorbed.
4. Mix lemon juice and honey together and add to pan.
5. Add pepper and cook for an additional 2 to 3 minutes.

Note: Brussels sprouts are entirely underutilized as a vegetable. This simple preparation turns an unwanted dish into an exciting choice.

Winter Squash with Apples and Pears

✓ *Makes 10 portions.*

2 lb butternut or acorn squash, ½-inch cubes
2 tart Granny Smith apples, peeled, cored, and diced
2 red Bartlett pears, cored and diced
4 oz spring onions, thinly sliced

½ cup white vegetable stock
2 oz sauternes wine
½ tsp cinnamon, ground
¼ tsp nutmeg, ground
¼ cup almonds, toasted

1. Place squash, apples, pears, and onions in sauté pan with vegetable stock.
2. Cover pan and cook until squash is tender and liquid is absorbed.
3. Add sauternes, cinnamon, and nutmeg.
4. Garnish with almonds.

Cauliflower Creole

✓ *Makes 10 portions.*

4 oz onions, fine dice
1 T garlic, finely chopped
4 oz green bell peppers, small dice
2 T virgin olive oil
2 cups tomatoes, concassé
1 tsp black pepper, coarse-ground

⅛ tsp red pepper, crushed
½ tsp lemon juice, freshly squeezed
2 tsp thyme, freshly chopped
2 tsp basil, freshly chopped
2 heads cauliflower, in bite-size pieces

1. Sauté onions, bell peppers, and garlic in oil until tender.

2. Add tomatoes, spices, herbs, and lemon juice.

3. Cook for 15 minutes.

4. Cook cauliflower separately in boiling water or in a steamer.

5. Place cauliflower in serving bowls and spoon sauce on top.

   Note: This type of preparation can be used with different vegetables: broccoli, carrots, brussels sprouts, cabbage, green beans, etc. A spicy side vegetable like this would be excellent with a baked chicken or fish, or even with roast pork or veal.

Red Cabbage with Apples and Sauternes

✓ *Makes 10 portions.*

2 T ginger, freshly chopped
1 oz corn oil
3 lb red cabbage, shredded
1 lb Granny Smith apples, peeled, cored,
    and diced

1 T cinnamon, ground
1 T white pepper, coarse-ground
4 oz sauternes wine

1. Sauté ginger in oil to release flavor into the oil.

2. Add cabbage, apples, cinnamon, and white pepper.

3. Cook together until cabbage is tender (about 10 minutes).

4. Add sauternes and cook an additional 5 minutes.

   Note: The use of the sauternes in this familiar recipe really makes the difference between a good vegetable dish and an excellent accompaniment.

Alabama Sweet Potato Home Fries

✓ *Makes 20 portions.*

4 lb sweet potatoes	2 tsp white pepper, coarse-ground
4 oz olive oil	1 T black pepper, coarse-ground
1 lb onions, medium dice	¼ tsp red pepper, crushed
1 T garlic, chopped	1 T thyme leaves

1. Blanch the sweet potatoes, in their skins, until a fork can easily penetrate the flesh; do not overcook them. Peel the potatoes and cut them into ½-inch dice.

2. In an iron skillet, or other heavy pan, heat the oil and add the diced potatoes. Cook until they begin to caramelize.

3. Add the onions and garlic and continue to cook until the onions are tender.

4. Add the peppers and thyme for the last 15 minutes of cooking. Fresh thyme, chopped, would make a good garnish because it would enhance the flavors.

Notes: Although sweet potatoes are relatively high in calories (200), they are full of vitamin A, fiber, and iron. When the potatoes are fried in hot oil their natural sugars caramelize, adding a sweet taste. Combined with the sharp taste of the fried garlic and the tang of the different peppers, these tastes blend to give a full flavor. The thyme leaves will add character and may be replaced by other leafy herbs to produce different tastes.

Sweet potatoes are also an excellent source of carotene, a yellow/orange color pigment that is a precursor for vitamin A.

Hash-brown Potatoes with Dill and Shallots

✓ *Makes 20 portions.*

4 lb russet potatoes, refrigerated, then peeled and grated into long, thin strips
4 T shallots, chopped
2 T dill, fresh, chopped
2 T Hungarian paprika

1 T white pepper, coarse-ground
1 T black pepper, coarse-ground
¼ tsp red pepper, ground
4 oz olive oil

1. Mix all ingredients together and allow to rest for 5 to 10 minutes. (It is better to cook these potatoes on top of a hot grill. If using a pan, cast-iron or a similar, thick-bottomed pan is needed.)
2. Lightly oil the grill with the olive oil and heat to 350°F.
3. Fry hash-browns on hot grill until well-browned, turn frequently.

Notes: Under refrigeration, the high starch content of the russets will convert partly to sugars. Caramelization thus will be more complete when they are cooked. Home-fried potatoes can be shaped using a variety of spooning methods, scoops, or ring molds. The starch content of the russet potatoes will hold them together when cooked.

Shallots will give a peppery, "onion" taste with a hint of garlic; combined with the fresh dill they will create a complete taste. The paprika will add color and a slightly sweeter taste to blend with the sharpness of the peppers and the shallots.

Potatoes are a good food supply. They have no fat and they are low in calories. The calories associated with potatoes are mostly from the fats used to prepare them. Potatoes are a plentiful source of potassium. The carbohydrates in potatoes provide energy for the body and the potato is also an excellent source of dietary fiber, vitamins, and minerals.

Cranberry Rice Pilaf with Peanuts

✓ *Makes 10 portions.*

2 oz peanut oil
1 cup fresh, whole cranberries
8 oz onions, small dice
1 tsp allspice, ground
½ tsp mace, ground
1 tsp fresh ginger, finely chopped

½ cup wild rice
1½ cups long-grain rice
2 oz dry sherry
4 cups clear vegetable stock
½ cup peanuts, unsalted, roasted, chopped

1. Sweat the onions and cranberries together in the oil until the onions are tender and the berry skins have burst.
2. Add the spices and the rice; stir everything very well.

3. Add the sherry and cook until dry, about 2 to 3 minutes.

4. Bring the stock to a quick boil and add to the rice mix; stir well.

5. Bring the whole mix to a boil on top of the stove; cover the pan, and finish cooking in a 350°F oven. Cooking time should be 20 to 22 minutes.

6. When rice is finished, there should still be a small amount of liquid in the pan. The hot rice will absorb this very quickly; do not stir at this point.

7. Add peanuts just before service.

Notes: Cranberries are native to North America. They were one of the first fruits used to make preserves and relishes in this country. Their subtle tartness is easily controlled by the addition of sweet flavors; in this case, those are supplied by the mace and the allspice. Orange juice or apples also blend very well with the distinctive cranberry flavor.

Peanuts are one of the best sources of niacin, which is required for the function of respiratory enzymes. Therefore, allowances are based on overall caloric intake. For every thousand calories, the body needs 6.5 mg to 6.6 mg of niacin.

Brown Rice Pilaf with Chick-peas and Pecans

✓ *Makes 10 portions.*

8 oz onions, small dice	2 tsp celery seeds
8 oz celery, peeled, small dice	1 T sage
8 oz carrots, small dice	1 T black pepper, coarse-ground
2 oz peanut oil	2 tsp white pepper, coarse-ground
2 cups brown rice	1 qt white vegetable stock
2 cups chick-peas, cooked	½ cup pecans, roasted, chopped

1. Cook onions, celery, and carrots in hot oil until lightly browned.

2. Add rice, chick-peas, and spices; stir well.

3. Boil the vegetable stock and add to mixture; bring to a full boil.

4. Cover the pot and cook in a hot oven (350°F) for approximately 20 to 25 minutes.

5. Stir in pecans just before service; use a kitchen fork so as not to mash the cooked rice kernels.

Notes: Anemia, caused by insufficient amounts of iron in the blood system, can make a person listless, irritable, and mentally sluggish. Chick-peas, an excellent source of iron, are also high in protein and fiber and have no cholesterol.

Brown rice is the whole kernel of rice with the bran still attached. Therefore, it naturally has more vitamins and minerals. Bran also has a high percentage of fiber, which aids in digestion.

Cinnamon Noodles with Toasted Almonds and Dates

✓ *Makes 10 portions.*

1 lb dry fettuccine noodles
2 oz safflower oil
2 T cinnamon, ground
1 T black pepper, coarse-ground

$\frac{1}{8}$ tsp red pepper, ground
$\frac{1}{4}$ cup dried dates, chopped
$\frac{1}{4}$ cup almonds, toasted, sliced

1. Cook the fettuccine in boiling water until tender; strain and chill.

2. In a sauté pan, reheat the noodles with safflower oil, cinnamon, peppers, and dates.

3. Add almonds just before service.

Notes: This recipe demonstrates how the use of spices, nuts, and fruits can transform a standard accompaniment. Cinnamon can awaken a sleepy palate; the almonds add a toasted crunch and the dates a natural sweetness to the final dish.

Dates are one of the oldest fruits known to play an important role in the human diet. From the tree of the date came its leaves, which were cooked much like a cabbage; the fruits, which were eaten fresh, or dried to last through the winter; and even the date pit, which was ground into a flour used to make biscuits and flat cakes.

Almonds, another very ancient food, give this dish a lot of nutritional value. Almonds contain a high percentage of calcium, protein, iron, and vitamin B_2. Toasting the almonds first brings out their nutty flavor, which goes a long way in any rice or pasta recipe.

17

Appetizers

Appetizers are an exciting and fun part of the menu. A selection of tasty tidbits designed to awaken the palate without overpowering it, they bridge the gap between hunger and the timing of the main course. Although usually highly seasoned, appetizers should not dictate an overall taste for the entire meal. Instead, they should have distinct and separate flavors.

Wild-Rice and Corn Fritters with a Sour Cream-Cinnamon Sauce

✓ *Makes 10 portions.*

1 cup buckwheat flour
2 tsp baking powder
1 T white pepper, coarse-ground
1 T vanilla
2 egg whites
2 T corn oil

2 cups wild rice, cooked
1 cup whole-kernel corn, cooked
2 oz celery, peeled, fine dice
12 oz low-fat sour cream
2 T cinnamon, ground

1. Dry-mix the flour, baking powder, and pepper.

2. Whip together vanilla, egg whites, and oil until well-mixed; add to dry ingredients.

3. Add corn, rice, and celery to the above mixture.

4. Pour batter onto a well-oiled grill or other suitable frying pan, making 4″ pancake-shaped fritters (approximately 2 oz each).

5. Cook fritters on one side until batter begins to show bubbles; flip over gently and cook the other side until firm.

6. Mix cinnamon with the sour cream and spoon 2-oz portions on each serving.

   Notes: Wild rice is found in fresh and brackish waters in Minnesota and Wisconsin. At one time, it was quite abundant, but overharvesting has nearly brought extinction in this country.

   It takes longer to cook wild rice than regular white or brown rice. The kernels will still have a slight bite when fully cooked, giving a nice texture to the final dish.

   One cup of raw wild rice has 22.6 g protein, 120.5 g carbohydrates, and a slight amount of fat. It has more than double the iron of brown rice.

   Buckwheat is grown extensively in Siberia and parts of Europe. It is also known by the name beechnut (because the seeds resemble beechnuts) and saracen (because of its dark color). Until the end of the nineteenth century, buckwheat was a staple food of northeastern Europe. Botanically, buckwheat is not a cereal, but because its seeds yield a flour it is correctly called a grain. Many farmers consider buckwheat a weed and use it as a fertilizing cover crop.

   Buckwheat is eaten more by animals than humans, which is unfortunate, because it is rich in minerals and B vitamins and has a lower caloric value than any of the cereal grains.

   Corn oil in this recipe helps to balance out the little bit of saturated fat in the low-fat sour cream. The amount of cholesterol in the recipe is insignificant—less than 25 mg.

Eggplant Pâté

✔ *Makes 10 portions.*

2 lb eggplant, peeled and diced
4 oz virgin olive oil
8 oz onions, small dice
4 oz green or red bell peppers, small dice
2 T garlic, finely chopped

2 cups tomato concassé
¼ cup basil, freshly chopped
½ cup ripe olives, chopped
1 T black pepper, coarse-ground
1 lemon, for its juice

1. Sauté eggplant in oil until lightly browned; remove from pan.
2. In same pan, sauté onions, bell peppers, and garlic for 2 minutes (vegetables should still have some texture, and garlic should not brown).
3. Mix everything together in a large bowl; squeeze the lemon for its juice, and add to eggplant.
4. Refrigerate overnight.
5. Serve a large scoop over a bed of leaf lettuce with toasted French-bread croutons.

Notes: Eggplant's nutritional virtue is its low amount of calories — only 24 in a 3½-oz portion. This beautiful fruit has been important to generations of Mediterranean and East Mediterranean cooks. Each fruit can weigh from 1 to 5 lb.

A 3½-oz portion of eggplant contains 92.7 g of moisture, 1.2 g of protein, 0.2 g of fat, and 5.5 g of carbohydrates. Almost a fifth of the carbohydrates are fiber. Although eggplant is not a great source for any one vitamin or mineral, it has small amounts of vitamins A, C, B_1, B_2, and B_3, calcium, chlorine, copper, iron, magnesium, manganese, phosphorous, potassium, and fluorine. (*Foods and Food Production Encyclopedia*, Douglas M. Considine, Glen D. Considine, Van Nostrand Reinhold, New York, 1982, pp. 593–596.)

Vegetable Pancakes with a Sour Cream-Horseradish Sauce

✓ *Makes 10 portions.*

8 oz carrots, shredded
8 oz zucchini, shredded
8 oz yellow squash, shredded
2 lb white potatoes, shredded
6 oz onions, fine dice
2 cups whole-kernel corn
2 T parsley, freshly chopped
1 T marjoram, freshly chopped

2 tsp savory, freshly chopped
2 tsp white pepper, fine-ground
½ tsp salt
2 egg whites
1½ pints low-fat sour cream
¼ cup horseradish, ground
10 oz peanut oil (for griddle)

1. Stir together all shredded vegetables with onions and spices.
2. Lightly beat egg whites and add to vegetables; stir well.
3. Oil a griddle with the peanut oil and pour ¼ cup of vegetable mix per pancake onto hot griddle; the starch from the potatoes and the egg whites will hold the vegetables together.
4. Brown on both sides.
5. Mix horseradish and sour cream together and serve with pancakes.

Popcorn Shrimp with Chili Sauce

✓ *Makes 10 portions.*

2½ lb medium shrimp (36 – 41 count), peeled and deveined

Batter:
2 bottles of a good-flavored beer
2 cups corn flour
2 cups all-purpose flour

2 T paprika
2 tsp white pepper, fine-ground

Sauce:
4 oz green bell peppers, small dice
6 oz onions, small dice
2 oz virgin olive oil
1 T garlic, finely chopped
1 T chili powder
1 tsp coriander, ground
1 tsp cumin, ground

2 bay leaves
1 T basil, freshly chopped
1 tsp black pepper, coarse-ground
¼ tsp red pepper, crushed
1 qt tomatoes, concassé
2 tsp lemon juice, freshly squeezed
Peanut oil (for deep fryer)

1. To make the sauce, sauté the onions and bell peppers in oil until tender.
2. Add garlic and spices and cook for 2 more minutes.
3. Add tomatoes and lemon juice; simmer for 1 hour.
4. To make batter, mix all dry ingredients together and slowly stir in beer; add only enough liquid for a pouring consistency.
5. Dip shrimp in batter and deep-fry in peanut oil until brown and crispy.
6. Serve with chili sauce on the side for dipping. (Remove bay leaves.)

Oyster Fritters with Apple and Raisin Chutney

✔ *Makes 10 portions.*

1 cup all-purpose flour
1 cup yellow cornmeal
4 tsp baking powder
4 egg whites, slightly beaten
1 tsp white pepper, fine-ground

1 T oregano, freshly chopped
2 pints select oysters, chopped (reserve oyster juice for batter)
Peanut oil (for frying)

Chutney:
4 baking apples, peeled, seeded, small dice
½ cup concentrated apple juice
½ cup water
1 cup golden raisins
2 tsp lemon zest

4 oz red bell peppers
1 T ginger, freshly grated
1 T cornstarch, dissolved in small amt. of water

1. To make chutney, place apples, apple juice, water, raisins, lemon zest, ginger, and bell peppers in a saucepan and bring to a boil.
2. Add cornstarch mixture and simmer until thickened.
3. Refrigerate chutney overnight.
4. To make fritters, mix cornmeal, flour, and baking powder thoroughly.
5. Add egg whites, white pepper, and oregano; mix until smooth.
6. Add oysters and just enough liquid to make a thick batter.
7. Using a small ice cream scoop, drop oyster batter in hot peanut oil until the fritters are golden-brown.
8. Drain fritters on paper towels to remove excess oil; serve with chutney.

Peppered Cornsticks with Mexican Lime Salsa

✔ *Makes 10 portions.*

2 cups yellow cornmeal
1 cup corn flour
2 tsp baking powder
½ tsp salt
2 tsp black pepper, coarse-ground

½ tsp white pepper, coarse-ground
⅛ tsp red pepper, ground
¼ cup corn oil
6 egg whites, slightly beaten
10 oz peanut oil (for frying)

Salsa:
4 oz onions, small dice
4 oz green or red bell peppers, small dice
4 oz celery, peeled, small dice
2 oz jalapeño peppers, seeded and chopped
1 qt tomatoes, concasseé

2 tsp cumin, ground
2 tsp coriander, ground
2 T parsley, freshly chopped
¼ cup fresh lime juice
1 T lime zest

1. To make the salsa, mix onions, bell peppers, celery, tomatoes, jalapeños, cumin, coriander, parsley, lime juice, and zest; refrigerate overnight.
2. To make the cornsticks, mix cornmeal, flour, baking powder, salt, and spices.
3. Add oil and egg whites; knead the dough until everything is well-incorporated.
4. Roll dough on lightly floured table top to ¼-inch thickness.
5. Cut dough into long strips and twist to make ribbons.
6. Cook ribbons in hot peanut oil until golden-brown.
7. Serve with salsa.

Corn Bread Pizza

✔ *Makes 10 servings.*

1 tsp dry yeast
2 cups warm water
2 cups cornmeal
2 cups all-purpose flour

¼ tsp salt
¼ cup corn oil
1 cup corn flour

Sauce:
4 oz onions, small dice
4 oz green bell peppers, small dice
1 T garlic, freshly chopped

2 oz corn oil
2 cups tomato sauce
2 tsp cumin, ground

Topping:
1 qt fresh tomatoes, small dice
4 oz red bell peppers, julienne
1 T jalapeño peppers, seeded and chopped

¼ cup fresh chives, chopped
12 oz monterey jack cheese, shredded

1. To make the dough, dissolve yeast in warm water and set aside until foam begins to rise.
2. Mix cornmeal, all-purpose flour, salt, and oil with water and yeast.
3. Add corn flour to dough until the dough is well-formed and dry to the touch.
4. Roll dough into a round ball and refrigerate overnight.
5. To make the sauce, sauté onions, bell peppers, and garlic in oil for 2 minutes.
6. Add tomato sauce and cumin and bring to a boil.
7. Simmer for 1 hour.
8. Roll out dough to ¼-inch thickness and place on lightly oiled pizza pan or other flat pan; crimp up the edges to help hold the sauce.
9. Pour sauce on top and spread as evenly as possible.
10. Cover with cheese and toppings.
11. Bake in hot (500°F) oven until crust is lightly browned and cheese is well-melted.
12. May be served with sour cream and/or guacamole.

Chicken Fingers with Sauce Anisette

✓ *Makes 5 portions.*

4 oz onions, fine dice	1 T lime juice
2 oz corn oil	2 oz anisette liqueur
20 chicken tenderloins	1 head Boston lettuce
1 tsp white pepper, coarse-ground	10 tomatoes, sliced

1. Sauté onions in hot oil until tender.
2. Add chicken tenderloins and sauté until lightly browned on both sides.
3. Add pepper, lime juice, and anisette; simmer for 3 to 4 minutes, or until sauce is slightly thickened and chicken begins to caramelize.
4. Serve on lettuce leaves with tomato slices.

Cajun Chicken Tenders

✓ *Makes 5 portions.*

2 T thyme, freshly chopped
1 tsp cumin, ground
½ tsp coriander, ground
2 tsp black pepper, coarse-ground
½ tsp white pepper, coarse-ground
⅛ tsp red pepper, ground

¼ tsp salt
20 chicken tenderloins
2 oz peanut oil
1 T lemon juice, freshly squeezed
1 head Boston lettuce
10 tomatoes, sliced

1. Mix all spices together and sprinkle liberally on chicken tenderloins.
2. Sauté chickens in hot oil until well-browned on both sides.
3. Squeeze lemon juice in pan with chicken and simmer for a few more seconds.
4. Serve with fresh lettuce leaves, sliced tomatoes, and a cold sauce (low-fat sour cream and chives is an excellent accompanying sauce).

Crab Coins Maryland

✓ *Makes 10 portions.*

2½ lb lump crabmeat, cleaned of all shells
2 oz virgin olive oil
2 egg whites, slightly beaten
4 oz onions, finely chopped
2 oz celery, peeled and finely chopped

2 T prepared mustard
2 T lemon juice, freshly squeezed
1 T Old Bay seasoning
½ cup fresh bread crumbs
corn oil for frying

1. Mix all ingredients together and shape into 1-oz, flat cakes; add extra bread crumbs if cakes do not hold their shape.
2. Pan-fry in hot corn oil until well-browned on both sides.
3. Serve with a spicy mustard or fresh horseradish.

Note: Although a very simple dish to prepare, this is full of flavor. The traditional recipe calls for mayonnaise as a binder, but here the egg whites and bread crumbs do the job just as nicely. The olive oil gives the cakes a different flavor from the usual one.

Fennel and Artichoke Hearts à La Grecque

✓ *Makes 10 portions.*

1 pint water
2½ lb fennel, peeled and french-fry cut
1 tsp fennel seeds
1 tsp coriander seeds
1 tsp black peppercorns, cracked
1 sprig fresh thyme

1 bay leaf
½ cup virgin olive oil
10 artichoke hearts, sliced
2 T lemon juice, freshly squeezed
1 T parsley, freshly chopped

1. Bring water to a boil and add spices and fennel (reserve parsley).

2. Simmer until fennel is tender; drain and discard bay leaf and thyme.

3. Heat olive oil in sauté pan and add fennel and artichoke hearts.

4. Heat for 2 to 3 minutes and add lemon juice and parsley.

5. Drain most of the oil and refrigerate the vegetables; serve cold.

Roasted Sweet Peppers Vinaigrette

✓ *Makes 10 portions.*

5 large red bell peppers
3 large green bell peppers
2 large yellow bell peppers
½ cup virgin olive oil
1 bunch spring onions, white and tender
  greens, thinly sliced
1 T basil, freshly chopped

1 T oregano, freshly chopped
1 tsp garlic, finely chopped
1 T red wine vinegar
1 T lemon juice, freshly squeezed
1 tsp white pepper, coarse-ground
¼ tsp salt

1. Rub bell peppers with a little of the oil and roast in 450°F oven until skin blisters, about 15 minutes.

2. Remove peppers and peel off the skins.

3. Remove seeds and cut peppers in juliennes.

4. Mix together all other ingredients and pour over pepper strips.

5. Refrigerate overnight.

6. May be served with hearts of lettuce or thinly sliced, fresh Italian bread, or both.

   Note: Bell peppers are naturally sweet; the roasting technique just helps to bring the sweetness to the surface. The spring onions are also sweet and tender and give this appetizer a rounded taste.

Chick-Pea Dip

✓ *Makes 1 pint.*

1 lb chick-peas, cooked
2 T garlic, freshly chopped
2 tsp black pepper, coarse-ground
½ tsp salt

6 oz virgin olive oil
2 oz lemon juice, freshly squeezed
2 T parsley, freshly chopped

1. Place chick-peas, garlic, pepper, salt, oil, and lemon juice in a blender; puree until smooth.

2. Add parsley and blend for 2 seconds only.

3. Serve with any fresh vegetable (celery, carrots, bell pepper strips) or dry crackers.

Note: This is a very tasty and nutritious dish that makes an excellent dip or a spread for a variety of canapés or open-faced vegetable sandwiches. Chick-pea spreads are a very popular Middle Eastern food used on all occasions in many ways.

Pear and Pineapple Relish

✓ *Makes 2 quarts.*

2 lb Kieffer pears, peeled and cored
1 ripe pineapple, peeled and cored
4 oz green bell peppers, fine dice

2 oz lemon juice, freshly squeezed
1 tsp white pepper, coarse-ground

1. Chop fruits in food chopper until they have a fine-dice consistency.

2. Add rest of ingredients.

3. Refrigerate overnight.

Note: Fruit relishes can be stored in sterilized jars for future use. They were developed as a way of preserving ripe fruit for use throughout the winter months. The addition of the bell peppers gives this relish a taste that will complement a variety of entrées and other appetizers.

Apple Pickles

✔ *Makes 2 quarts.*

12 baking apples, Rome Beauties or Macintosh, peeled, cored, sliced
12 oz apple juice concentrate
12 oz water

2 T lemon juice, freshly squeezed
2 tsp whole cloves
2 cinnamon sticks

1. Place all ingredients in a saucepan and bring to a boil.
2. Immediately remove from the fire and place in refrigerator overnight.

  Notes: Other interesting variations can be made by adding different fruits to this recipe: apple and pear pickles, apple and cranberry pickles, apple and orange pickles. The terms "pickles" and "relish" are interchangeable in these preparations; either can be used as an appetizing snack with crackers and cheese, or as an accompaniment to poultry and meats.

Barbecued Fruit with Honey and Poppyseed Dressing

✔ *Makes 10 portions.*

1 ripe pineapple, peeled, cored, in bite-
size pieces
5 kiwi fruits, peeled, in bite-size pieces
40 large whole strawberries

5 large peaches, peeled, in bite-size pieces
½ cup honey
2 T lemon juice, freshly squeezed
2 T poppy seeds

1. Skewer the fruit, using alternating colors.
2. Lay skewers on a hot broiler for 1 minute; turn on the other side for an additional minute.
3. Mix together honey, lemon juice, and poppy seeds and brush lightly on broiled fruit.

  Notes: This interesting appetizer can use any firm-fleshed fruit. The amount of honey for each kabob is very slight and, therefore, the caloric value is still relatively low. These kabobs should be served hot off the grill or they will lose their appeal.

18

Desserts

Substitutions can be made in baked goods and pastries just as easily as in other foods to transform glutinous products into nutritious ones. Although some recipes still contain large amounts of sugar, butter, and eggs, the individual portion sizes are such that the amounts actually given to customers are well below objectionable levels. The problems in desserts come from the traditional, fatty icings and cream fillings used liberally in various pastries and cakes. These are used to keep cakes from staling and to give moisture to a dry product. Freshly baked cakes and muffins do not need that kind of preservative covering. Most cakes and pies can have toppings made from fruit purees or whipped mousses.

Cinnamon Oat-Bran Muffins

✓ *Makes 1 dozen.*

1¾ cups skim milk
1½ cups oat-bran cereal, uncooked
1 egg
¼ cup light-brown sugar
1½ tsp cinnamon, ground

1 tsp vanilla
4 tsp vegetable oil
1 cup all-purpose flour
2 tsp baking powder

1. Combine milk and cereal.

2. Add egg, sugar, cinnamon, vanilla, and oil; mix well.

3. Combine baking powder and flour and add to mixture.

4. Lightly mix until dry ingredients are moistened.

5. Fill muffin cups two-thirds full and bake at 400°F for 20 minutes.

Notes: A simple muffin formula can be changed to better meet the body's nutritional needs while still satisfying the taste buds. The oat bran adds both flavor and fiber. Chopped pecans, walnuts, or raisins could be added for variety.

Tea Muffins

✓ *Makes 1 dozen.*

¾ cup all-purpose flour, sifted
¼ tsp salt
2 tsp baking powder
½ tsp cinnamon
1 cup bran flakes

1 egg
½ cup water
1 tsp sugar substitute
1 T vegetable oil
3 T raisins, chopped

1. Sift together dry ingredients, except for sugar substitute and raisins.

2. Add bran flakes.

3. Beat egg, water, oil, and sugar substitute together until well-blended.

4. Stir into dry ingredients.

5. Add raisins.

6. Fill muffin cups two-thirds full and bake at 400°F for 20 minutes.

Note: This basic formula can be easily changed to produce a variety of muffins. Add applesauce and pineapple chunks for a fruitier muffin, or dates and pecans for a more traditional kind.

Orange-Spice Cupcakes

✓ *Makes 1 dozen.*

1½ cups all-purpose flour, sifted
½ tsp baking soda
1 tsp baking powder
¼ tsp salt
½ tsp cinnamon, ground
¼ tsp allspice, ground
¼ tsp nutmeg, ground

¼ tsp ginger, ground
2 egg whites
6 oz concentrated, unsweetened orange juice
1½ T vegetable oil
1 tsp orange zest, grated

1. Sift together dry ingredients.
2. Whip egg whites, juice, oil, and zest together.
3. Stir wet ingredients into dry ones just until dry are blended.
4. Fill muffin pans two-thirds full; bake at 350°F for 20 minutes.

Note: This recipe demonstrates that oil can be substituted for butter or margarine, orange juice for water and sugar, and egg whites for whole eggs.

Yogurt and Banana Mousse

✓ *Makes 10 portions.*

2 cups skim milk
1 oz unflavored gelatin
6 ripe bananas, slice two and reserve
2 tsp vanilla

6 egg whites
2 oz sugar, fine granulated
2 cups plain, low-fat yogurt
¼ cup almonds, sliced, toasted

1. Combine gelatin and skim milk to soften the gelatin granules.
2. Add 4 bananas and heat together thoroughly.
3. Puree bananas and milk together until very smooth; set aside to cool.
4. Beat egg white until soft peaks form.
5. Add sugar to egg whites and mix for 30 more seconds.
6. Fold whipped egg whites into cool banana mixture.
7. Fold in yogurt and remaining sliced bananas.
8. Garnish with more yogurt and almonds.

Notes: This dessert can be served by itself or used as a topping for muffins, cakes, and pies. Other yogurt-fruit mousses can be made simply by substituting equal parts of fresh fruit for the bananas.

Meringue-Pie-Crust Fruit Tarts

✓ *Makes 10 portions.*

10 egg whites
10 oz sugar, fine granulated
½ pint fresh strawberries

½ pint fresh raspberries
½ pint fresh blueberries
1 qt plain, low-fat yogurt

1. Whip egg whites until very fluffy.
2. Slowly add sugar while continuing to whip egg whites.
3. Continue to whip egg whites until soft peaks are formed.
4. Using a pastry bag with a star tip, pipe 4-inch diameter plates with high decorative edges on a parchment-paper-lined sheet pan.
5. Bake in 200°F oven for 2 hours, or until well-dried, but not browned.
6. Reserve one-quarter of the fruit, sliced for garnishes.
7. Puree the rest with the plain yogurt in a blender at high speed.
8. Spoon fruited yogurt into dry meringue shells and cover with fresh, sliced berries.

Note: Meringue pie shells can take the place of more traditional flour pie crusts in many presentations. The meringue shells contain no fat and only enough sugar to give them solid structure. The rest of the sweetness comes from the fruit.

Apple and Oatmeal Crisp

✓ *Makes 8 portions.*

10 Granny Smith apples, peeled, cored, and sliced
2 oz apple juice concentrate
1 T cornstarch
1 tsp cinnamon, ground
¼ tsp nutmeg, ground

½ tsp vanilla
1 cup rolled oats
¼ cup all-purpose flour
¼ cup light-brown sugar
¼ cup pecans, chopped
2 oz butter

1. Dissolve cornstarch in apple juice and pour over sliced apples.
2. Add spices and stir well.

3. Mix together oats, flour, sugar, and pecans.

4. Melt butter and add to oat mixture; stir until mixture crumbles in the hand.

5. Place apples in baking dish.

6. Cover with topping, spreading evenly and to the sides of the pan.

7. Bake in 350°F oven until crust is brown and the apple juice bubbles through the sides.

Note: Pies that do not have bottom crusts can be just as satisfying as traditional pies when served with this interesting oatmeal topping. The oats have the added advantage of supplying some fiber. This dessert can be served hot or cold, by itself or with ice cream.

White Fluffy Cake with Peaches and Nectar

✓ *Makes 12 portions.*

½ cup butter
½ cup sugar, granulated
2½ cups cake flour, sifted
3 tsp baking powder
1 cup skim milk
1 tsp vanilla extract

½ tsp almond extract
4 egg whites, whipped to firm peaks
8 fresh peaches, peeled and sliced thin
½ cup peach nectar
2 oz peach brandy

1. Cream butter and sugar together until very light and fluffy.

2. Sift together all other dry ingredients and fold into creamed mixture, alternating with milk, vanilla, and almond extract.

3. Fold in the egg whites.

4. Pour into buttered and floured cake pan and bake at 350°F for 45 to 60 minutes. (Cake is done when sides pull away from the pan and cake springs back when pressed with a finger.)

5. In a sauté pan, heat the peaches with the nectar and reduce liquid by half.

6. Add brandy and cool sauce.

7. Sauce can be served cold or warm over cake and low-fat ice cream, if preferred.

Date, Applesauce, and Walnut Torte

✓ *Makes 12 portions.*

1 cup dates, pitted, chopped
¾ tsp baking soda
½ cup boiling water
½ cup apple juice concentrate
½ cup applesauce

3 T vegetable oil
1 egg
1 cup all-purpose flour, sifted
½ cup walnuts, chopped

1. Place dates in saucepan and sprinkle with baking soda.
2. Pour boiling water over dates and put aside to rest.
3. In a large bowl, mix apple juice, applesauce, oil, and egg until well-mixed.
4. Add the dates and water and stir well.
5. Add flour and walnuts; stir until smooth.
6. Bake in a lined cake pan at 375°F for 30 to 35 minutes, or until toothpick comes out clean, and sides of cake pull away from pan.
7. Serve plain or with fruit.

Fresh Berry Streusel

✓ *Makes 12 portions.*

5 cups fresh blueberries
5 cups fresh strawberries
1 tsp fresh lemon juice

½ cup light-brown sugar
½ cup oat flour
½ cup butter, melted

1. Add lemon juice to berries and allow to sit for 15 minutes.
2. Blend together sugar, flour, and butter; the mixture should be very crumbly, but will hold together when pressed.
3. Place berries in baking dish and top with streusel.
4. Bake in 400°F oven for 20 minutes.

Poached Pineapple and Plums

✓ *Makes 10 portions.*

1 ripe pineapple, peeled, in bite-size pieces
10 to 12 plums, peeled and sliced

2 cups concentrated pineapple juice
2 cups water

1. Put plums, pineapple, juice, and water in a large saucepan.
2. Heat fruit and simmer for about 40 minutes, or until sauce begins to thicken.

   Note: This simple poaching recipe can be used on most fruits to create various sauces for sponge cakes and brownies.

Broken Meringue Parfait with Black Currants and Yogurt

✓ *Makes 10 portions.*

10 egg whites
10 oz sugar, granulated
1 cup black currants, dried
¼ cup water
2 oz kirsch

1 qt plain, low-fat yogurt
12 mint leaves
2 egg whites, slightly beaten
¼ cup sugar, fine-granulated

1. Whip egg whites until soft peaks form.
2. Continue to whip, slowly adding sugar.
3. Pipe whipped meringue onto parchment-lined sheet pan and bake in 200°F oven for 2 hours (any left-over broken pieces of meringue can be used for another dessert).
4. Heat currants with water until they come to a quick boil.
5. Remove from the heat and add kirsch.
6. Allow to cool completely.
7. Fold currants and sauce into yogurt.
8. Place some of the currant yogurt in the bottom of parfait glasses and cover with broken meringue.
9. Cover with more yogurt and more meringue.
10. Make at least four layers, topping the last layer off with yogurt.
11. Dip mint leaves in lightly whipped egg whites and then in fine granulated sugar. Serve as garnish.

Vegetarian Mincemeat Pie

✓ *Makes 16 slices.*

1½ cups raisins or currants
2 oz dry sherry
3 cups Rome Beauty or Macintosh
    apples, peeled, cored, small dice
½ orange, with peel, ground
1 T fresh lemon juice

1¼ cups sugar, fine-granulated
1 tsp cinnamon, ground
½ tsp allspice
¼ tsp cloves, ground
¼ tsp ginger, freshly grated
4 oz butter, melted

Dough:
2 cups all-purpose flour
⅔ cup butter

6 T cold water

1. Pour sherry over raisins and allow to sit for 15 minutes.

2. Using a pastry knife, cut butter into flour until the butter is pea-sized.

3. Add cold water to make a pastry dough.

4. Roll out dough to line a large baking pan or two, 9-inch pie pans.

5. Mix together all ingredients for the filling, including the melted butter.

6. Pour into pie shell(s).

7. Bake at 450°F for 25 minutes.

Bibliography

Brillat-Savarin, Jean-Anthelme, 1984, *The Philosopher in the Kitchen*, Middlesex, England, Penguin Books, Ltd.

Brown, Elizabeth Burton, 1977, *Grains, an Illustrated History*, Englewood Cliffs, New Jersey, Prentice Hall.

Chalmers, Irena, 1988, *Good Old Food*, New York, Barron's.

Coyle, L. Patrick, Jr., 1982, *The World Encyclopedia of Food*, New York, Facts on File, Inc.

Davis, Frank, 1983, *The Frank Davis Seafood Notebook*, Gretna, Louisiana, Pelican Pub. Co.

De Sélincourt, Aubrey, trans., 1959, *Herodotus, The Histories*, Baltimore, The Penguin Press.

Ensminger, Ensminger, Konlande, Robson, 1983, *Foods and Nutrition Encyclopedia*, *Vol. 1 and 2*, 1st Edition, Clovis, Calif., Pegus Press.

Freeman, Margaret, 1948, *Herbs for the Medieval Household*, 2nd Edition, New York, Huxley House.

Furnas, C. C., and Furnas, S. M., 1937, *The Story of Man and His Food*, New York, The New Home Library.

Hartbarger, Janie Coulter, and Hartbarger, Neil J., 1983, *Eating for the Eighties, A Complete Guide to Vegetarian Nutrition*, New York, Berkley Publication Group.

Hillman, Howard, 1981, *Kitchen Science*, Boston, Houghton Mifflin Co.

Hunter, Beatice Trum, 1972, *The Natural Foods Primer*, New York, Simon and Schuster.

MacNeil, Karen, 1981, *The Book of Whole Foods Nutrition and Cuisine*, New York, Vintage Books.

Martin, Ethel Austin, 1963, *Nutrition in Action*, 3rd Edition, New York, Holt, Rinehart and Winston, Inc.

McCormick and Co., 1984, *Spices of the World Cookbook*, New York, McGraw-Hill Book Co.

Null, Gary, 1987, *The Vegetarian Handbook*, New York, St. Martin's Press.

Parry, J. W., 1953, *The Story of Spices*, New York, Chemical Publishing Co.

Ritchie, Carson I. A., 1981, *Food in Civilization*, New York, Beaufort Books, Inc.

Rodale Press Editors, 1985, *Nuts and Seeds, The Natural Snacks*, Emmaus, Penn., Rodale Press, Inc.

Stare, Frederick J., M.D.; Olson, Robert, M.D.; Whelan, Elizabeth M., Sc.D.; 1989, *Balanced Nutrition Beyond the Cholesterol Scare*, Holbrook, Mass., Bob Adams, Inc.

Stobart, Tom, 1982, *Herbs, Spices and Flavorings*, New York, The Overlook Press.

Tannahill, Reay, 1973, *Food in History*, New York, Stein and Day, Inc.

Nutrition bibliography

Adams, C., 1986, *Handbook of the Nutritional Value of Foods in Common Units,* U.S.D.A., New York, New York, Dover Publications.

Addes, P., 1990, "Coronary Heart Disease, An Update with Emphasis on Dietary Lipid Oxidation Products," *Food and Nutrition News,* 62 (2), Chicago, Illinois, National Live Stock and Meat Board.

Agricultural Research Service, 1977, "Fat in Food and Diet," U.S.D.A., Bulletin No. 361, U.S. Government Printing Office, p. 5.

Allegrini, M., Pennington, J., and Tanner, J., 1983, Total Diet Study: "Determination of Iodine Intake by Neutron Activation Analyses," *Journal of American Dietetic Association,* 83 (1), 18–23.

Alpers, D., Clouse, R., and Stenson, W., 1983, *Manual of Nutritional Therapeutics,* Boston, Massachusetts, Little, Brown and Company.

American Institute for Cancer Research Newsletter, 1988, "Good Grades for Lean Beef Update," 21, p. 10.

Anderson, A., 1988, "Chromium in Human Health and Disease," *Nutrition and the M.D.,* 14 (3).

Anonymous, 1980, "Atherosclerosis and Auto Oxidation of Cholesterol," *Lancet,* 1:946–965.

Ballentine, C., 1985, "The Essential Guide to Amino Acids," *FDA Consumer, HHS Publication Number 86-1124,* Rockville, Maryland, Department of Health and Human Services.

Bosco, D., 1980, *The Peoples Guide to Vitamins and Minerals from A to Zinc,* Chicago, Illinois, Contemporary Books.

Call, D. L., 1988, "Animal Product Options in the Marketplace," *Food and Nutrition News,* 60 (4).

Chandra, R., 1986, "Nutrition and Immunity," *Contemporary Nutrition,* Minneapolis, Minnesota, General Mills, 11 (11) and 11 (12).

Cook, J., 1983, "Nutritional Anemia," *Contemporary Nutrition,* 8 (4), Minneapolis, Minnesota, General Mills.

Council on Scientific Affairs American Medical Association, 1988, *Contemporary Nutrition,* Minneapolis, Minnesota, General Mills, 13 (3, 4).

Department of Health and Human Services, 1983, "Potassium—Keeping a Delicate Balance," *FDA Consumer, HHS Publication 83-2170,* Rockville, Maryland, U.S. Government Printing Office.

Division of Agricultural and Food Chemistry of the American Chemical Society, 1982, "Symposium: Unconventional Sources of Dietary Fiber," Washington, D.C., American Chemical Society.

The Encyclopedia of Organic Gardening, 1978, Emmaus, Pennsylvania, Rodale Press.

Etherton, P. M., Krummel, D., Dreon, D., Mackey, S., and Wood, P., 1988, "The Effect of Diet on Plasma Lipids, Lipoproteins, and Coronary Heart Disease," American Dietetics Association, 88 (11).

Friedman, R., 1987, "Calcium Supplements: Don't Depend on Them," *University of California, Berkeley Wellness Letter,* 3 (6), New York, New York, Health Letter Associates.

Gorringe, J., 1986, "Why Blame Butter: discussion paper," *The Royal Society of Medicine,* 79:661 – 663.

Grant, A., 1979, *Nutritional Assessment Guidelines,* Seattle, Washington, Anne Grant.

Grosvenor, M., 1989, "Diet and Colon Cancer," *Nutrition and the M.D.,* 15 (4), 1 – 2.

Grundy, S. M., 1989, "Recent Research on Dietary Fatty Acids: Implications for Future Dietary Recommendations," *Food and Nutrition News,* 61 (5).

Guthries, 1980, "Atherosclerosis and Auto-oxidation of Cholesterol," *Lancet,* 1:964 – 965.

Halberg, F., 1983, "Chronobiology and Nutrition," *Contemporary Nutrition,* 8 (9), Minneapolis, Minnesota, General Mills.

Harris, W. S., 1985, "Health Effects of Omega 3 Fatty Acids," *Contemporary Nutrition,* 10 (8), 1 – 2.

Hartmann, P., and Bell, E., 1984, "Nutrition for the Athlete," *Sports Medicine for the Primary Care Physician,* East Norwalk, Connecticut, Appleton-Century-Crofts, pp. 105 – 121.

Heaney, R., 1986, "Calcium Bioavailability," *Contemporary Nutrition,* 11 (8), Minneapolis, Minnesota, General Mills.

Heinz International Research Center and Heinz Research Fellowship of Mellon Institute, 1963, *Nutritional Data,* Pittsburgh, Pennsylvania, H. J. Heinz Company.

Heishman, J., 1988, "Iodine Intake Deficiency, Excess, and Hypersensitivity," 14 (5).

Hideshige, I., Werthessen, N., and Taylor, B., 1976, "Angiotoxicity and Atherosclerosis due to Contaminants of USP-Grade Cholesterol," *Archives Pathological Laboratory Medicine,* 100, 565 – 572.

Hodges, A., 1989, *Culinary Nutrition for Foodservice Professionals,* New York, New York, Van Nostrand Reinhold.

Hoeg, J. M., 1987, "Managing the Patient with Hypercholesterolemia," *Nutrition and the M.D.,* 13 (9).

Holly, H., 1982, "Diet and Hypertension, An Update on Recent Research," *Contemporary Nutrition,* 7 (11), Minneapolis, Minnesota, General Mills.

Howard, R., Herbold, N., 1978, *Nutrition in Clinical Care,* New York, New York, McGraw-Hill Book Company.

Hulley, S., Cohen, R., and Widdowson, G., 1977, "Plasma High Density Lipoprotein Cholesterol Level," *Journal of the American Medical Association,* 238 (2), pp. 2269 – 2271.

Hunter, Beatrice, 1978, *The Great Nutrition Robbery,* New York, New York, Charles Scribner's Sons.

Imai, H., et al, 1976, "Angiotoxicity and Arteriosclerosis due to Oxidized Cholesterol," *Arch. Path. Lab. Med.,* 100:565 – 572.

Institute of Shortening and Edible Oils, Inc., 1988, *Food Fats and Oils,* Washington, D.C.

Johnson, J., 1980, "The Molybdenum Cofactor Common to Nitrite Reductions, Xanthine Dehydrogenase and Sulfite Oxidase," *Molybdenum and Molybdenum Containing Enzymes,* New York, New York, Pergamon Press.

Kinsella, J., 1989, "Dietary Polyunsaturated Fatty Acids, Eicosanoids, and Chronic Diseases," *Contemporary Nutrition,* 14 (2), Minneapolis, Minnesota, General Mills.

Kurtz, T., Hamoudi, A., Al-Bander, and Curtis, R., 1987, "Salt Sensitive Essential Hypertension in Men — 'Is the Sodium Ion Alone Important?'," *New England Journal of Medicine,* 317:1043.

Lukaski, H., Johnson, P., Bolonchuk, W., and Lykken, G., 1985, "Assessment of Fat-free Mass Using Bioelectrical Impedance Measurements of the Human Body," *American Journal of Clinical Nutrition,* 41, 810.

Lyons, P., Truswell, A., Mira, M., Vizzard, J., and Abraham, J., 1989, "Reduction of Food Intake in the Ovulatory Phase of the Menstrual Cycle," *American Journal of Clinical Nutrition,* 49 (6).

Martin, D., Mayes, P., and Rodwell, V., 1983, *Harpers Review of Biochemistry,* 19th edition, Los Altos, California, Lange Medical Publication.

Maryland Dietetic Association, 1987, "The Omega Families," *Chesapeake Dietetic Lines,* 40 (4), Lutherville, Maryland, Maryland Dietetic Association.

Mayer, J., 1988, "Vitamin E has as many mysteries as it does unsubstantiated claims," Baltimore, Maryland, Sun Paper.

Mitchell, M., 1990, *Instructors Manual and Test Bank to Accompany Wardlaw, G., Insel, P., Perspectives in Nutrition,* Boston, Massachusetts, Times Mirror, Mosby College Publishing.

Monsen, E., 1988, "Iron Nutrition and Absorption: Dietary Factors which Impact Iron Bioavailability," *Journal of the American Dietetic Association,* 88, 786.

Monty, K., and McElroy, W., 1959, *Food, the Yearbook of Agriculture,* pp. 122–129, Washington, D.C., USDA Government Printing Office.

Multiple Risk Factor Intervention Trial, 1982, Patient Package, Baltimore, Maryland.

National Dairy Council, 1977, *Guide to Good Eating — A Recommended Daily Pattern,* Rosemont, Illinois.

Nutrition and the M.D., 1987, "Clinical Assessment of Mild Iron-Deficiency Anemia," 13 (3).

———, 1987, "Dietary Boron and Osteoporosis," 13 (3).

———, 1989, "Dietary Guidelines for Individuals with Diabetes," 15 (9), 4.

———, 1988, "Enhancing Calcium Absorption," 15 (1) 8.

———, 1987, "Estimating Adult Energy Needs," 13 (12).

———, 1989, "Fish Oil Supplements and Hypertriglyceridemia," 15 (9) 3–4.

———, 1989, "More on Meal Frequency," 15 (12).

———, 1988, "Hypervitaminosis A," 14 (9) 1.

———, 1989, "Palm Oil," 15 (9) 4–5.

———, 1989, "Pharmacologic Management of Hyperlipidemia," 15 (9) p. 2.

———, 1987, "Use of the Harris/Benedict Equation in Determining Energy Expenditure," 13 (3).

———, 1987, "Vitamin A and Photoaged Skin," 13 (10).

Nutrition Close-Up, 1988, "Dietary Guidelines: Recent Developments in Information," Washington, D.C., Egg Nutrition Center 5 (2).

————, 1989, "Exercise, Weight Loss, and Heart Disease," Washington, D.C., Egg Nutrition Center, 6 (1).

————, 1989, "LDL Metabolism and Incorporation into Atherosclerotic Plaques," 6 (2), Washington, D.C., Egg Nutrition Center.

————, 1989, "Lipid Metabolism and Heart Disease," Washington, D.C., Egg Nutrition Center, 6 (1).

————, 1988, "Surgeon General's Report on Nutrition and Health — Recommendations on Dietary Fat and Cholesterol," Washington, D.C., Egg Nutrition Center, 5 (3).

————, 1989, "The Role of Abnormal Apoproteins in Atherosclerosis," Washington, D.C., Egg Nutrition Center, 6 (2).

————, 1989, "Today's Egg Contains 25% Less Cholesterol," Washington, D.C., Egg Nutrition Center, 6 (2).

————, 1990, "Hydrogenated Vegetable Fats Shown to Increase Serum Cholesterol," Washington D.C., Egg Nutrition Center, 7 (3).

Nutrition Reviews, 1989, "Dietary Beans, a Risk Factor for Cholesterol Gallstones," 47:369.

Offenbacher, E., and Xavier, F., 1983, "Temperature and pH Effects on the Release of Chromium from Stainless Steel into Water and Fruit Juices," *Journal of Agricultural and Food Chemistry,* 31 (89 – 92).

Pike, R., and Brown, M. L., 1975, *Nutrition, An Integrated Approach,* 2nd Edition, New York, New York, John Wiley & Sons.

Pozefsky, T., 1986, *Concepts and Controversy in Management of Obesity — Lecture,* Baltimore, Maryland, Union Memorial Hospital.

Proudfit, F., and Robinson, C., 1958, *Nutrition and Diet Therapy,* New York, New York, The Macmillan Company.

Rajagopalan, K., 1987, "Molybdenum — An Essential Element," *Nutrition Reviews,* 45 (11) 321.

Randal, J., 1990, "Fluoride in the Water — A New Animal Study Suggests It Can Cause Cancer," Washington, D.C., *Washington Post.*

Rankin, C., 1990, *Eating Disorders Lecture,* Baltimore, Maryland, Mercy Hospital.

Recher, R., 1983, "Osteoporosis," *Contemporary Nutrition,* 8 (5), Minneapolis, Minnesota, General Mills.

Savaiano, D., and Kotz, C., 1988, "Recent Advances in the Management of Lactose Intolerance," *Contemporary Nutrition,* 13 (9, 10), Minneapolis, Minnesota; General Mills Nutrition Department.

Seminars in Nutrition, 1989, "Diet and Exercise in the Prevention and Control of Chronic Disease," pp. 2 – 12, Littleton, Colorado.

Sherwin, R., 1982, "Obesity as a Rick Factor," lecture to staff, Baltimore, Maryland, University of Maryland Department of Epidemiology.

Simonson, M., 1982, "Advances in Research and Treatment of Obesity," *Food and Nutrition News,* 53 (4), 1 – 4.

Smith, R., 1988, "Nutrition, Brain and Behavior," *Sierra Pacific Seminars* (April 24), Baltimore, Maryland, The New England Center for Nutrition Education.

————, 1989, *Nutrition, Hypertension and Cardiovascular Disease,* Portland Oregon, The Lyncean Press.

Solomons, N., Guerrero, A., and Torun, B., 1985, "Dietary Manipulation of Postprandial Colonic Lactose Fermentation: Effect of Solid Foods in a Meal," *Clinical Nutrition,* 41, p. 199.

Stamler, J., "Cutting Cholesterol," *Nutrition Action Health Letter,* Washington, D.C., Center for Science in the Public Interest, 16 (7), 5–7.

Taylor, F., 1978, "Iodine—Going from Hypo to Hyper," *FDA Consumer, HHS (FDA) 81-2153,* Rockville, Maryland, U.S. Government Printing Office.

Tolstoi, L. G., 1989, "The Role of Pharmacotherapy in Anorexia Nervosa and Bulimia," *Journal of the American Dietetic Association,* 89 (11).

Watson, R., 1989, "Nutrition and Cancer," *Food and Nutrition News,* 61 (3), Chicago, Illinois, National Live Stock and Meat Board.

Wenck, D., Baren, M., and Dewan, S., 1983, *Nutrition,* Englewood Cliffs, New Jersey, Simon and Schuster.

Whiteside, L., 1984, *The Carob Cookbook,* Wellingborough, Northamptonshire, Great Britain, Thorsons Publishers Limited.

Whitney, E., and Hamilton, E., 1977, *Understanding Nutrition,* Saint Paul, Minnesota, West Publishing Co.

Wilson, E., Fisher, K., and Pilar, A., 1979, *Principles of Nutrition,* 4th Edition, New York, New York, John Wiley & Sons.

Zeman, F., 1983, *Clinical Nutrition and Dietetics,* Lexington Massachusetts, The Collamore Press, pp. 164–165.

Index

Broiled Tuna with Chili-Garlic Sauce, 161–162
Broken Meringue Parfait with Black Currants and Yogurt, 237
Brown fat theory of obesity, 107
Browning, versus sweating, 32
Brown Rice Pilaf with Chick-peas and Pecans, 217
Brussels sprouts, 213
Buckwheat, 220
    as amino acid source, 58
Bulgur-clam stuffing, 155–156
Bulimia, 109
Burgers, chicken, 151
Butter
    as flavoring, 35
    versus margarine, 118
B vitamins, 78–81, 173–174, 196–197, 220

Cabbage, 143, 146, 174, 177, 208
Cabbage and Broccoli Soup with Chick-peas, 197–198
Cajun Bean Salad, 182–183
Cajun Chicken Burgers with Jack Cheese Pockets, 151
Cajun Chicken Tenders, 226
Cajun cooking, 48, 162
Calamari and Eggplant Stew, 122
Calcium, 85–87
California cooking, 48
Calories
    counting, 105
    in foods, 110
    recommended amounts, 108
    recommended sources, 104–105
Calvados, 204–205
Canola oil, 162–163
Caramelization, 33, 215
Caraway, 14
Caraway Beef with Pearl Onions, 136
Carbohydrates, 61–68
    digestion of, 62–63
    enzyme deficiency, 63–64
Cardamom, 15
Cardiovascular disease, and fatty foods, 70–74
Carrots, 210–211
Cashews, 172
Casseroles. *See* Stews and casseroles

Cassia, 14
Catfish, 162
Cauliflower, 188, 200
Cauliflower Creole, 214
Cayenne pepper, 15
Celery, 31
Celery seed, 15
Chambord, 132–133
Cheese, 119, 151
Chef, role in menu planning, 49
Cherries, 138
Cherry and Peach Soup, 205
Chervil, 16
Chianti, 158
Chicken, 129, 130–131, 148–154, 191, 201, 202, 226
    Baked Chicken in Cucumber-Lime Sauce, 153
    Broiled Sesame Chicken Breast with Basil Marinade, 148
    Cajun Chicken Burgers with Jack Cheese Pockets, 151
    Chicken Fingers with Sauce Anisette, 225
    Chicken Indienne, 152
    Chicken Paprika, 150
    Country Chicken and Shrimp, 202
    Forester Chicken Soup, 201
    Georgia Chicken, 154
    Grilled Chicken Salad, 191
    Italian Peasant Chicken, 154–155
    Roasted Sage Chicken, 149–150
    Smothered Chicken and Onions, 152–153
Chicken Fingers with Sauce Anisette, 225
Chicken Indienne, 152
Chicken Paprika, 150
Chicken Piedmont, 131
Chick-Pea Dip, 228
Chick-Peas, 197–198, 217
Chili, 161–162, 203
Chili Macaroni, 128
Chili sauce, 222–223
Chlorine, 99–100
Chocolate, and stearic acid, 70
Cholent (Braised Beef and Dumplings), 127
Cholesterol, 69–70
    in breakfast foods, 111
    in butter and margarine, 118